CHORDS For Guitar

Transposable Chord Shapes using the CAGED system

By Gareth Evans

ISBN 978-0-9928343-1-9

Written by Gareth Evans

Photography, Diagrams and Cover design by Gareth Evans

www.guitar-book.com

Introduction

This book is designed as a reference to give you various shapes for different types of chord. These shapes are based on the C A G E D system, which derives from the basic chords that beginners often start with, enabling you to learn how to locate chords yourself. All you have to do is move the chord shape up or down the fret-board. To make sure you're on track each chord type has a question with answers at the back of the book.

You will not find the same shape repeated for any chord type within this book. Rather than give you 1000's of chords, many of which are the same shape, this book gives you more chord types, just over 60, for which there are over 200 unique shapes.

The simpler chords that we often start with (such as major chords) are not always necessarily the easiest to finger on the fret-board. Perhaps ironically an A13sus4 pattern 2 (page 61) is easier to play than for instance a C major open chord (page 6). When playing any chord for the first time it can help to play one string at a time to make sure all the notes are clear. This can apply to all chords within this book.

Although this is primarily a reference for movable chord shapes, relevant music theory has also been included later on in the book.

Contents

How to use Fret-board Diagrams

Fret-board diagrams for chords are usually shown vertically because chords tend to span less frets than scales. The following diagram on the left names the different parts, while the one on the right shows how chords are displayed within the diagram.

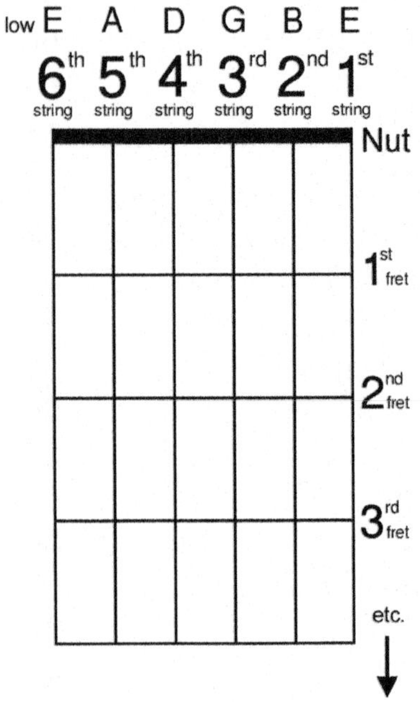

On the example to the right, the dots on the frets show us where to place our fingers.

The "X" symbols above the nut indicate those strings are not played. The "O" symbols above the nut indicate those strings are played open (open means the string is played with no frets used.)

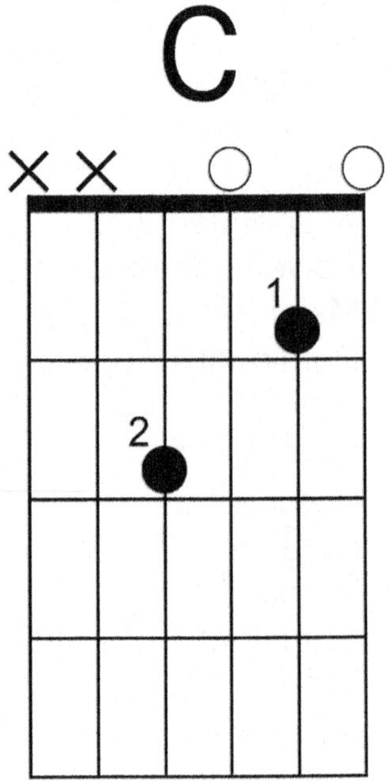

The numbers added next to each dot advise which fingers to use. The fingers are numbered as shown in the picture below.

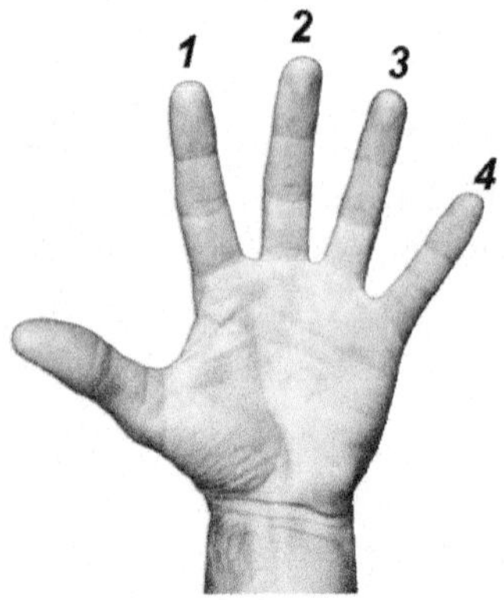

The fret-board diagram above indicates that you would use the index (1) and middle (2) finger for the chord. As shown to the right…

When further up the fret-board and away from the nut, a fret number is used. Here we can see the 3rd fret is referred to on the right of the diagram, so we would play the chord from that location.

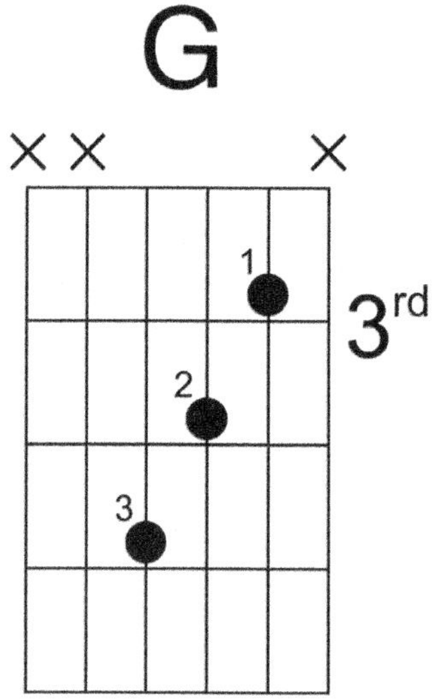

The chord would be played like this…

Root Notes & CAGED Chords

All chords are based from a root note. This could be any note of the musical alphabet, as shown below.

A	A♯ B♭	B	C	C♯ D♭	D	D♯ E♭	E	F	F♯ G♭	G	G♯ A♭

The notes with symbols are sharps (♯) and flats (♭). These are different names for the same note known as *enharmonic equivalents*. For instance C♯ and D♭ are the same.

When a chord's name is indicated with *only* the root note, such as "G" or "E♭", this is for the most fundamental chord type; the major chord. So "G" would mean the chord of G major and "E♭" would mean the chord of E flat major. Other types of chords are indicated with symbols after the root note. For example a small "m" tells us it's a minor chord, such as "Gm" for G minor or "E♭m" for E flat minor.

The CAGED system is named after the following major chords of the same names, these are "open chords" meaning there are open strings played within them. The purpose of the CAGED system is to keep the fretting hand in the same area of the fret-board.

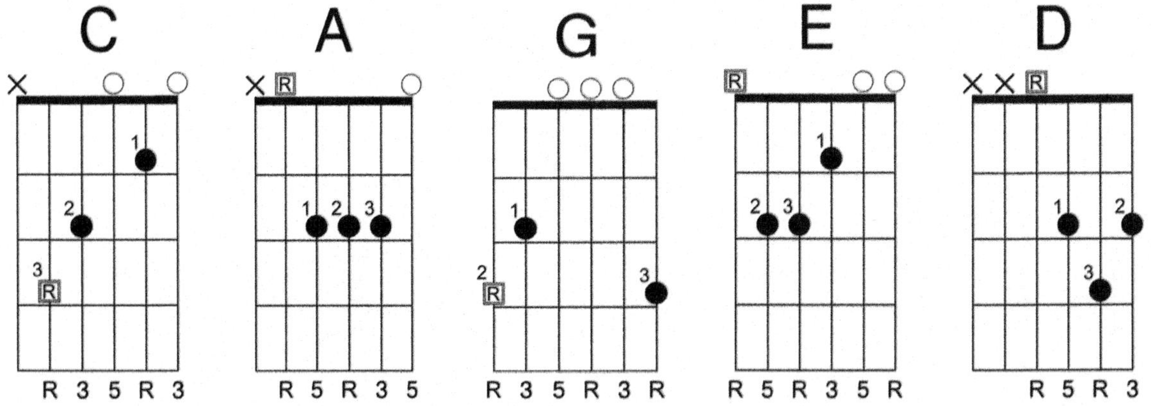

The Root note is indicated with an "R" in a small square box, for example on the C chord we can see that the Root note of "C" is on the 5th string 3rd fret. In the case of A, E and D major the root note is on the open string hence why the "R" in the small square is shown behind the nut (the root note is in other locations, known as other *octaves*, but this is the one we need to focus on.)

Note: The figures underneath the fret-board diagrams (such as R 3 5) indicate what intervals the notes within the chords are, which relates to the structure of the chord, beyond and including the root note itself. This is primarily a reference book for transposable chords, but if you understand or want to learn about intervals now or at a later date, then their locations are noted underneath the chords for your future reference. There is a fuller explanation toward the back of the book starting on page 62.

These 5 chord shapes are the basis behind many other chords, not just the ones shown, because of this we can name them generically as patterns 1 to 5.

C = **Pattern 1** (Root on 5th string)

A = **Pattern 2** (Root on 5th string)

G = **Pattern 3** (Root on 6th string)

E = **Pattern 4** (Root on 6th string)

D = **Pattern 5** (Root on 4th string)

These chords aren't only played around the bottom of the fret-board; their shapes can be moved up and down it too. This is where the *Barre chord* can become useful. Let's say we want to make a B major chord, using pattern 4. Here is the original E open chord for pattern 4.

E

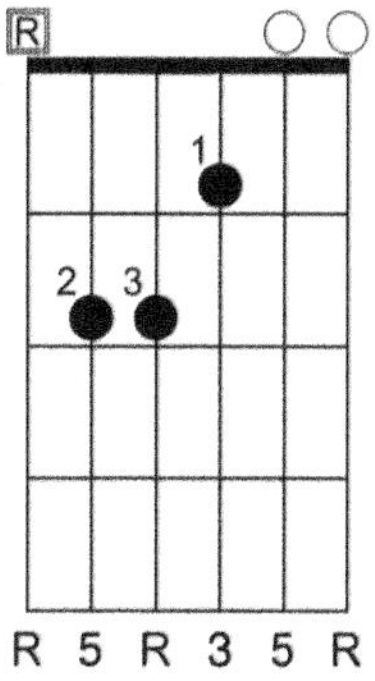

The root note for pattern 4 is on the 6th string, so this is the string on which we need to find the note of B for the root note (you can use the fret-board diagram to the right for this) and therefore from where we place the chord shape.

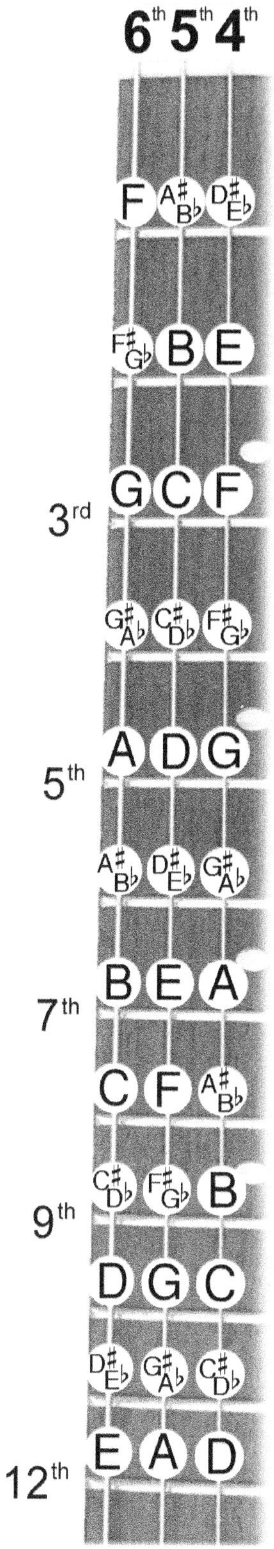

The note of B can be found on the 7th fret of the 6th string. Here is our new B major chord. The curved line across the 7th fret represents a 1st finger barre.

B

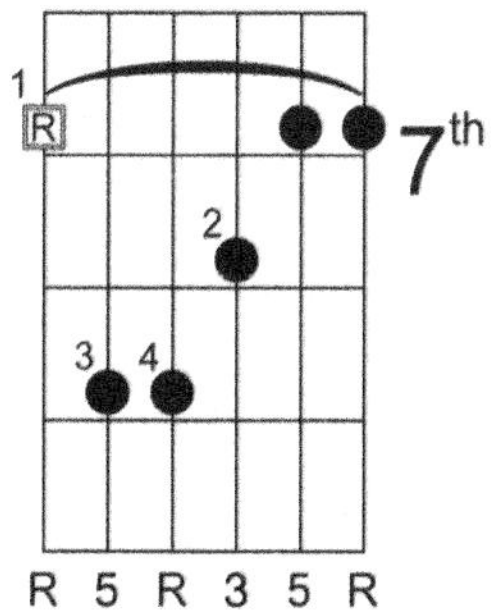

So we have made B major pattern 4. Notice the similarity between the shape of this chord and the E major from which it originated. The 1st finger barre of the B major chord takes the role of the notes on open strings that were in the E major chord.

This chord was chosen because being further up the fret-board it is easier to play. F major on the other hand, with its root note on the 1st fret of the 6th string would be trickier as it needs more pressure for the barre due to it being next to the nut which holds the strings up (if you can play an F major chord pattern 4 then even better). Either way the principle would have been the same; moving the chord shape so that the root note and therefore the chord is different. We can call this ***Transposing by the Root Note.***

In music, transposition refers to the process of moving a collection of notes up or down in pitch by a constant interval. In simple terms this is what we have just done by moving a chord shape, the chord type didn't change (i.e. constant interval).

Let's try another example. Making a C sharp major chord with pattern 2. Below left is the original A major open chord for pattern 2.

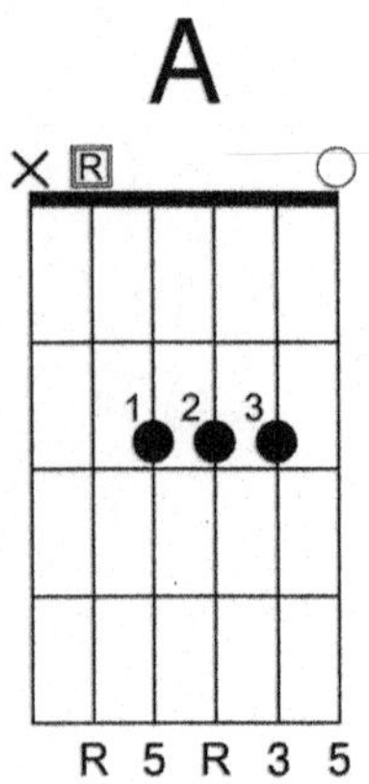

The root note for pattern 2 is on the 5th string, so this is the string on which we need to find the note of C♯ for the root note (you can use the previous fret-board diagram to find this) and therefore from where we place the chord shape.

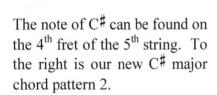

The note of C♯ can be found on the 4th fret of the 5th string. To the right is our new C♯ major chord pattern 2.

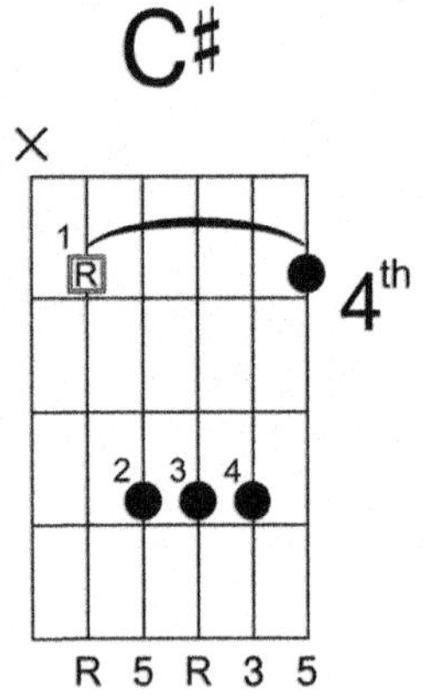

Note: In this book, numerical names are used for the strings (i.e. 1st, 2nd string etc.) rather than their note names (i.e. low E, A string etc.) because the root note is always referred to by its letter name (i.e. E, F♯, D♭ etc.) therefore making the terms used to identify the strings and the root notes on them different.

Here are all 5 patterns as barre chords. Chords where less than all of the strings are spanned by the barre are known as a *partial-barre* (such as for pattern 1 and pattern 3). They are shown on no particular fret because they all work whichever fret you place the Root note.

Pattern 1 **Pattern 2** **Pattern 3** **Pattern 4** **Pattern 5**

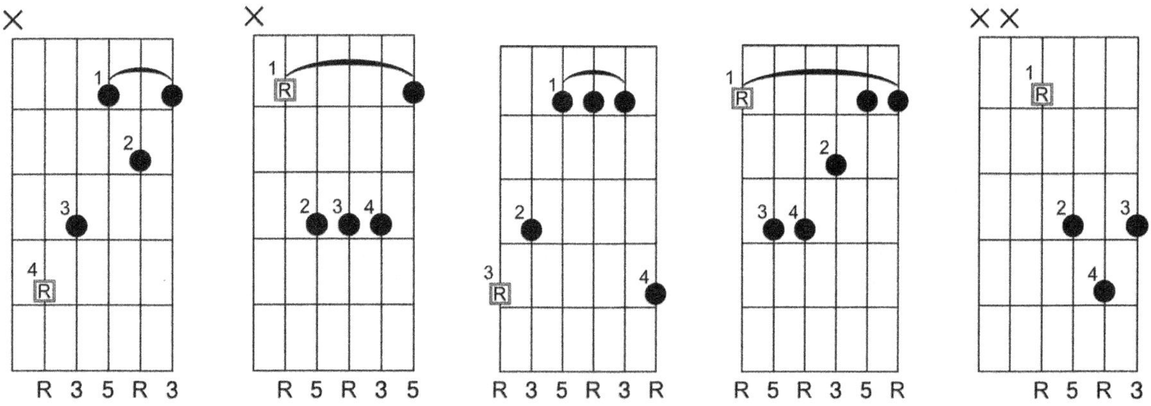

Pattern 1 and 3 are not as practical to play so are not used as often as the others. Pattern 5 may also be trickier than 2 and 4. You aren't expected to be able to play all of these straight away; the real point of this is to understand the principle of how chord shapes can be moved up and down the fret-board. In fact, major chord pattern 3 would more often be played as shown below left. Pattern 4 can also be played as a fragment of itself by leaving out the 6th and 5th strings; when doing so the string we can refer to for the root note is now the 4th, as shown below right.

Pattern 3

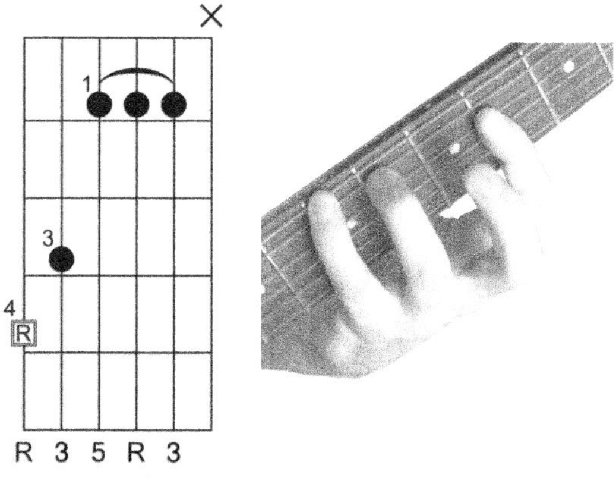

Pattern 4 (root on 4th)

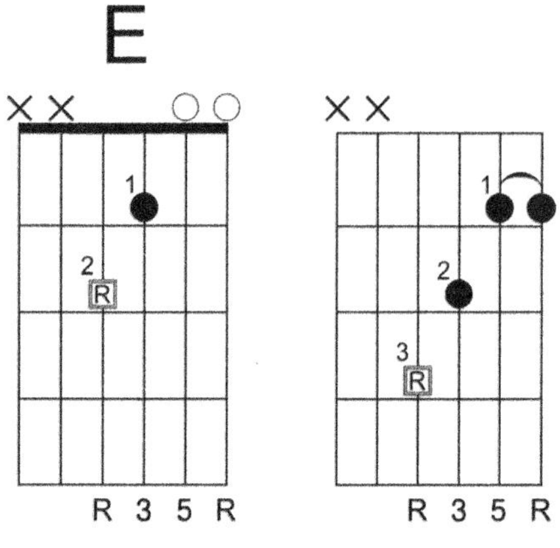

Here are a few for you to work out / play. You can refer to the diagram on page 7 to find the root note for whichever string it is on…

Q1) F major pattern 2
Q2) B♭ major pattern 4
Q3) A major pattern 4 (root on 4th string)
Q4) G♯ major pattern 5
Q5) C major pattern 3
Q6) F♯ major pattern 1

(answers at back of book)

So to conclude; you can take CAGED patterns 1 to 5 anywhere up or down the fret-board depending where you locate the root note. This principle actually works for all chord types not just the major chords covered so far.

For the chords within this book the versions with the root note of C, A, G, E or D are shown on the left for each pattern (most of which are open chords), followed by the transposable version to its right. In some cases not all 5 patterns are practical to play so only the ones that are, are shown.

Minor (R ♭3 5)

Pattern 2

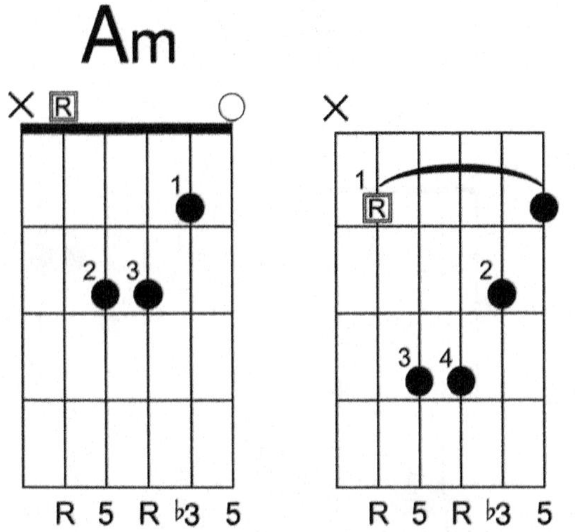

Pattern 3

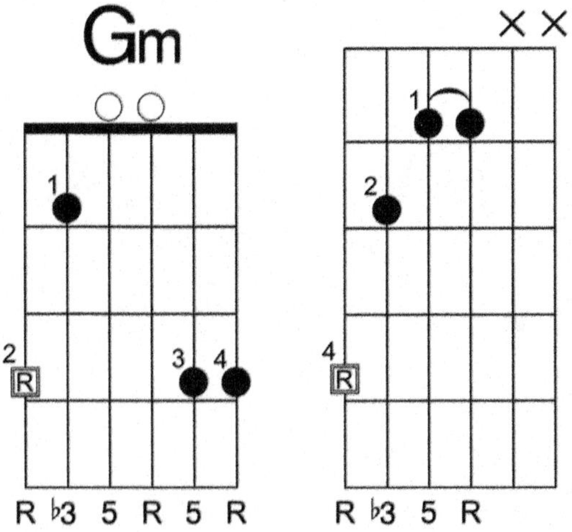

Pattern 4

Em

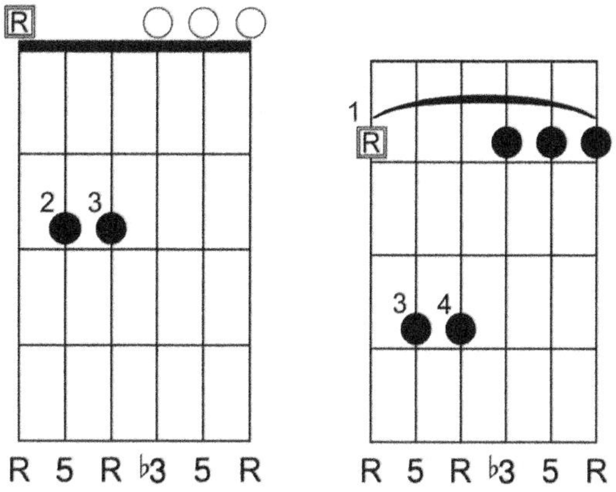

Pattern 4 (root on 4th)

Em

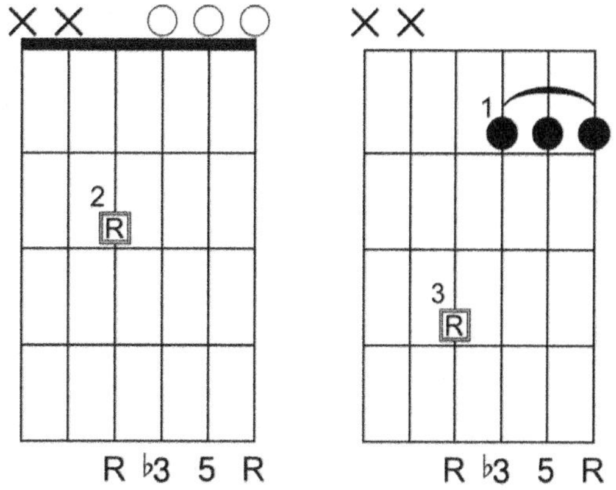

Pattern 5

Dm

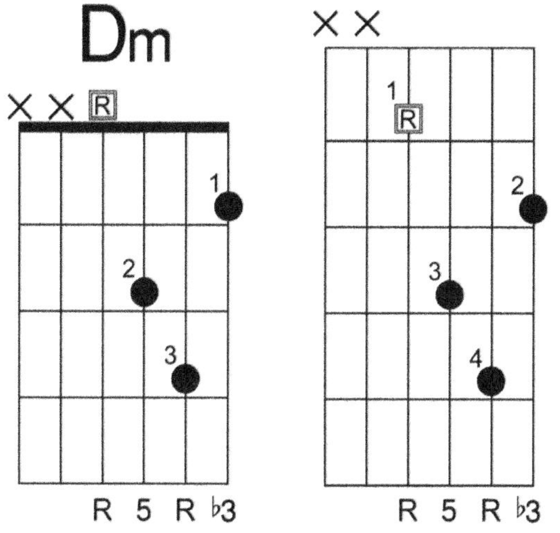

For each chord type there's a question for you to test yourself on.

Q7) Can you work out / play Fm pattern 2?

You can refer to the diagram on page 7 to find the root note. If you would like a fret-board diagram, which is separate from this book, there is also one at www.guitar-book.com/guitar-fretboard-notes.htm or go to the home page www.guitar-book.com and find it from there.

Pattern 1 is not included for minor chords due to being impractical to play and rarely used. For some chord types pattern 1 *is* practical to play, such as for the following augmented chords.

Augmented (R 3 #5)

Pattern 1

Caug

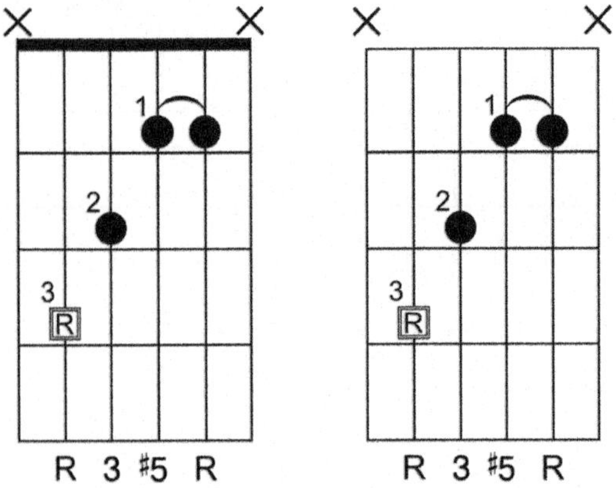

Pattern 2

Aaug

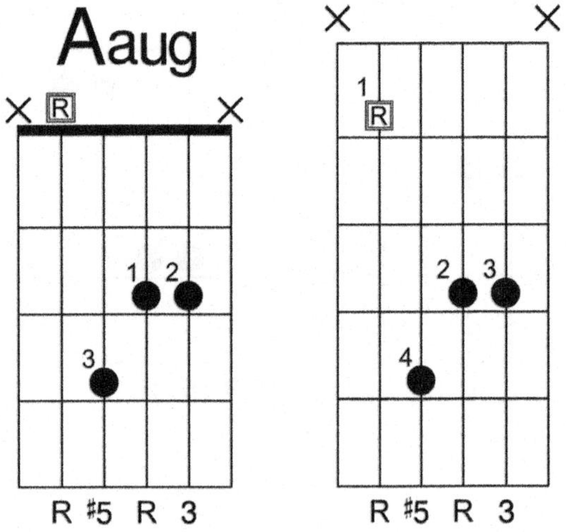

For Eaug pattern 4 below, the bracket to the right of the "O" for the open 1st string means this note is optional; played or not, it will still be an augmented chord. The same applies to the bracketed note on the transposable version, in which there is also an "X" behind this optional note, meaning that if the note isn't used then the string should not be played at all.

Pattern 3

Gaug

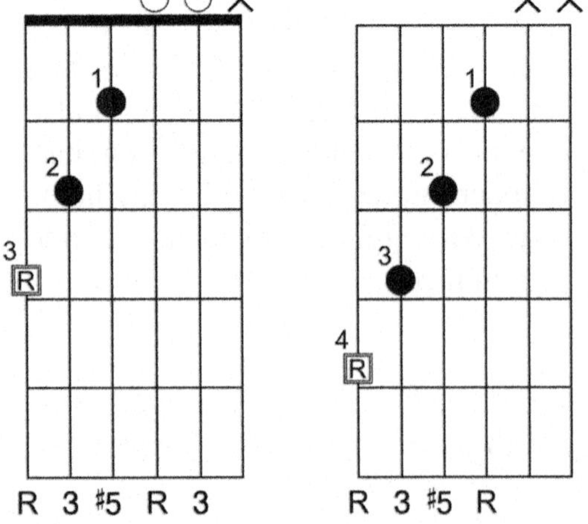

Pattern 4

Eaug

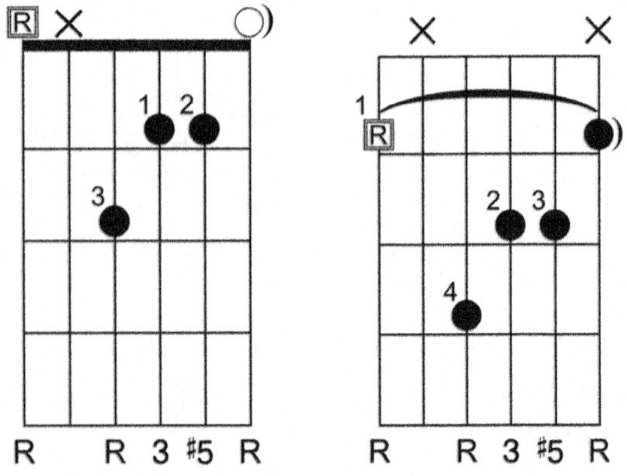

Chords such as the previous pattern 4 can also be played finger-style (often used in Jazz) by the plucking hand using the thumb for the bass note and fingers for the others, making it easier to miss the 5th string.

Pattern 4 (root on 4th)

Eaug

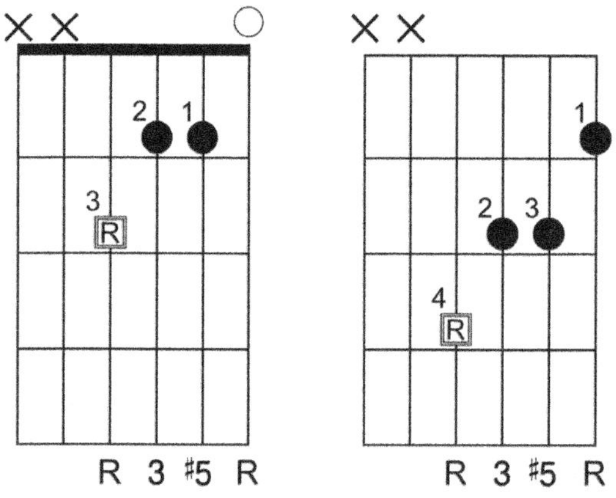

Pattern 5

Daug

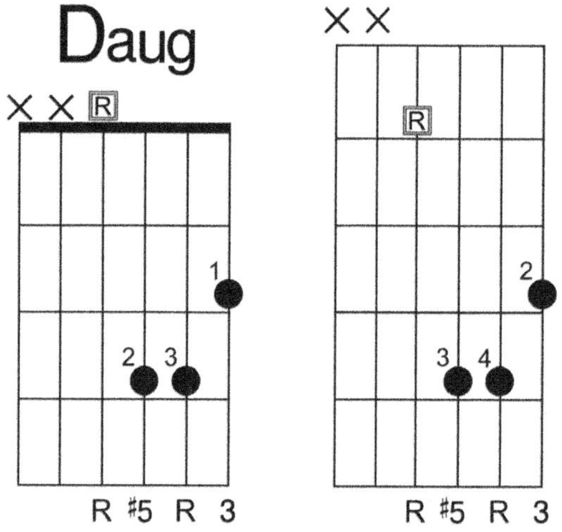

Diminished (R b3 b5)

Pattern 2

Adim

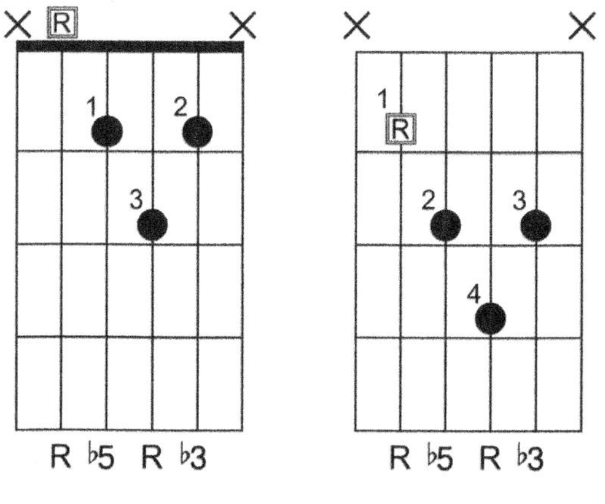

Pattern 4

Edim

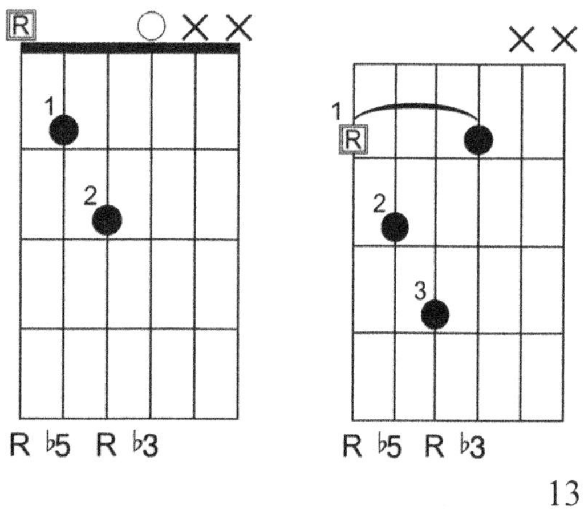

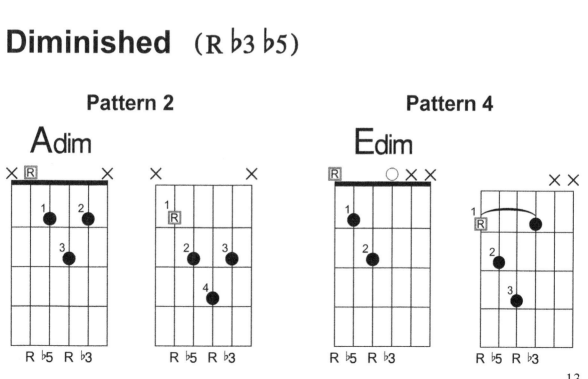

Pattern 5

Ddim

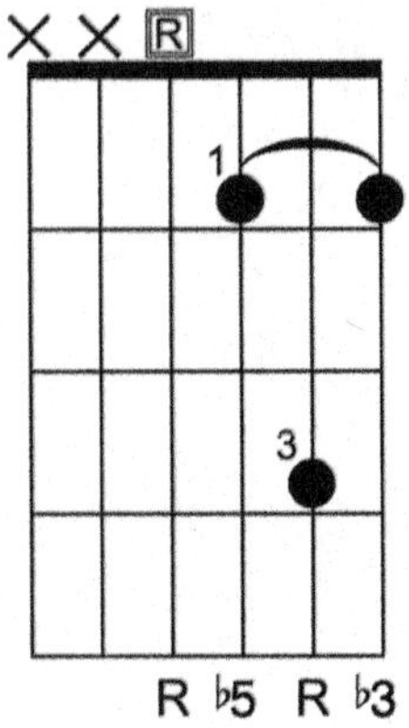

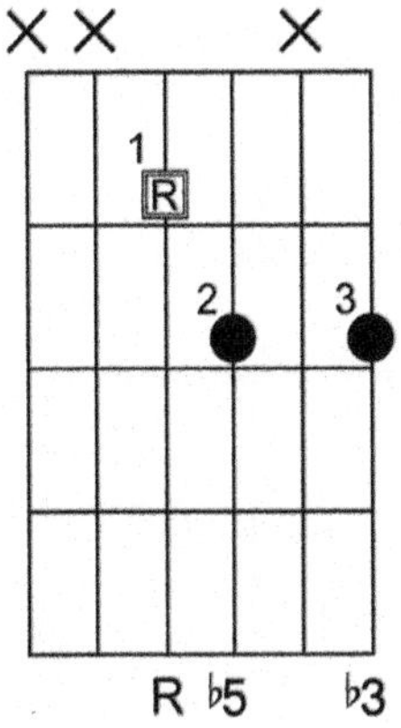

Q8) Can you work out / play D♯aug pattern 1?

Q9) Bdim pattern 4?

Suspended (R 4 5)

Sometimes the transposable version of an open chord is impractical to play. In such cases this will be indicated in the space where it would normally go.

Pattern 1

Csus⁴

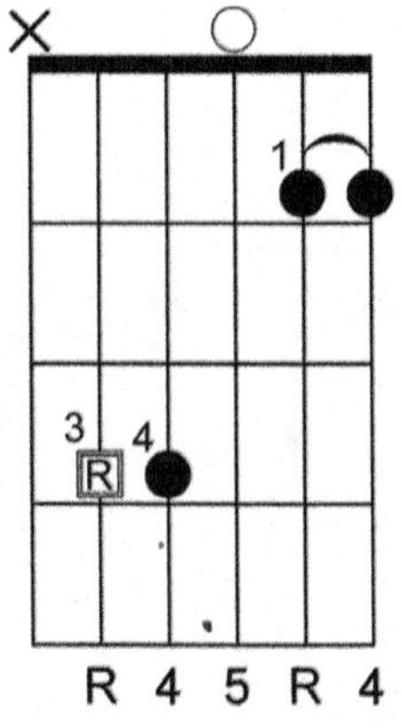

Transposable version impractical

Pattern 2

Asus⁴

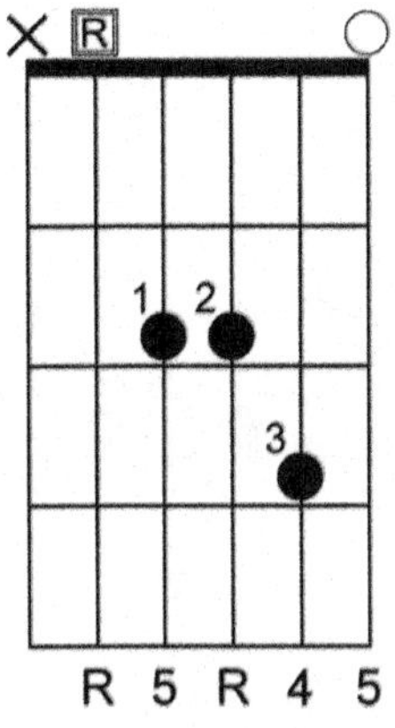

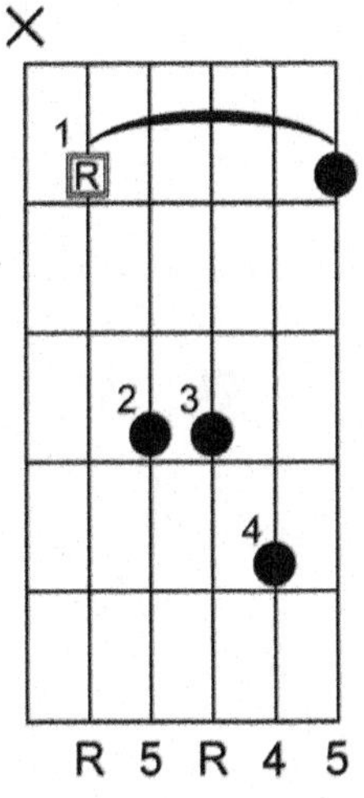

Pattern 3

Gsus4

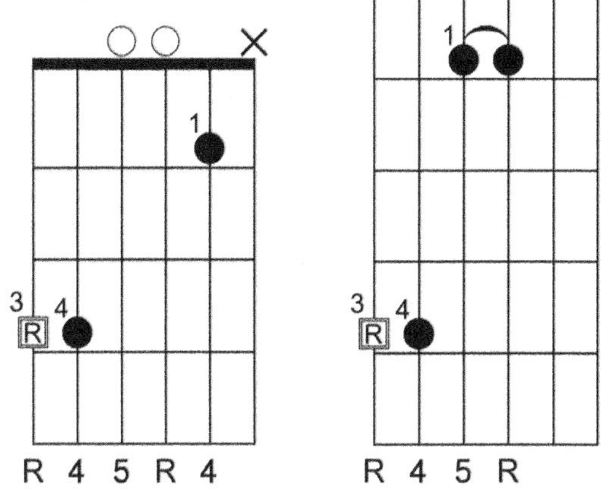

Pattern 4

Esus4

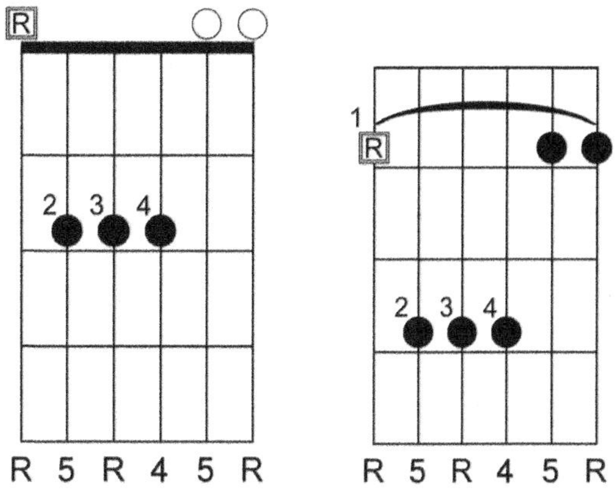

Pattern 4 (root on 4th)

Esus4

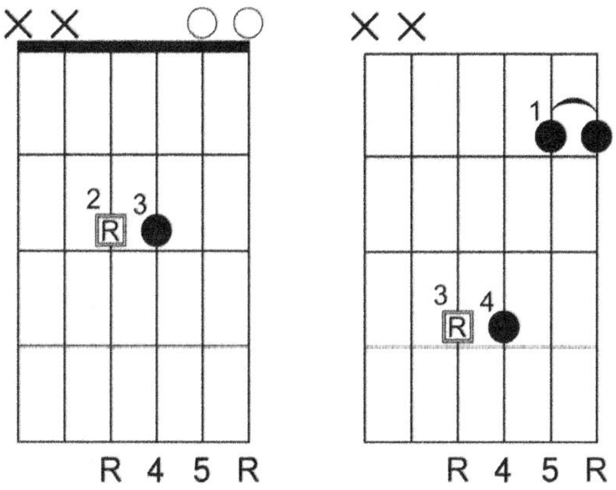

Pattern 5

Dsus4

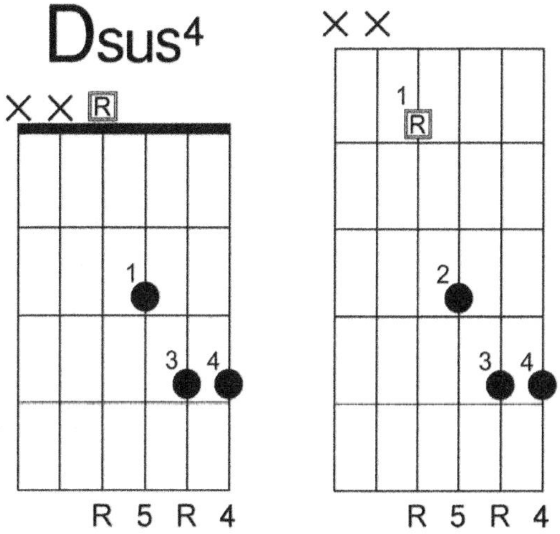

The 1st, 3rd and 4th fingers are used in the Dsus4 chord (rather than 1st, 2nd and 3rd) because often it is played in succession with a D major chord.

Suspended 2nd (R 2 5)

Pattern 1

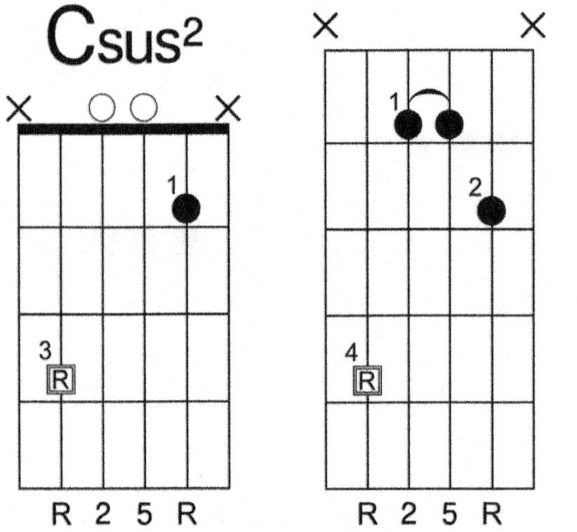

Pattern 2

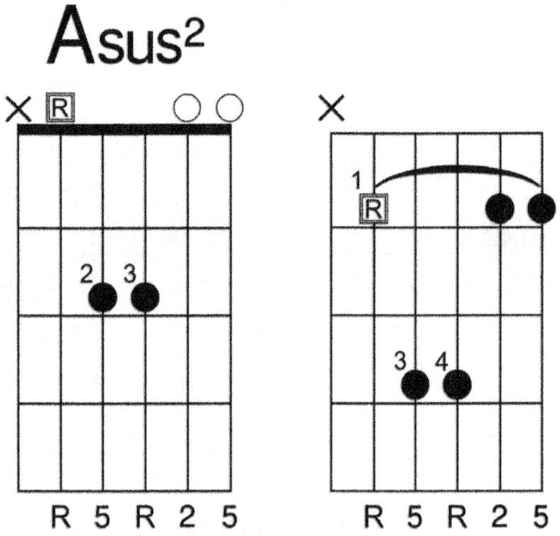

Pattern 3

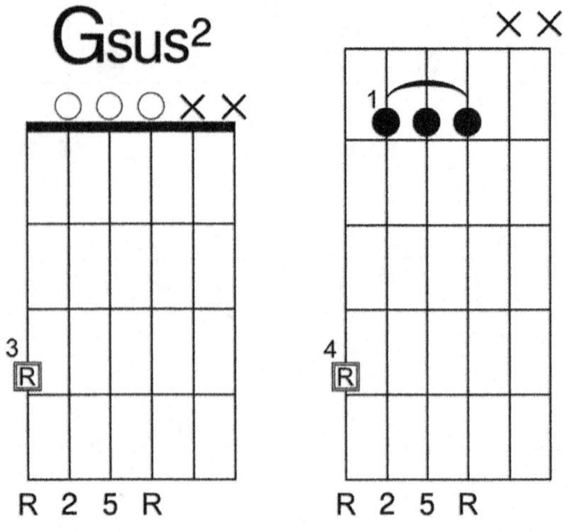

Pattern 4

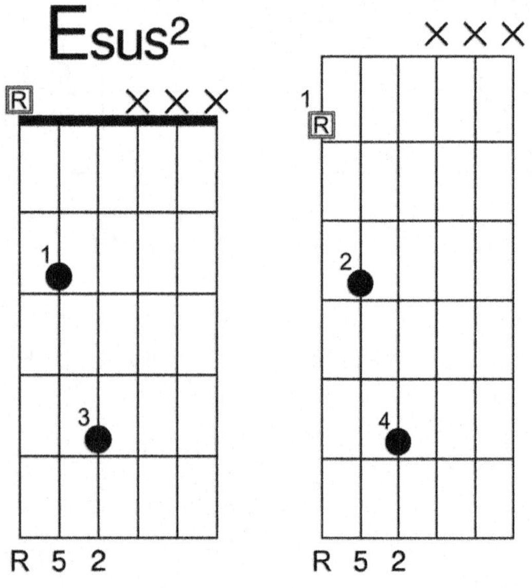

Pattern 5

Dsus2

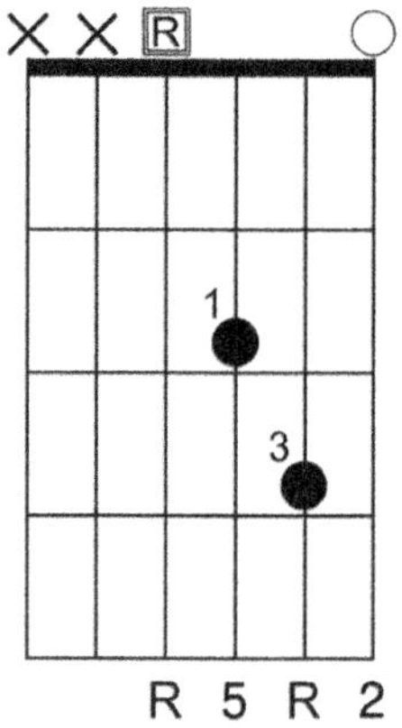

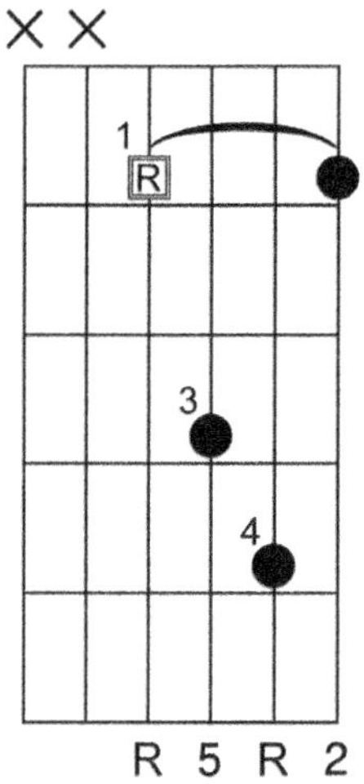

Q10) Can you work out / play Gsus4 pattern 5?

Q11) B♭sus2 pattern 4?

The 1st and 3rd fingers are used in the Dsus2 chord because often it is played in succession with a D major chord.

Power Chords (R 5)

Pattern 2

A5

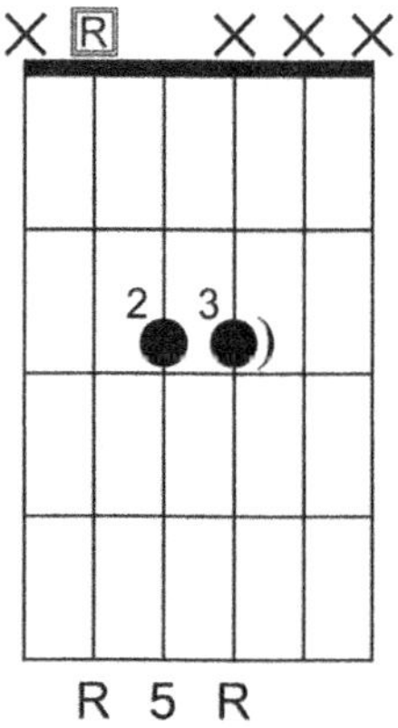

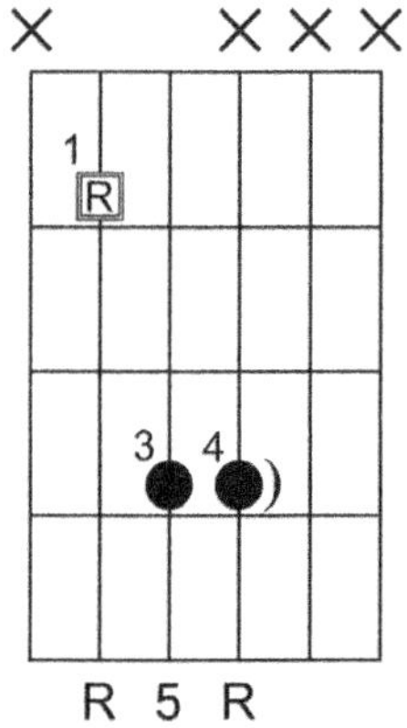

Pattern 4

E5

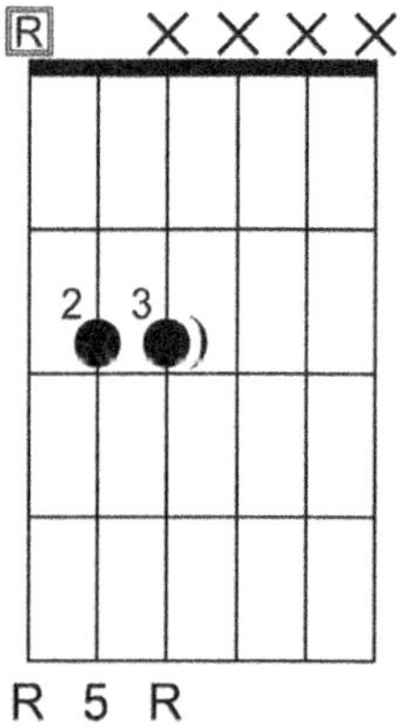

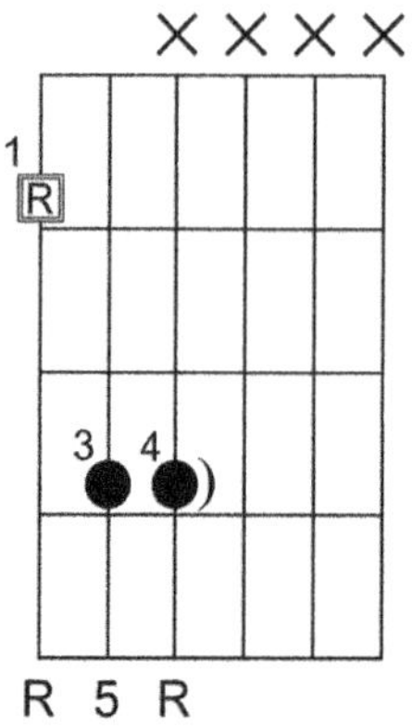

Pattern 5

D^5

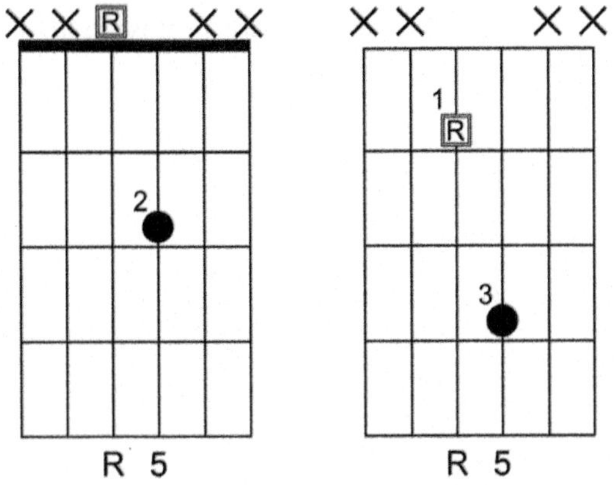

Q12) Can you work out / play F♯5 pattern 4?

Major 7th (R 3 5 7)

Pattern 1

$Cmaj^7$

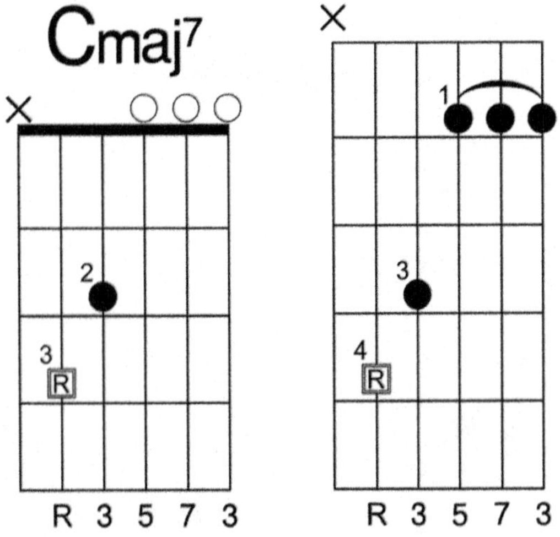

Pattern 2

$Amaj^7$

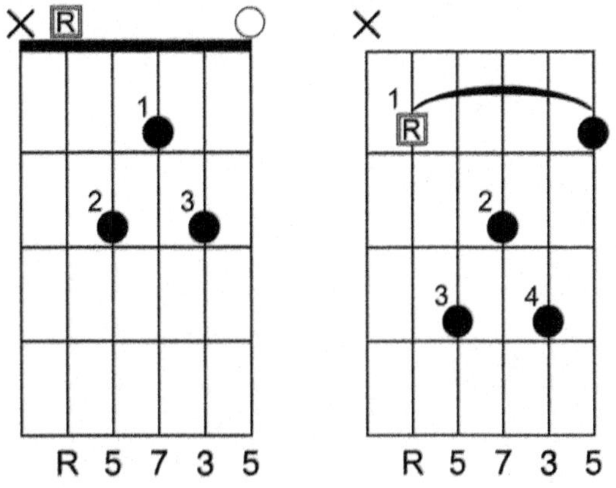

For Pattern 4 there are two different ways to play the transposable version.

Pattern 4

Emaj7

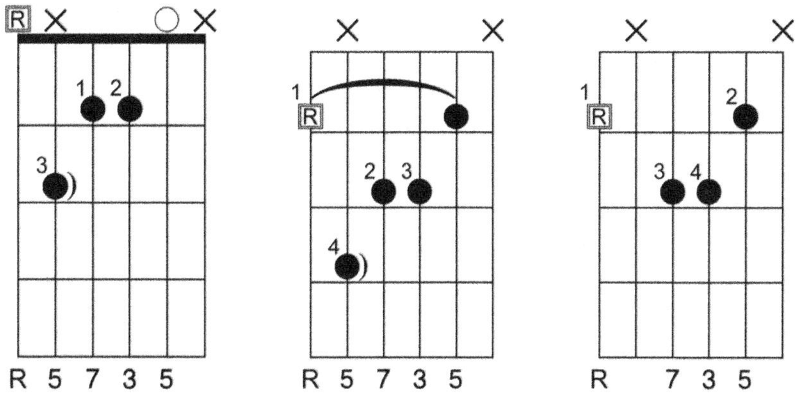

Pattern 4 (root on 4th)

No open chord version for E root

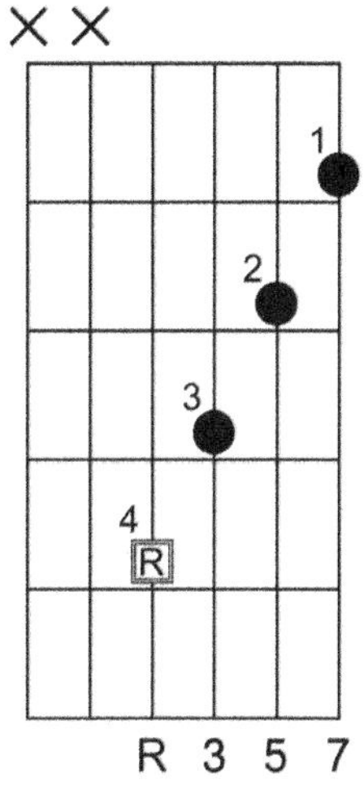

Pattern 5

Dmaj7

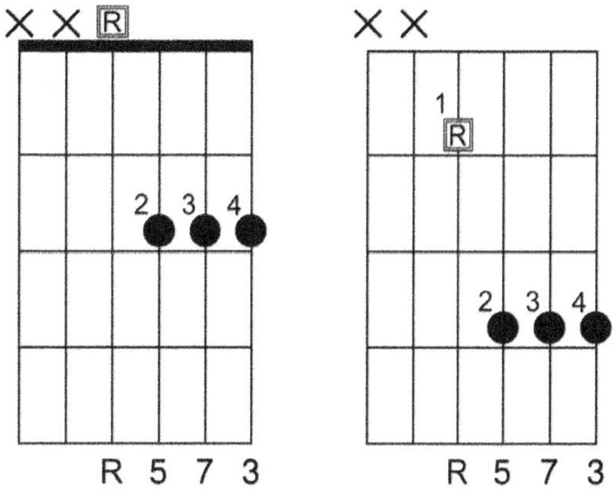

Pattern 5 could also be played with a half-barre using the 3rd finger across the 3rd, 2nd and 1st strings.

Dominant 7th (R 3 5 ♭7)

Pattern 1

C7

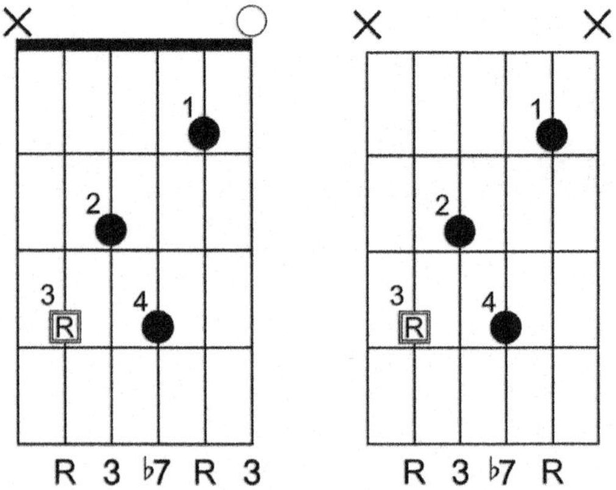

Pattern 2

A7

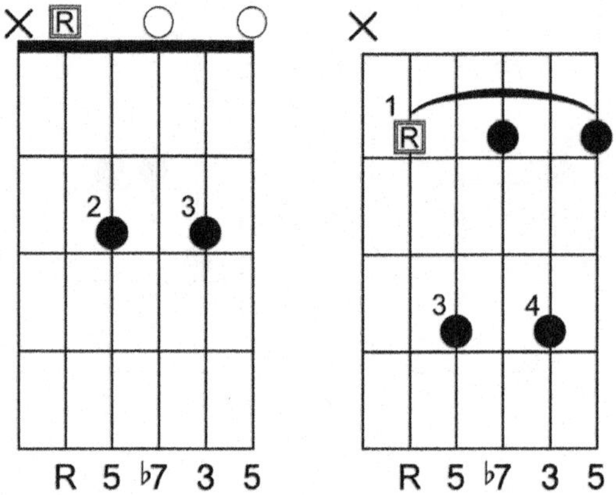

For Pattern 4, below right, if the optional note is not played then the one behind it can be used. For E7 that would be the open 2nd string and for the transposable version that would be part of barre on the 2nd string.

Pattern 3

G7

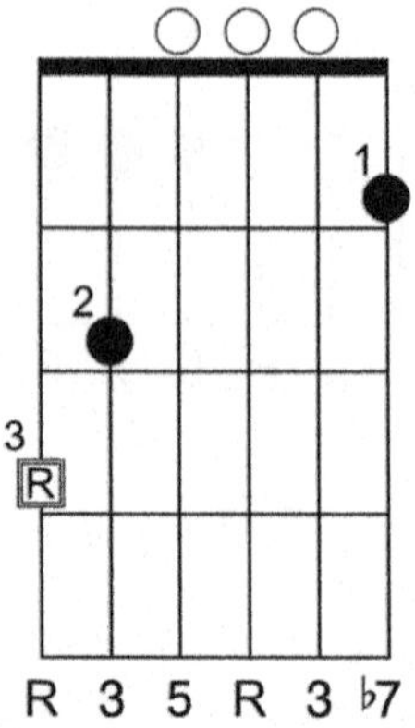

Transposable version impractical

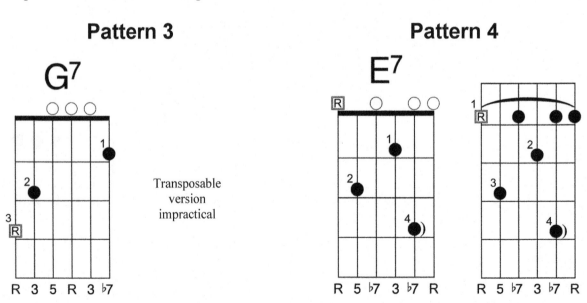

Pattern 4

E7

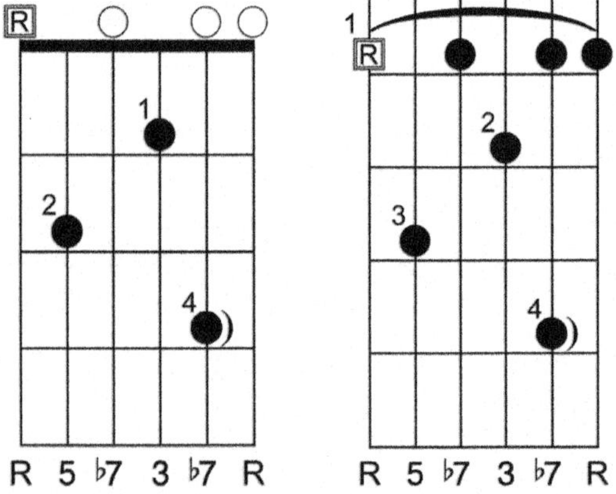

Pattern 5

D7

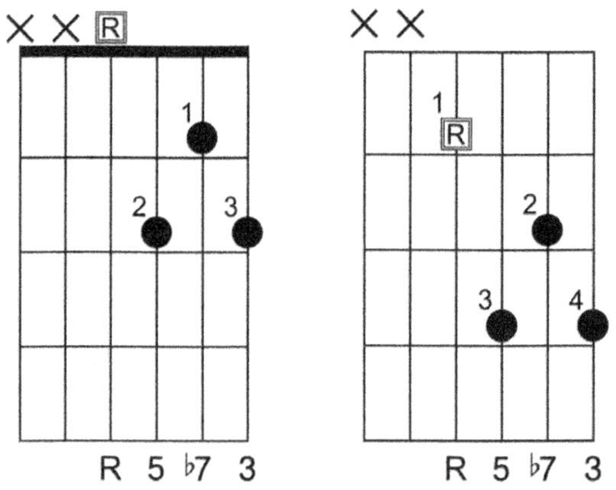

Q13) Can you work out / play Fmaj7 pattern 4 (root on 4th)?

Q14) C7 pattern 5?

Minor 7th (R ♭3 5 ♭7)

Pattern 2

Am7

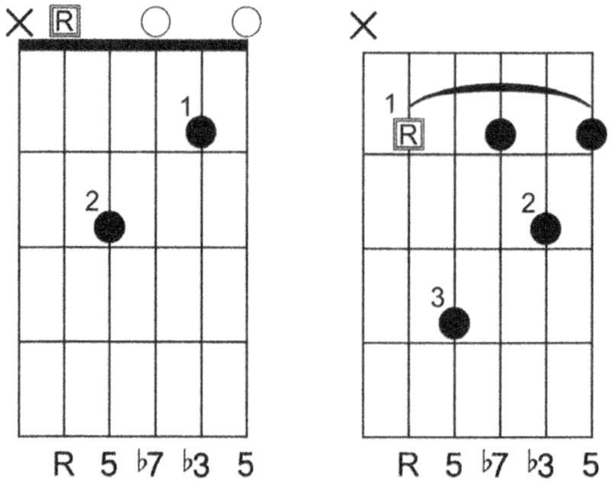

Pattern 4

Em7

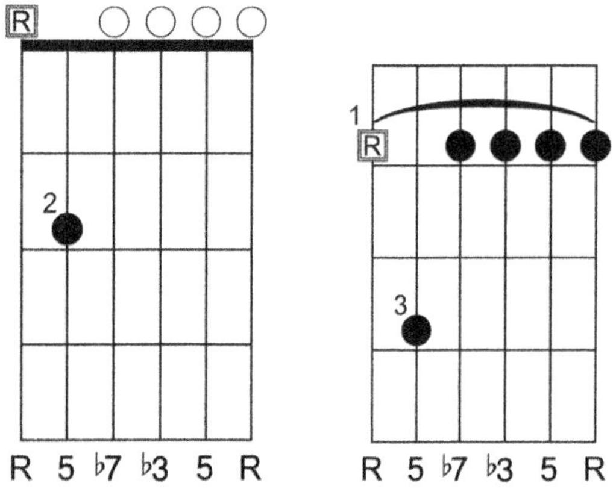

Below left is a Jazz version for pattern 4. Its transposable version could also be played with a 1st finger barre.

Pattern 4

Em7

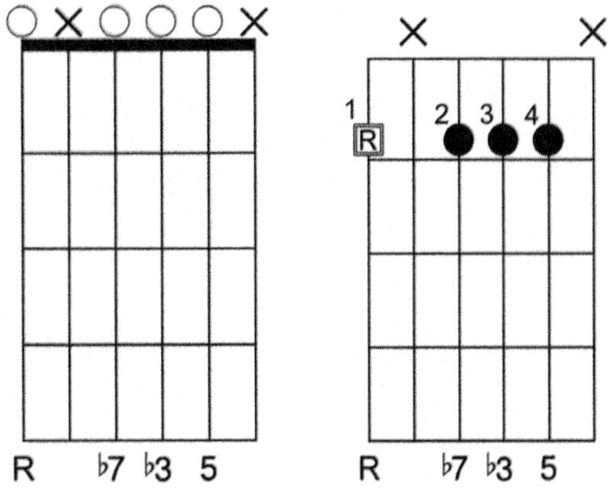

Pattern 5

Dm7

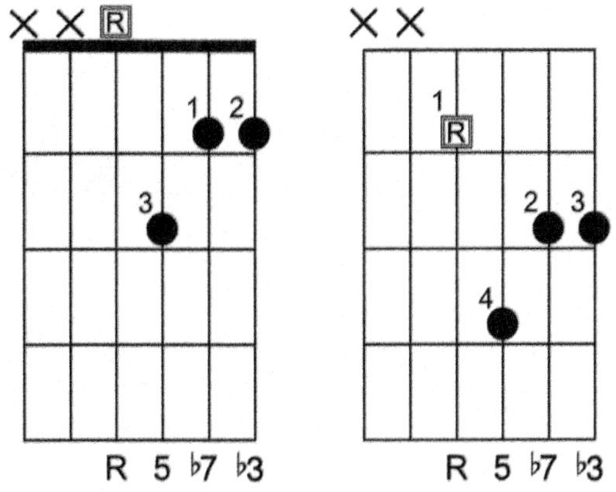

Minor 7th ♭5 (R ♭3 ♭5 ♭7)

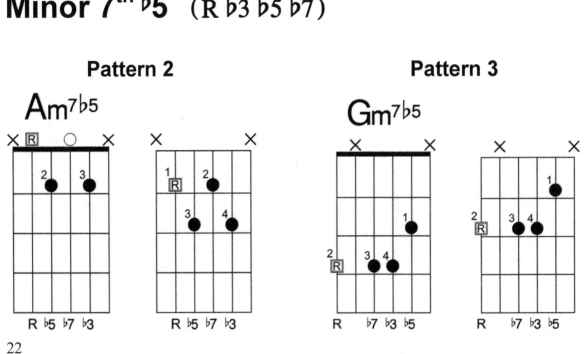

Pattern 2

Am7♭5

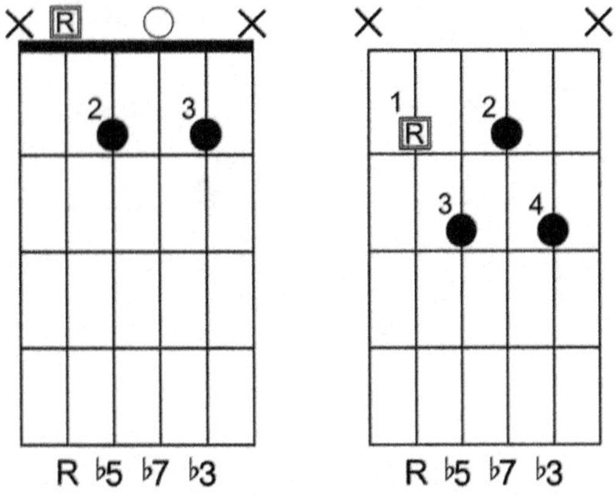

Pattern 3

Gm7♭5

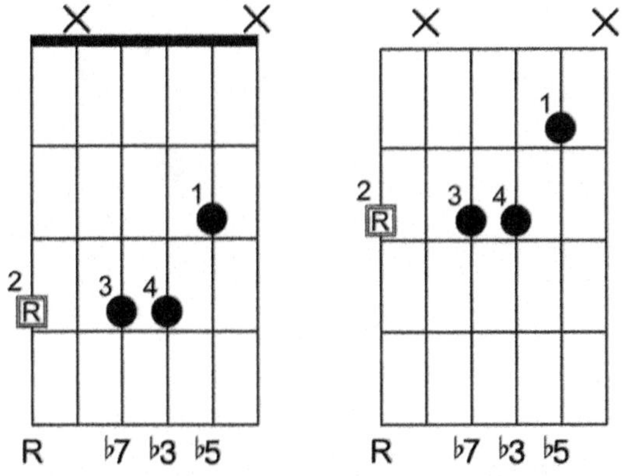

Pattern 4

$\mathrm{Em}^{7\flat 5}$

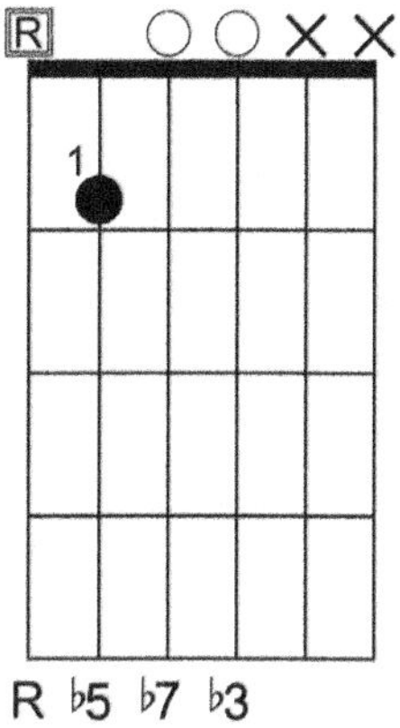

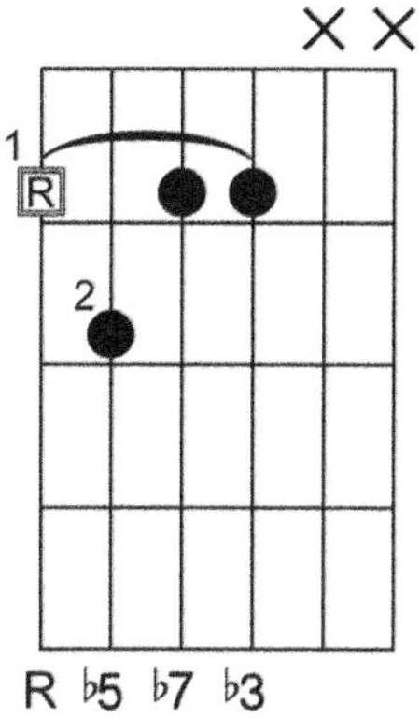

Pattern 5

$\mathrm{Dm}^{7\flat 5}$

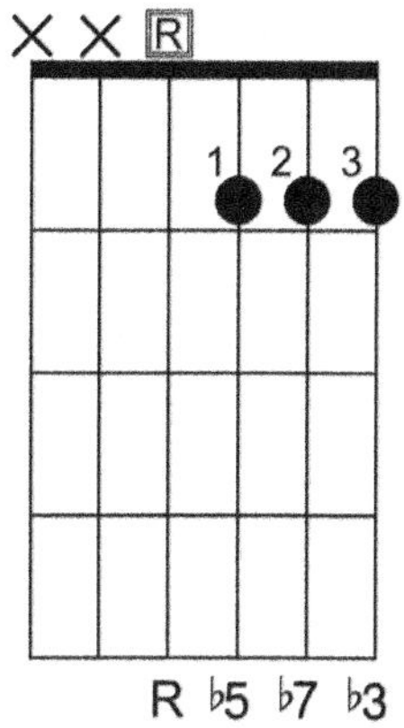

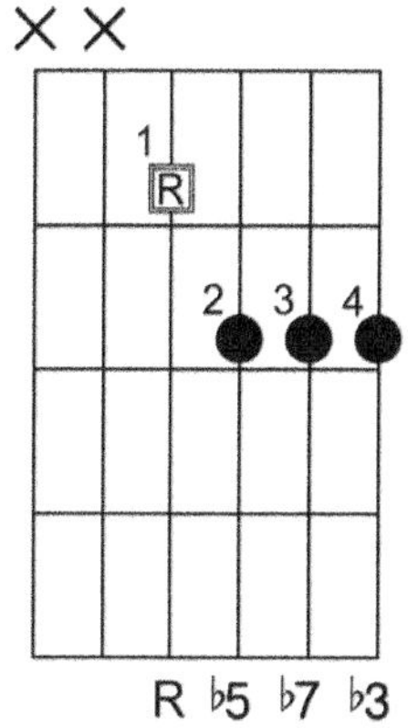

Pattern 5 could also be played with a partial-barre.

Major 9th (R 3 5 7 9)

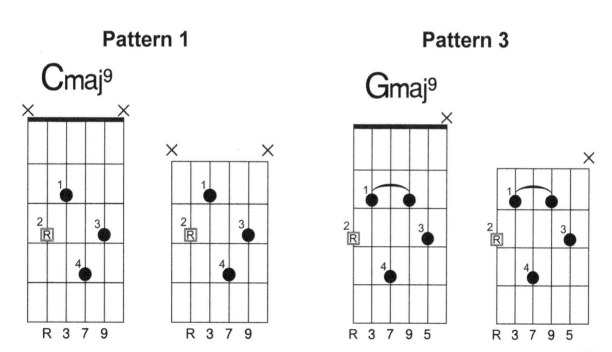

Pattern 1

Cmaj^{9}

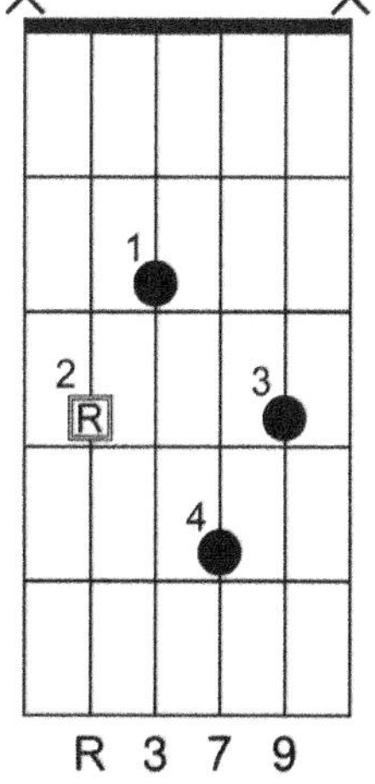

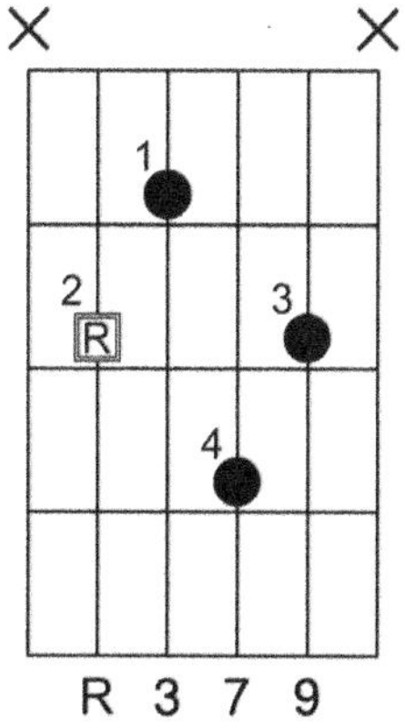

Pattern 3

Gmaj^{9}

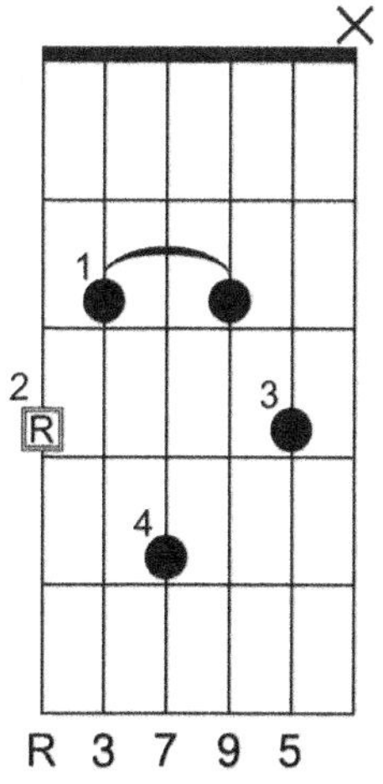

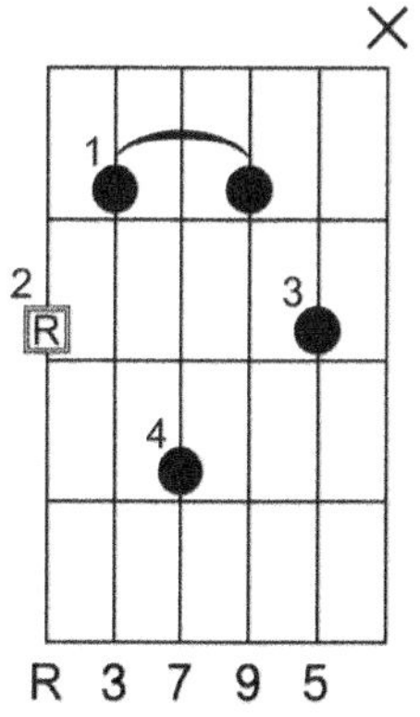

Below left is an easier version for pattern 3 with the 5th interval omitted. Pattern 5 to the right is tricky because of how far the 4th finger needs to stretch; therefore it will be easier further up the fret-board where the frets are closer together.

Pattern 5

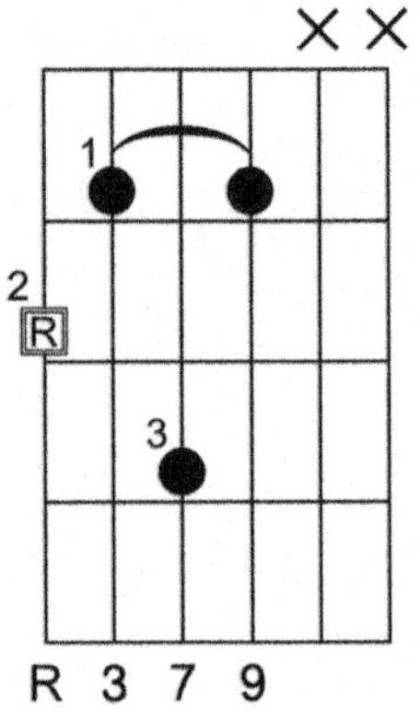

No open chord version for D root

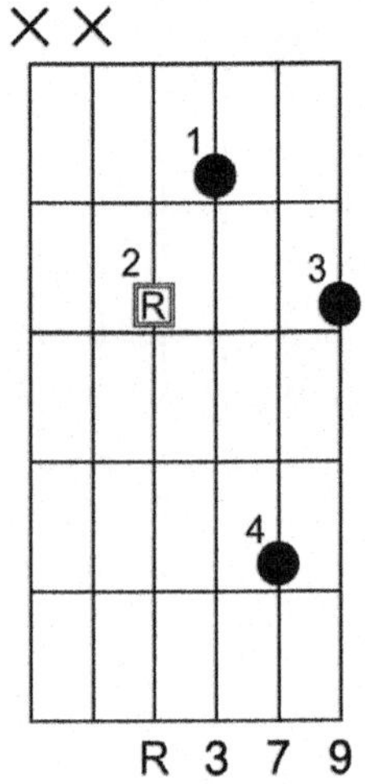

Dominant 9th (R 3 5 ♭7 9)

Pattern 1

C9

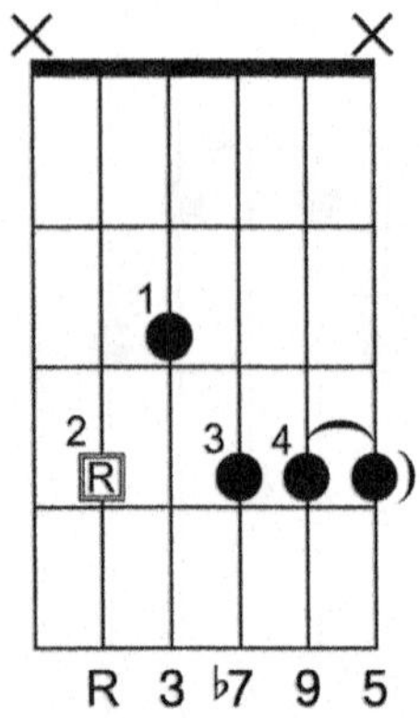

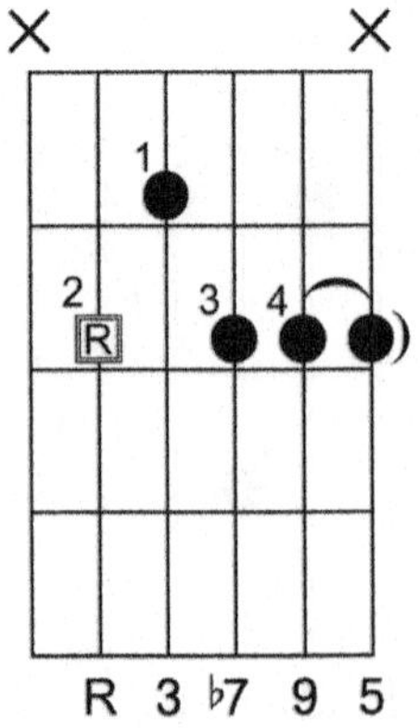

Pattern 3

G9

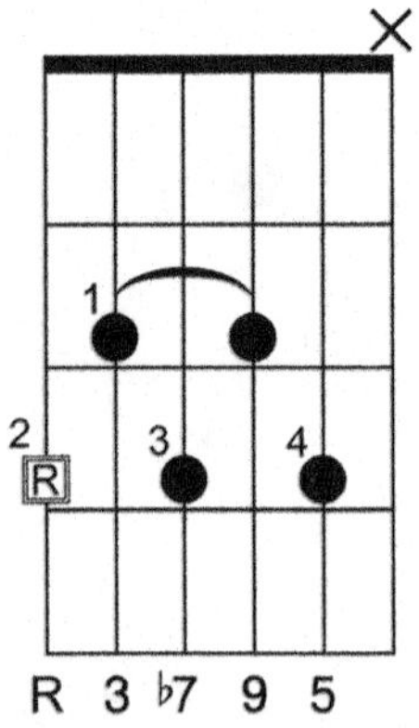

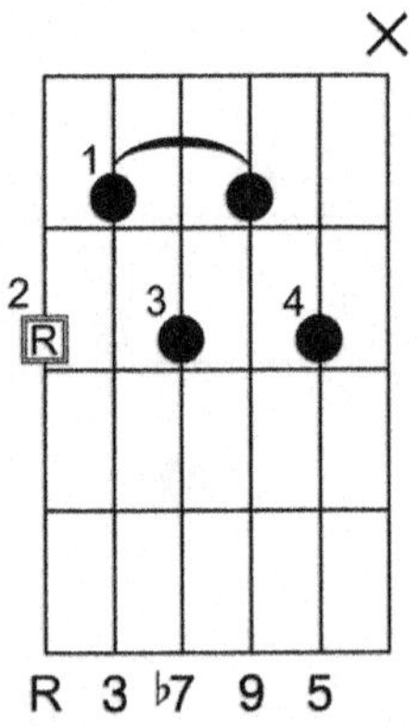

Pattern 4 (root on 4th)

E9

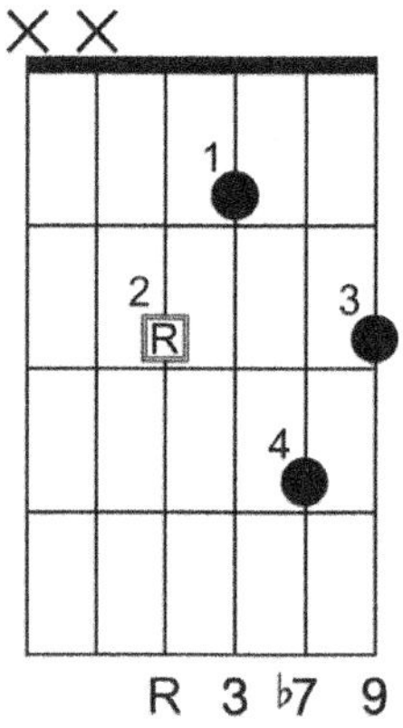

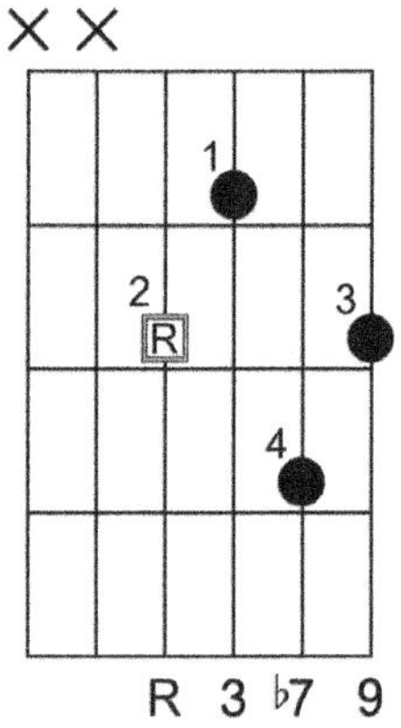

Q15) Can you work out / play D♭m7 pattern 2?

Q16) Am7♭5 pattern 3?

Q17) Emaj9 pattern 1?

Q18) G♯9 pattern 4 (root on 4th)?

Minor 9th (R ♭3 5 ♭7 9)

Pattern 1

Cm9

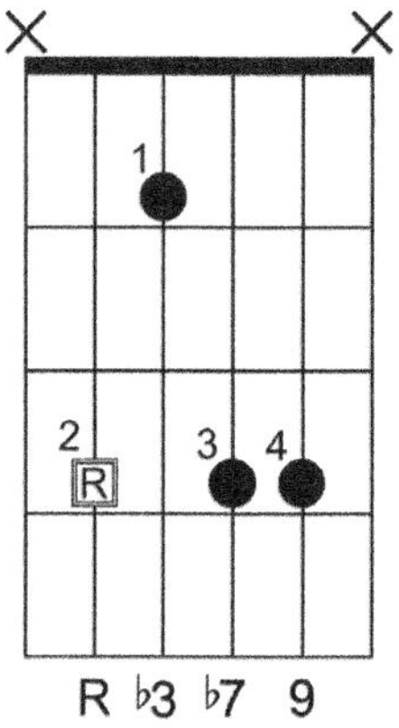

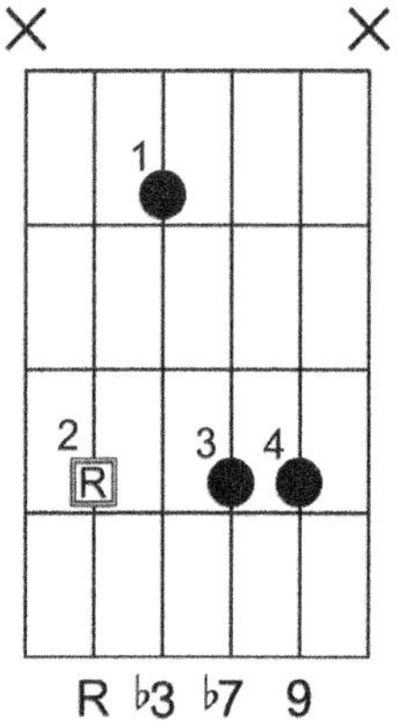

Pattern 4

Em9

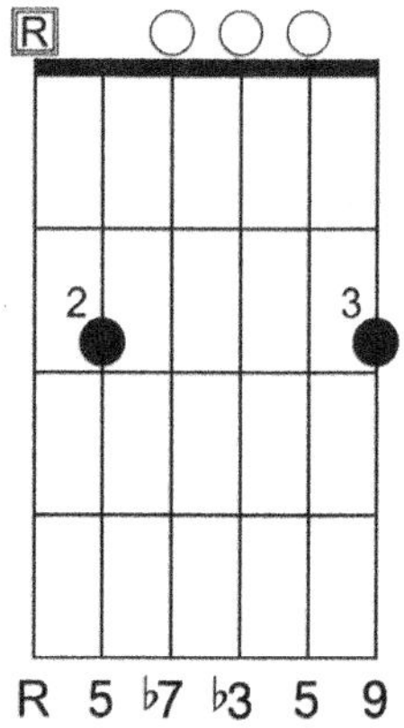

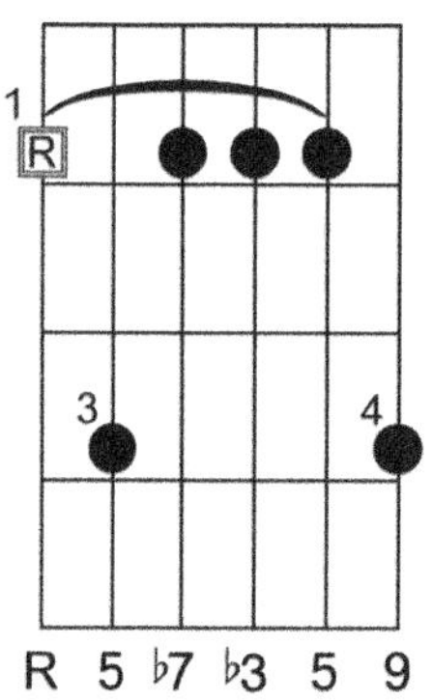

Pattern 4 (root on 4th)

Em9

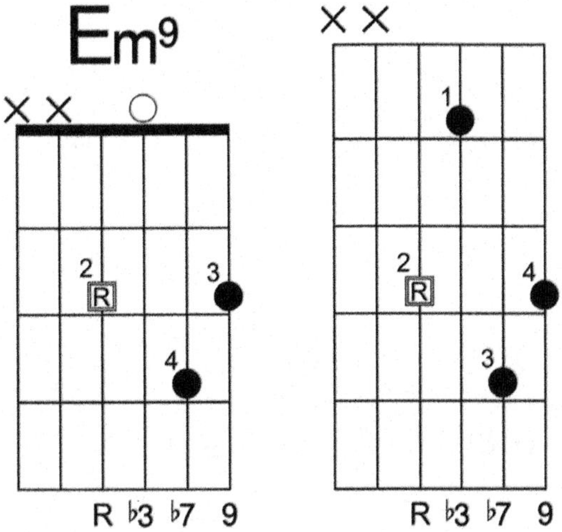

Q19) Can you work out / play Dm9 pattern 1?

Dominant 11th (R 3 5 ♭7 9 11)

Pattern 1

C11

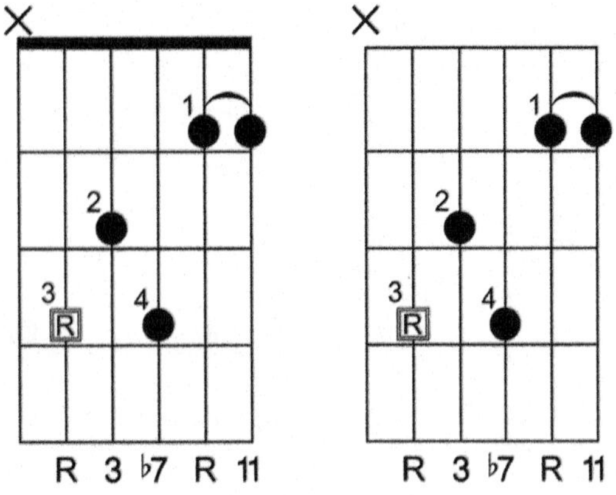

Pattern 2

A11

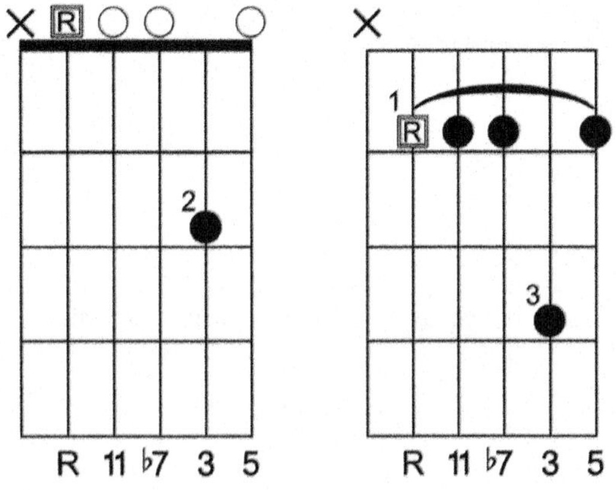

Pattern 3

G^{11}

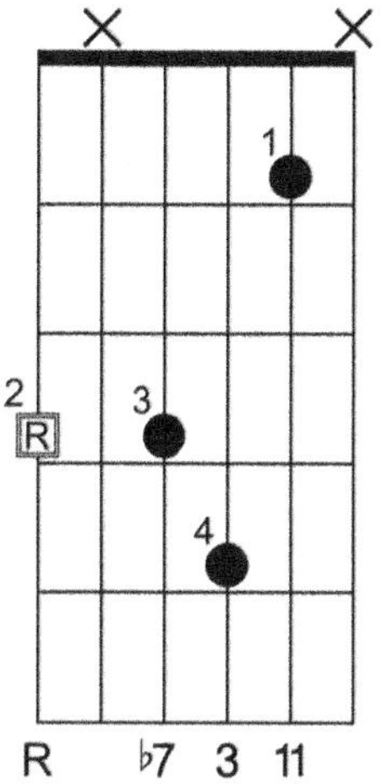

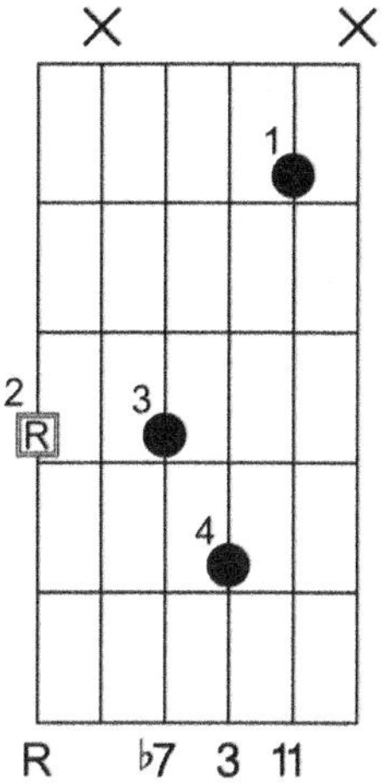

Q20) Can you work out / play E♭11 pattern 1?

Minor 11th (R ♭3 5 ♭7 9 11)

Pattern 1

Cm^{11}

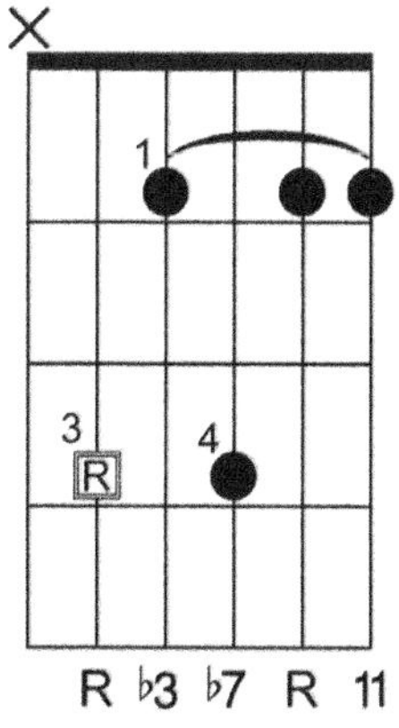

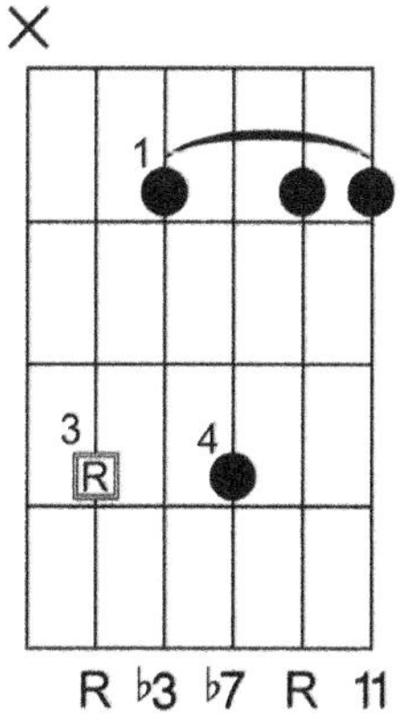

Pattern 2

Am^{11}

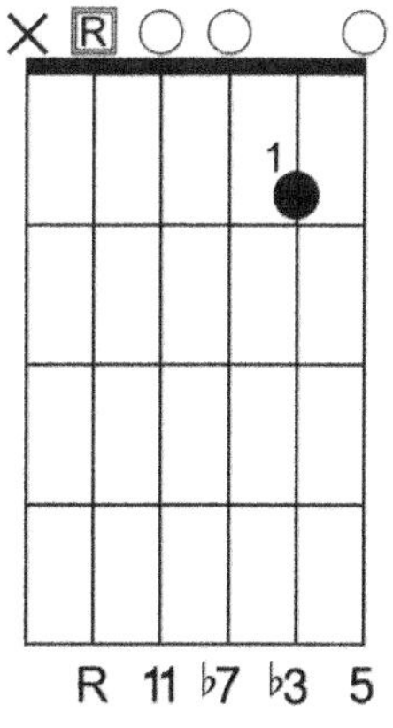

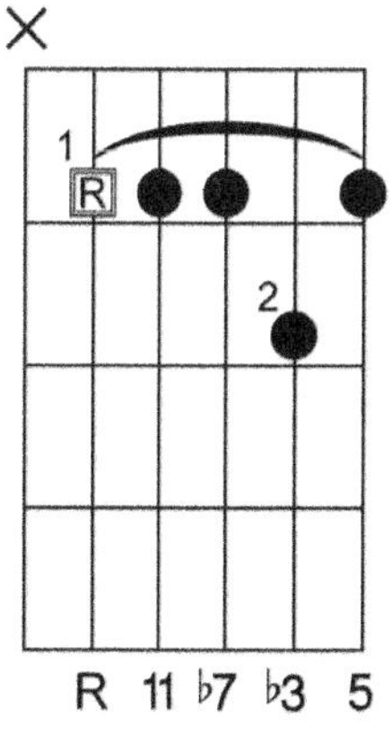

Pattern 3

Gm11

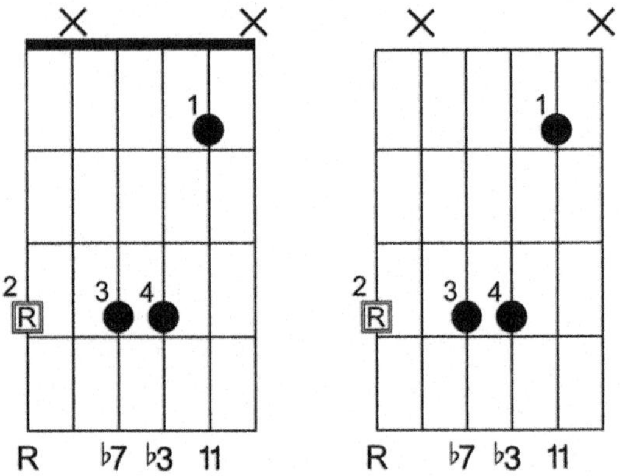

Q21) Can you work out / play Am11 pattern 3?

Major 13th (R 3 5 7 9 11 13)

Pattern 1

Cmaj13

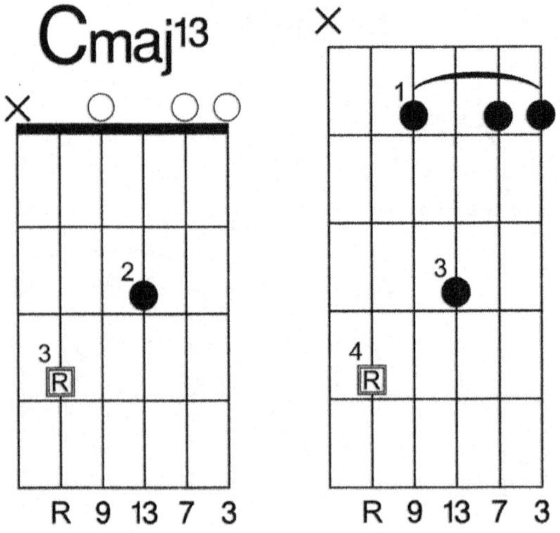

Pattern 2

Amaj13

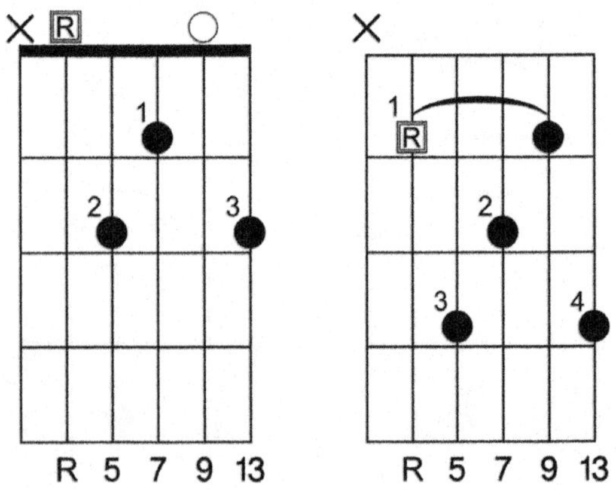

Pattern 3

Gmaj13

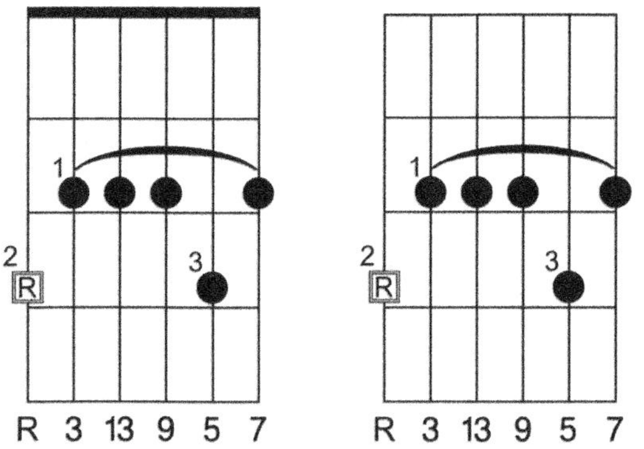

Pattern 4

Emaj13

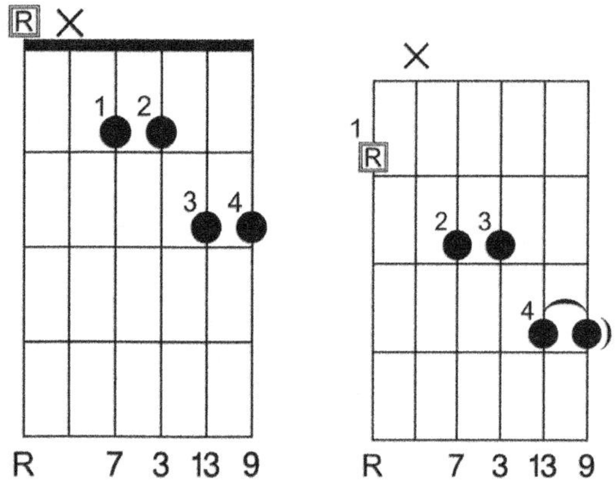

Dominant 13th (R 3 5 ♭7 9 11 13)

Pattern 1

C13

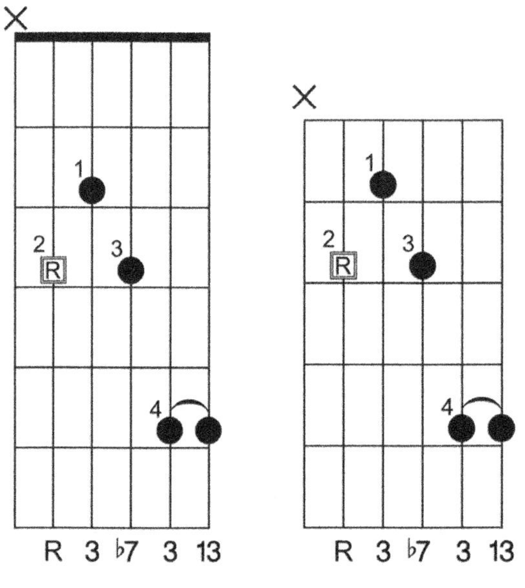

A different fingering for Pattern 1

C13

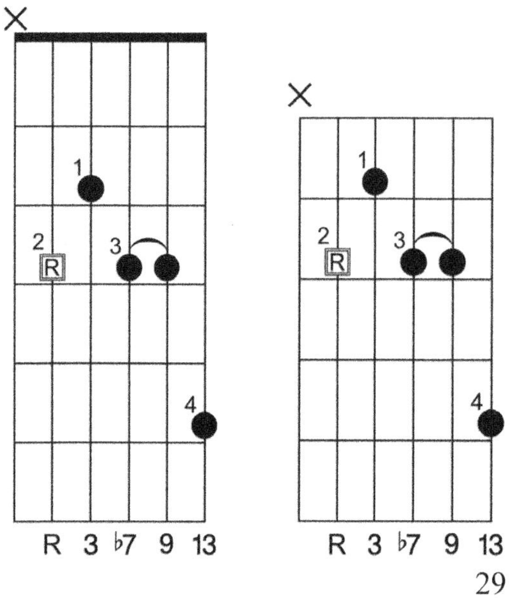

Pattern 2

A13

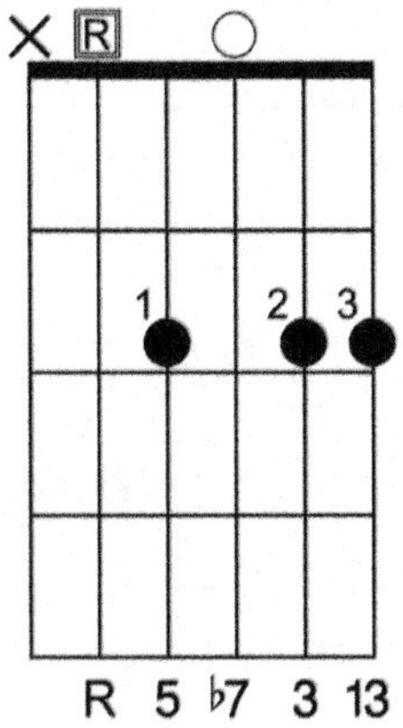

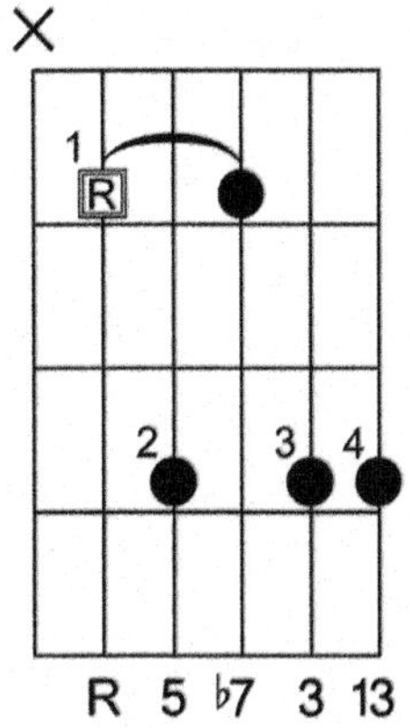

Pattern 3

G13

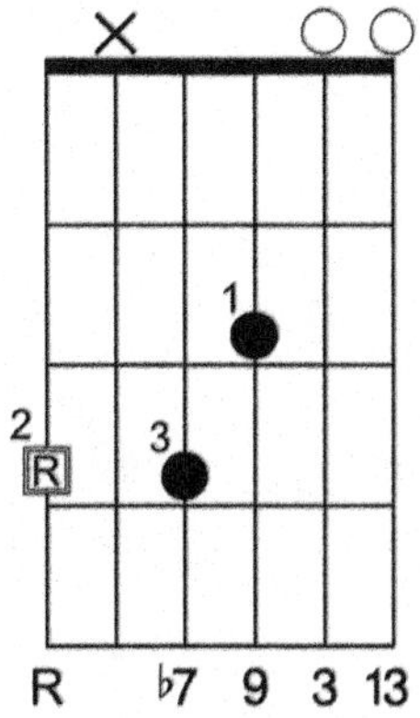

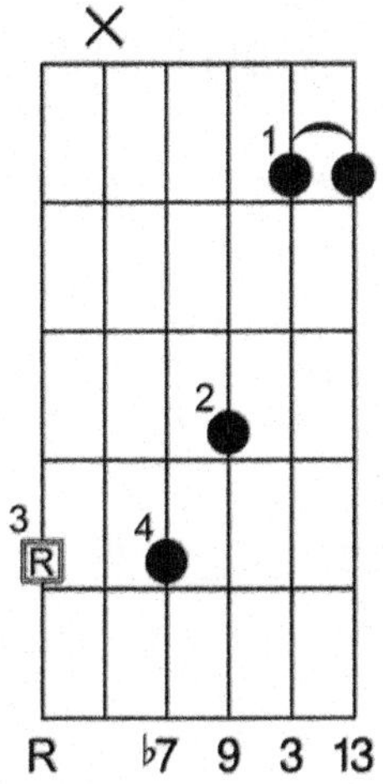

Pattern 4

E13

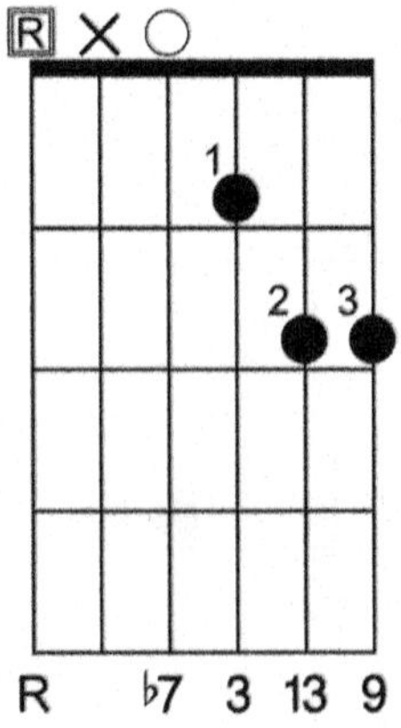

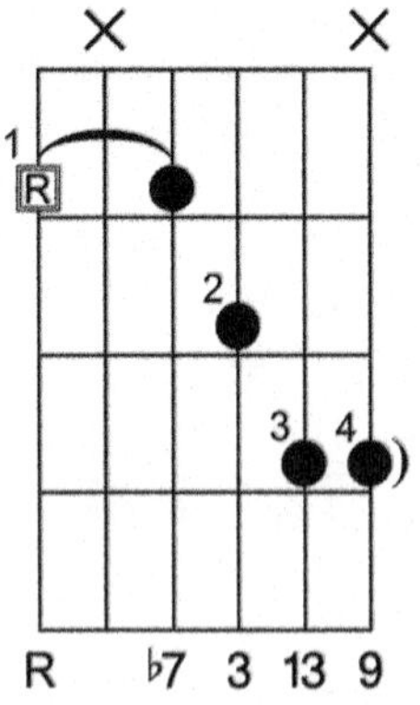

A different fingering for Pattern 4

E13

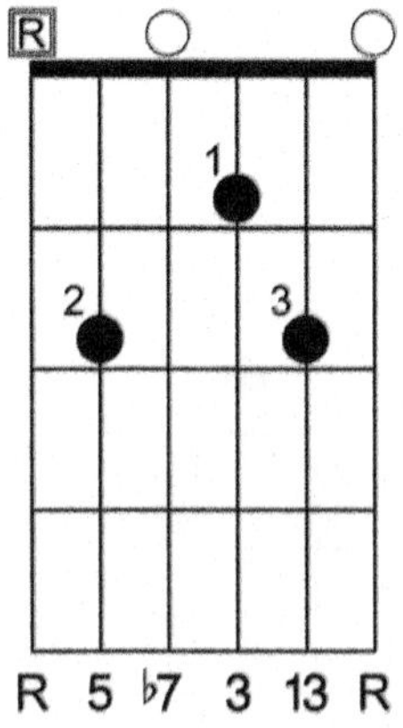

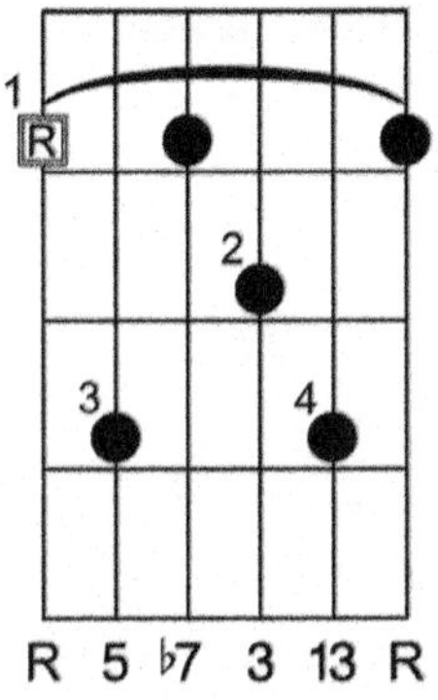

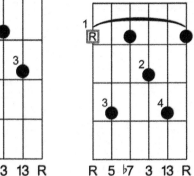

Minor 13th (R ♭3 5 ♭7 9 11 13)

Pattern 2

Am13

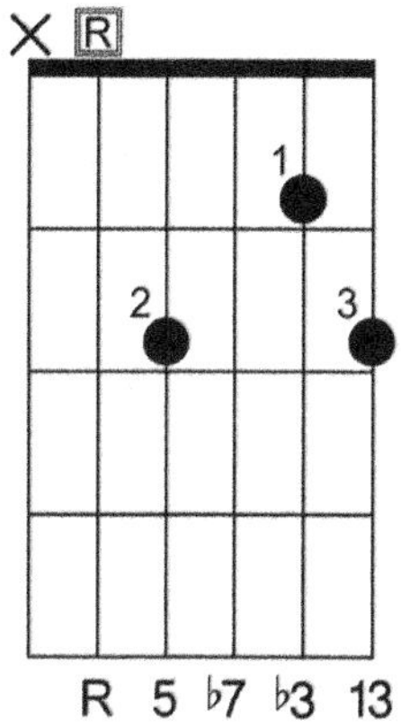

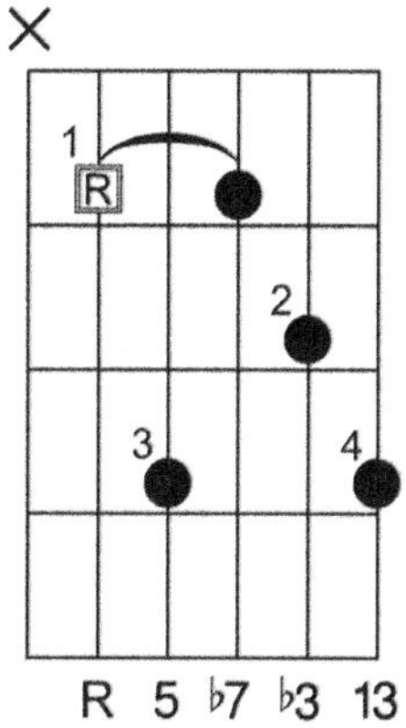

Pattern 3

Gm13

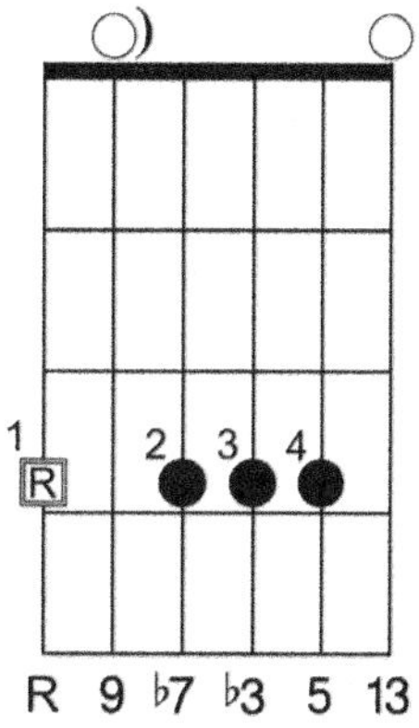

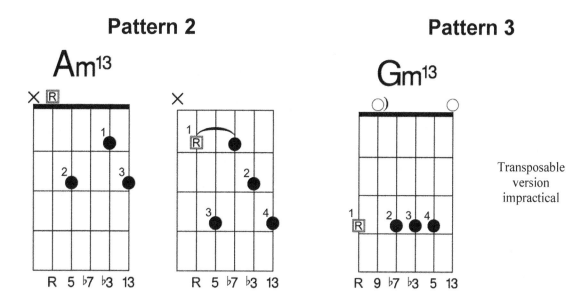

Transposable version impractical

Pattern 4

Em13

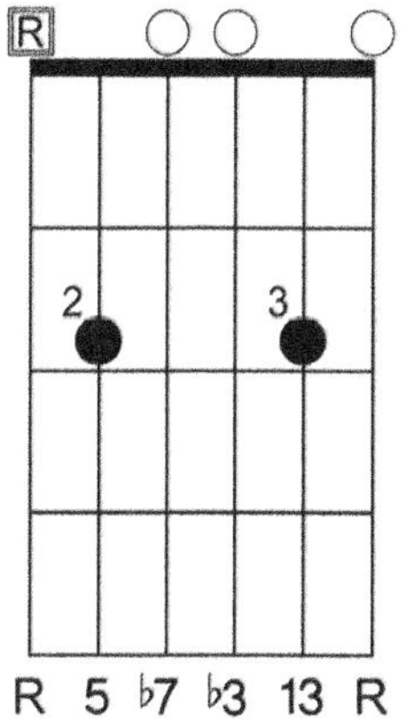

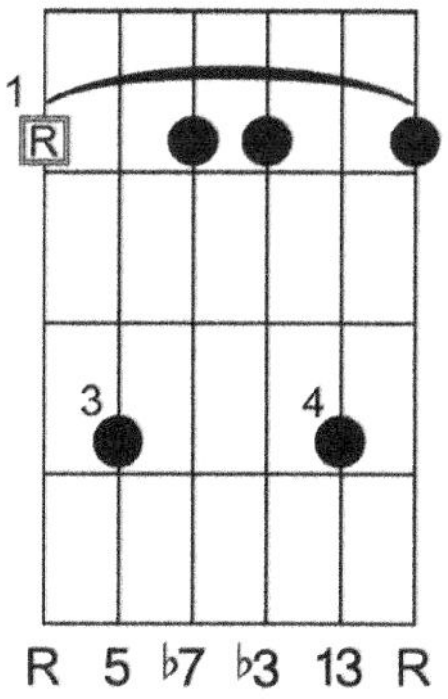

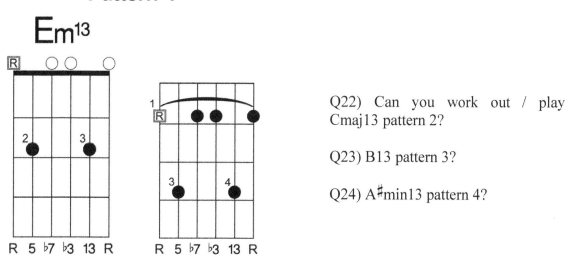

Q22) Can you work out / play Cmaj13 pattern 2?

Q23) B13 pattern 3?

Q24) A♯min13 pattern 4?

Major 7th #5 (R 3 #5 7)

Pattern 1

Cmaj7#5

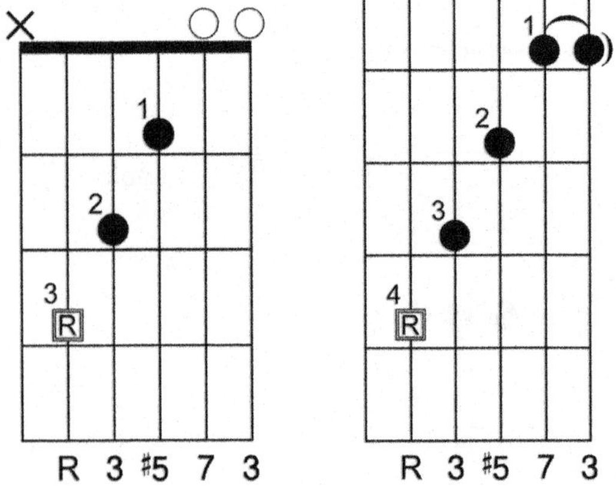

Pattern 2

Amaj7#5

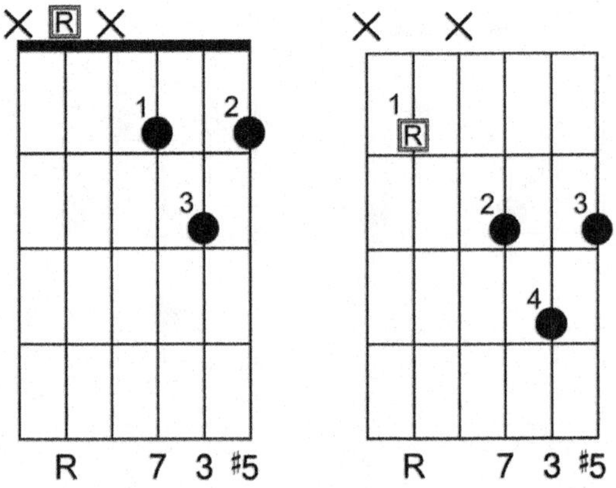

Pattern 4

Emaj7#5

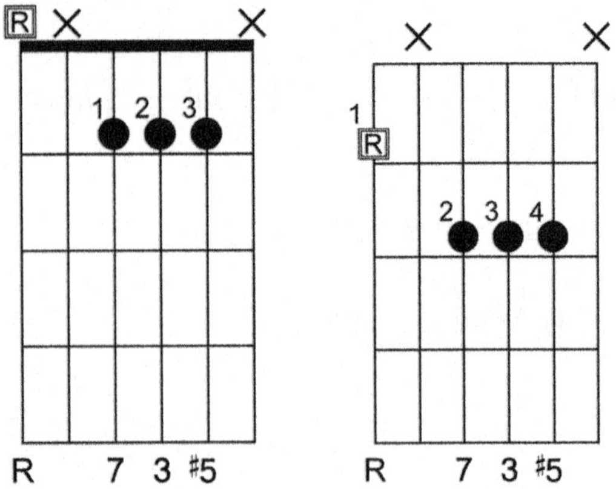

Q25) Can you work out / play C#maj7#5 pattern 1?

Major 7♯11 (R 3 5 7 ♯11) & Major 7♭5 (R 3 ♭5 7)

The difference between these two chords is that major 7th ♯11 has a 5th whereas major 7th ♭5 does not. Otherwise they are similar because although the ♭5 is a *simple interval* and ♯11 is a *compound interval*, they can be played in each other's place (simple and compound intervals are explained on pages 62-67, and playing them in each other's place explained on page 72).

The chord to the left can only be a major 7th ♯11 as it has both a 5th and ♯11 within it. The 5th can be omitted from the maj7♯11 for easier fingering; doing so will make it identical to maj7♭5. In such a case, whether the chord is a maj7♯11 or a maj7♭5 depends on the musical piece in which it is being used and therefore what name it is given.

The following chords are named maj7♭5 but could be maj7♯11 by regarding the ♭5 as ♯11.

Pattern 1

Cmaj7♯11

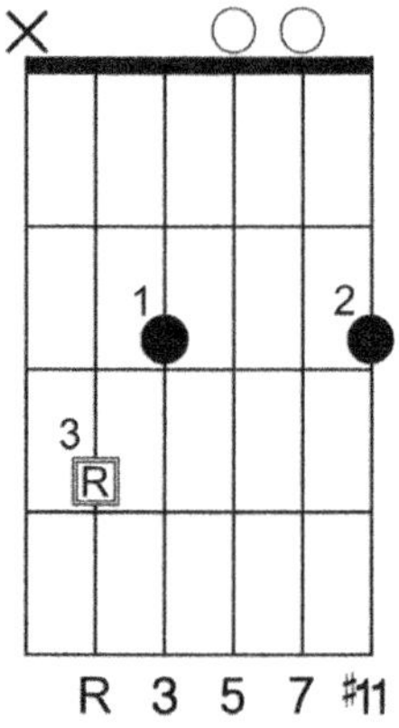

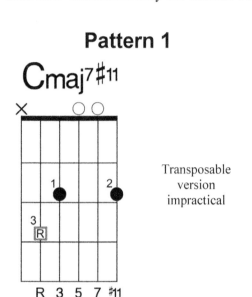

Transposable version impractical

Pattern 1

Cmaj7♭5

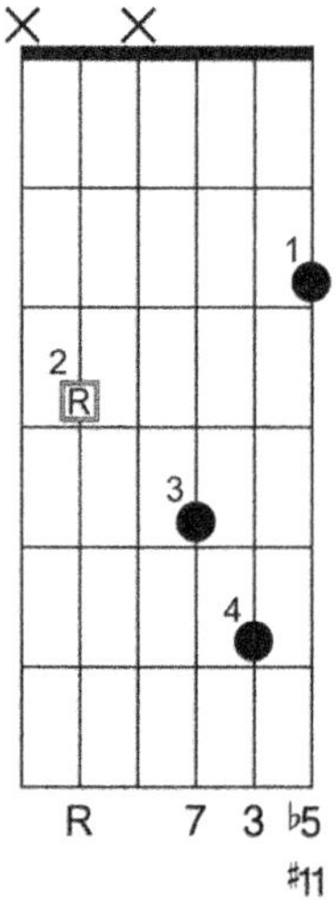

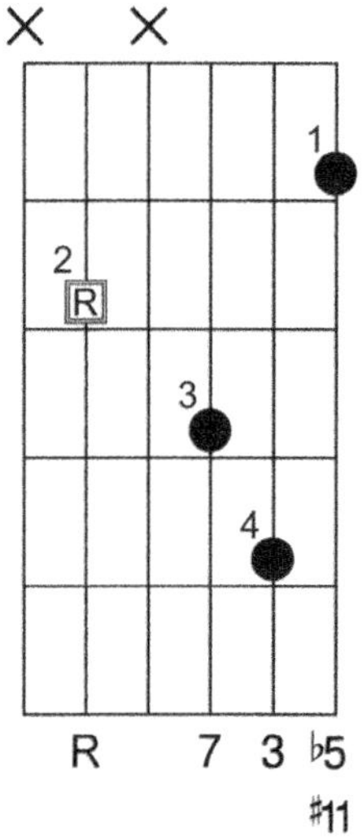

Pattern 2

Amaj7♭5

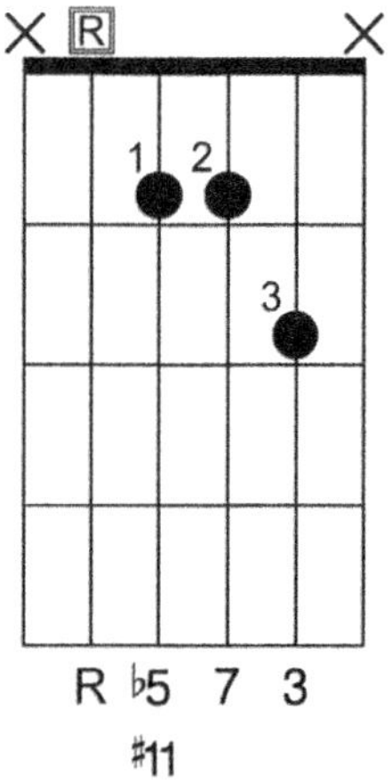

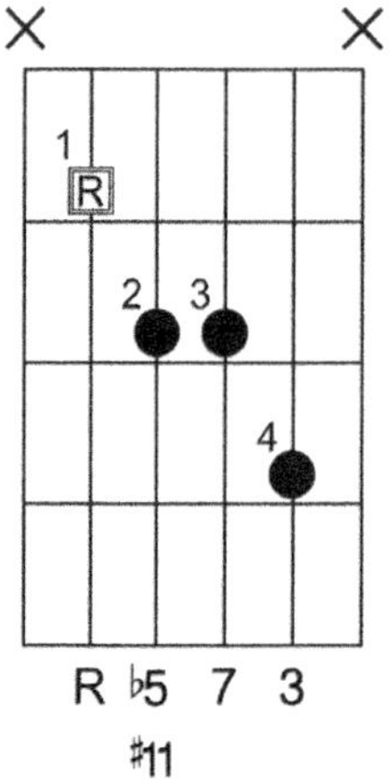

Pattern 3

Gmaj7♭5

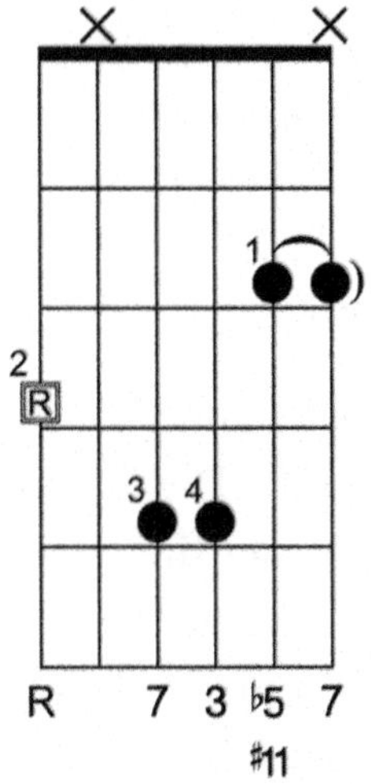

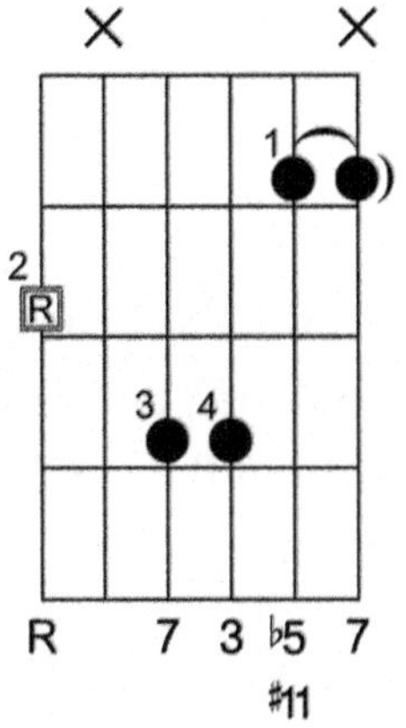

Pattern 4 (root on 4th)

No open chord version for E root

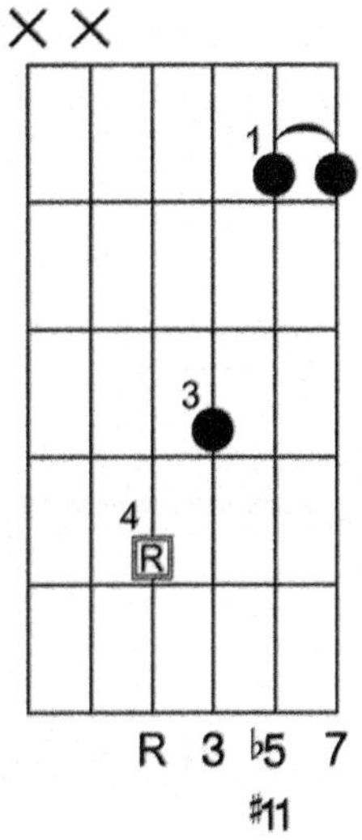

Pattern 5

Dmaj7♭5

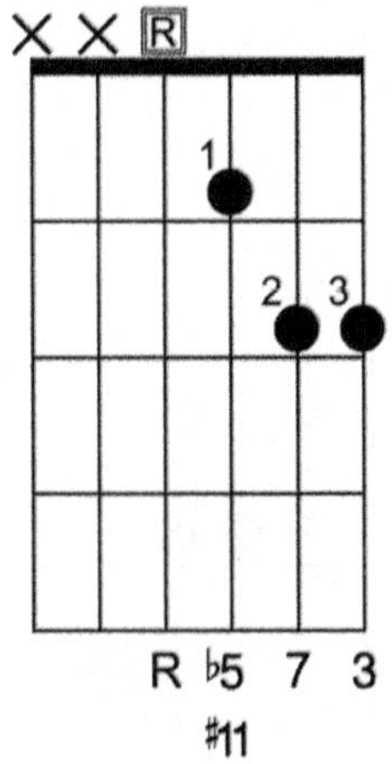

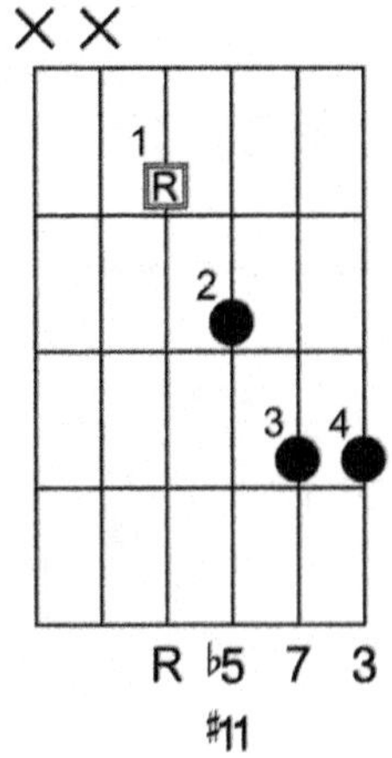

Q26) Can you work out / play Dmaj7♭5 pattern 2?

Dominant 7th #5 (R 3 #5 b7)

For Pattern 2 there are two different ways to play the transposable version.

Pattern 2

A7#5

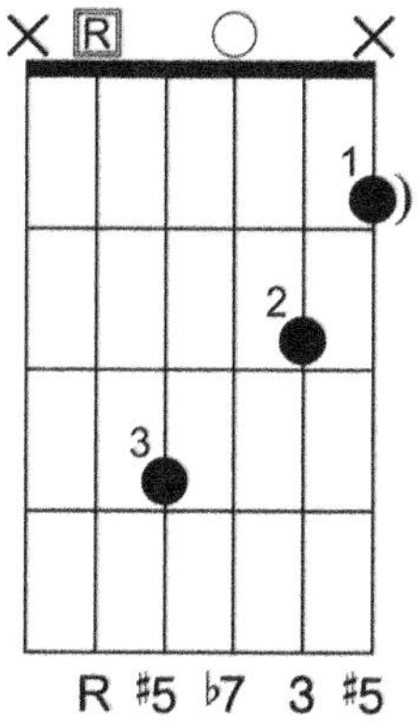

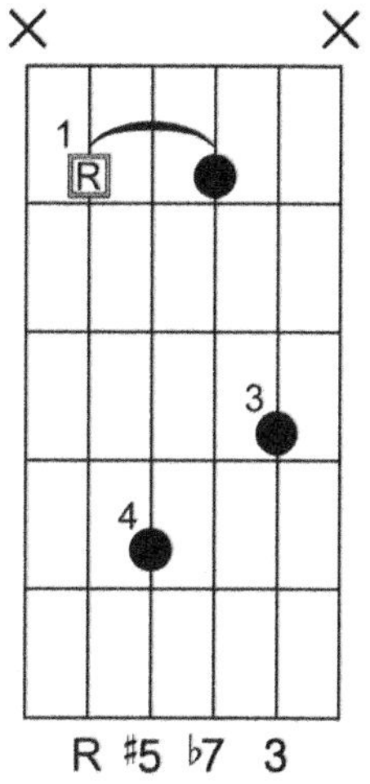

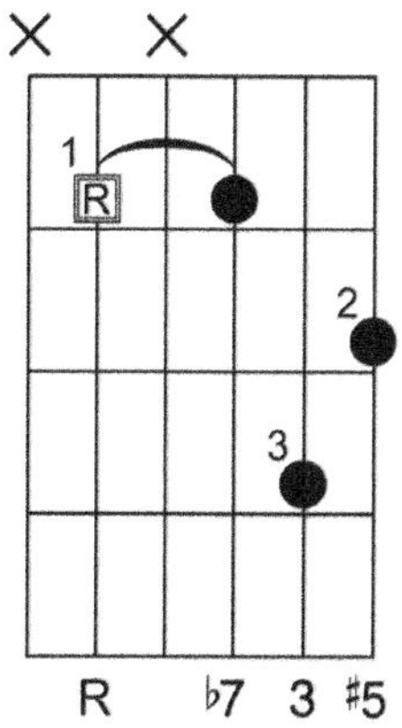

Pattern 4

E7#5

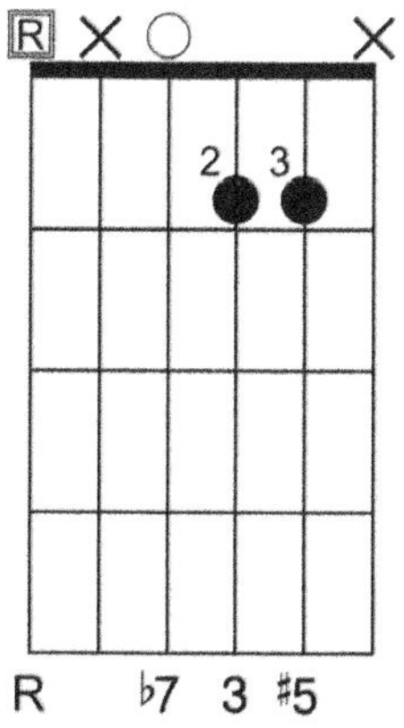

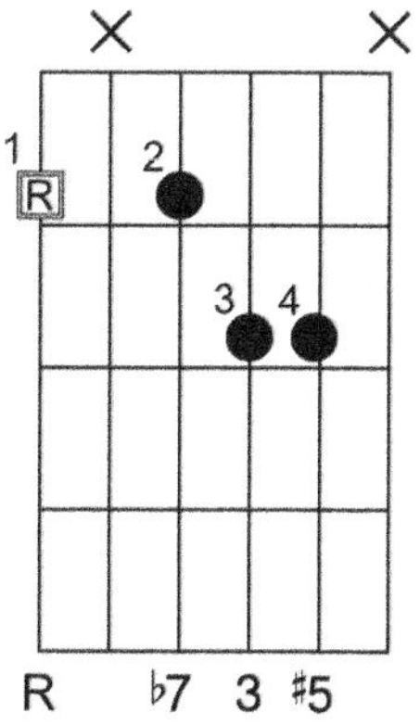

Pattern 5

D7#5

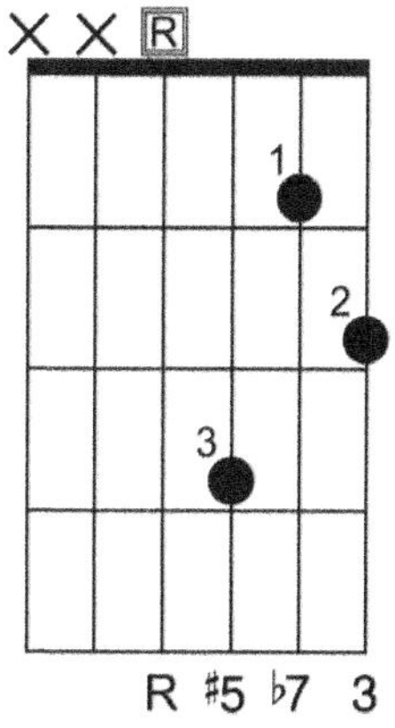

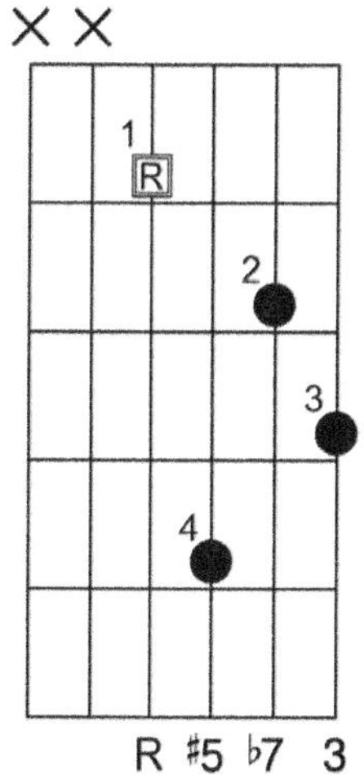

Dom 7♯11 (R 3 5 ♭7 ♯11) & Dom 7♭5 (R 3 ♭5 ♭7)

The difference between these two chords is that Dominant 7th ♯11 has a 5th whereas Dominant 7th ♭5 does not. Otherwise they are similar because the ♭5 and ♯11 can be played in each other's place.

The 5th can be omitted from the Dom7♯11 for easier fingering; doing so will make it identical to Dom7♭5. In such a case, whether the chord is a Dom7♯11 or a Dom7♭5 will depend on the musical piece in which it is being used and therefore what name it is given.

Therefore the following chords are named Dom7♭5 but could also be Dom7♯11 by regarding the ♭5 as ♯11.

Pattern 2

A7♭5

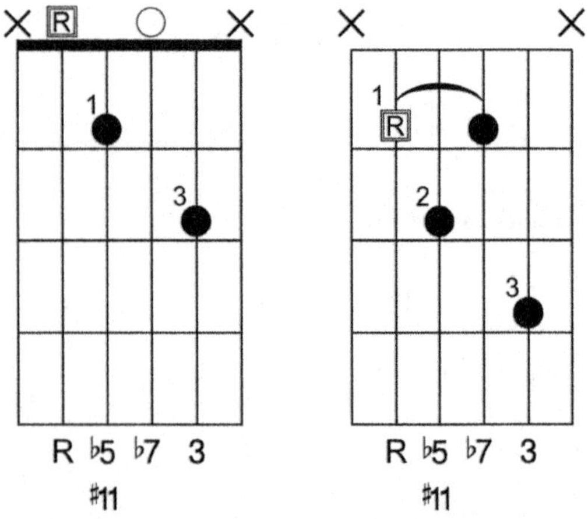

Pattern 3

G7♭5

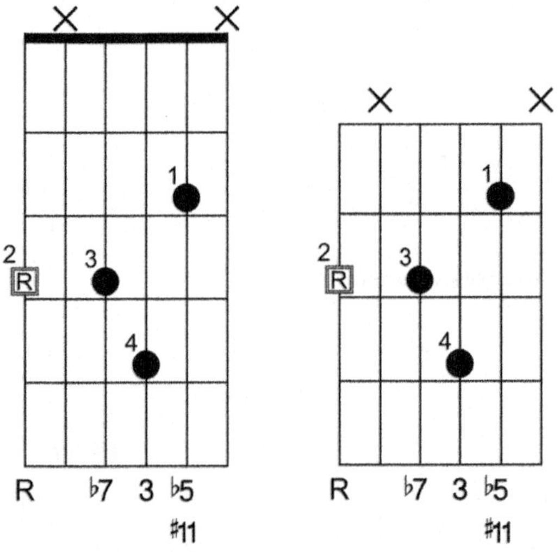

Pattern 4

$E^{7\flat 5}$

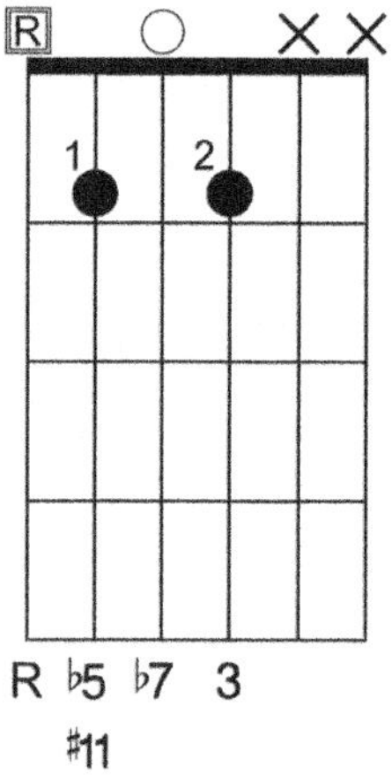

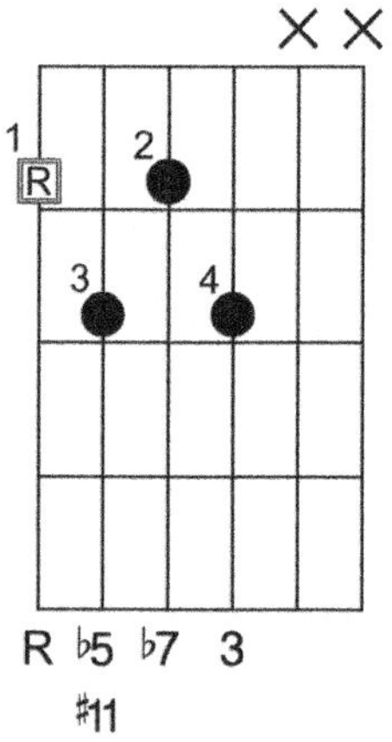

Pattern 5

$D^{7\flat 5}$

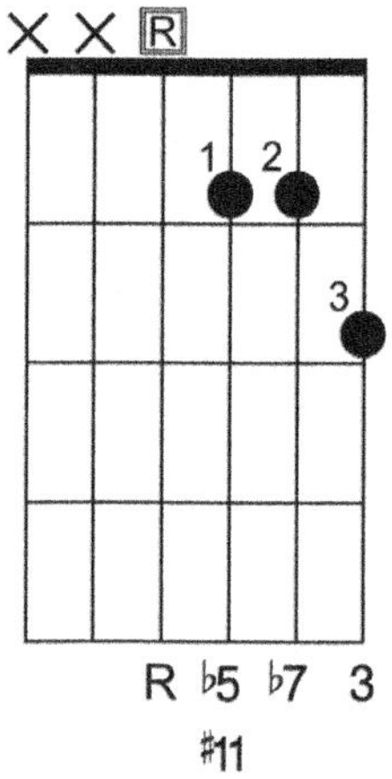

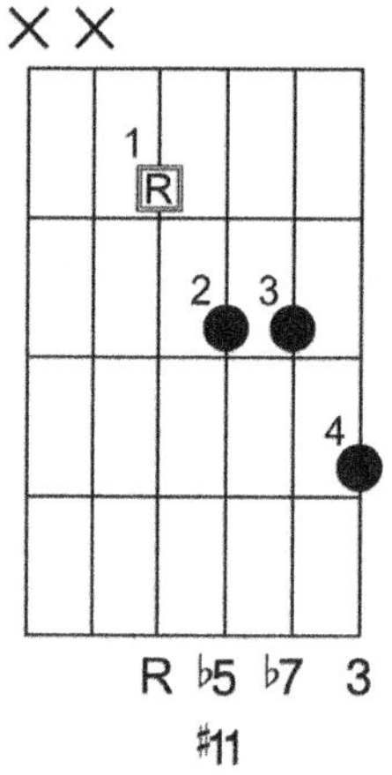

Dominant 7th ♯9 (R 3 5 ♭7 ♯9)

Pattern 1

$C^{7\sharp 9}$

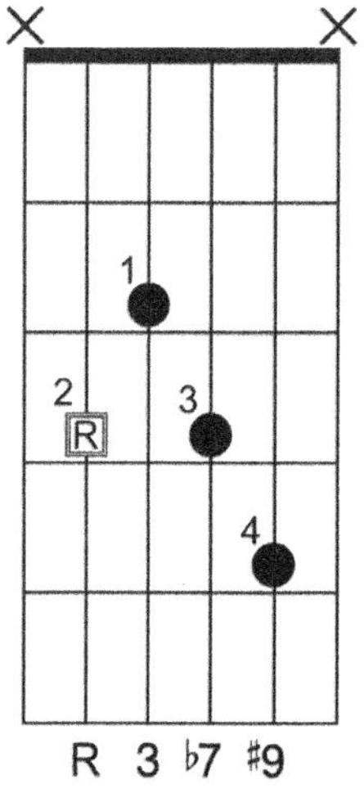

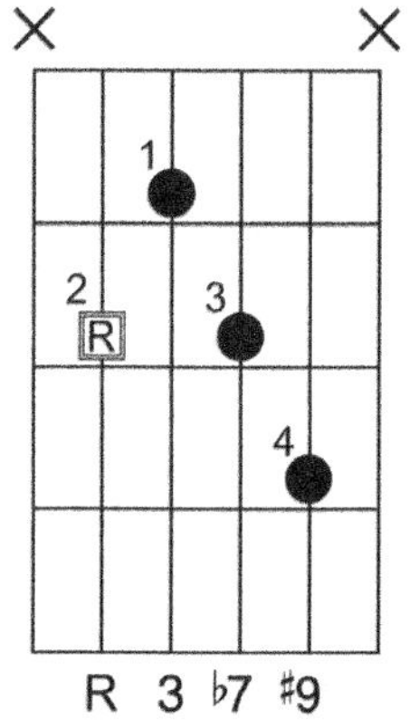

Pattern 3

$G^{7\sharp 9}$

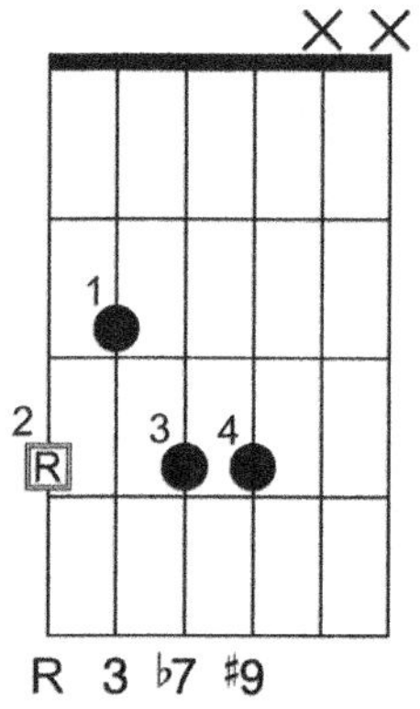

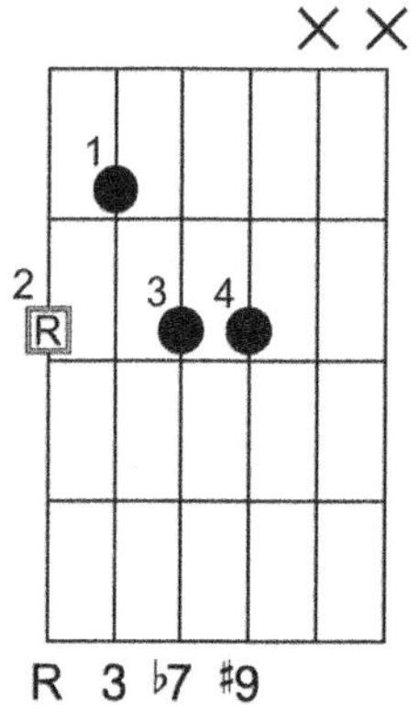

Pattern 4

$E^{7\sharp 9}$

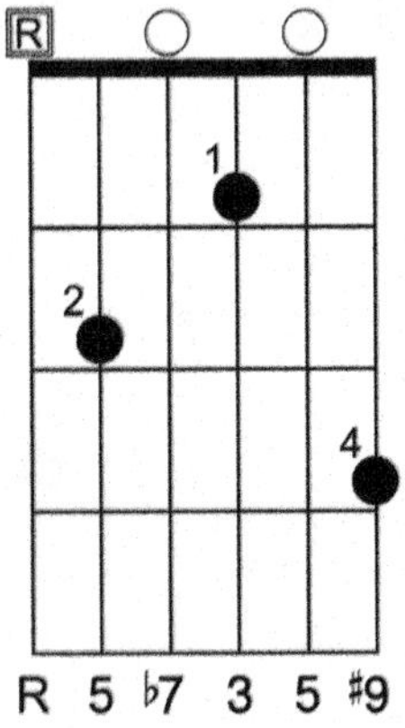

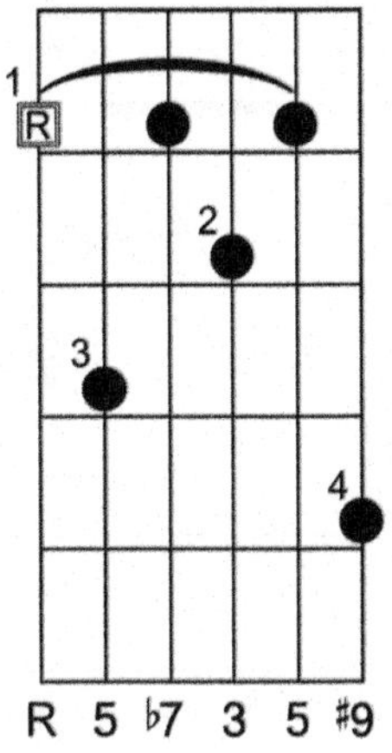

Pattern 4 (root on 4th)

$E^{7\sharp 9}$

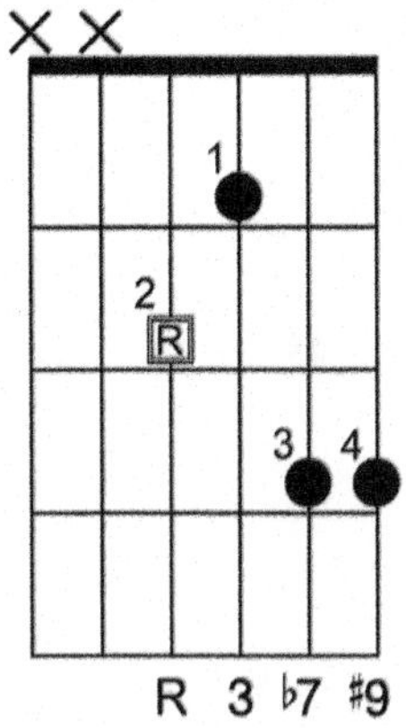

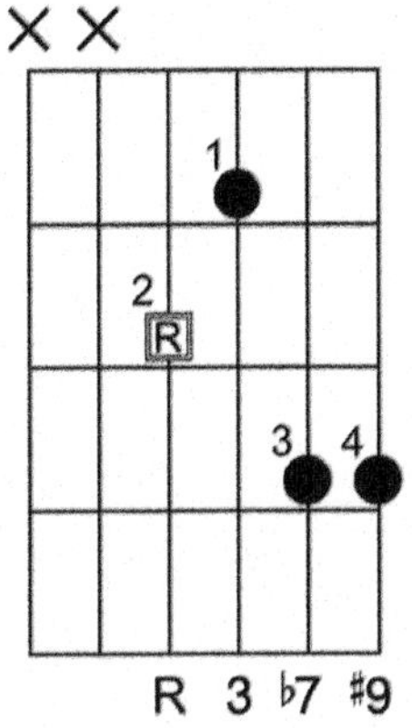

Dominant 7th ♭9 (R 3 5 ♭7 ♭9)

Pattern 1

$C^{7\flat 9}$

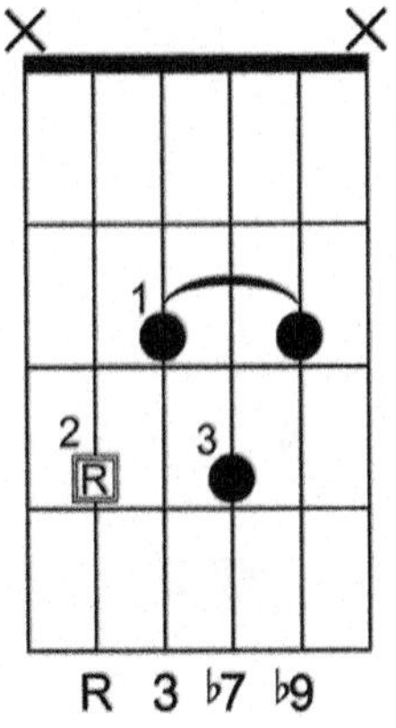

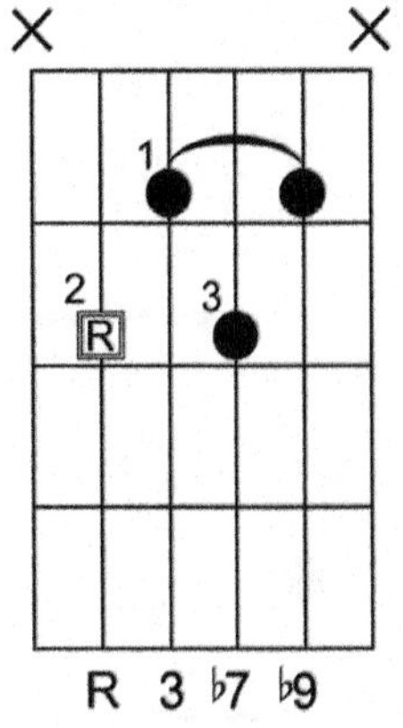

Pattern 3

$G^{7\flat 9}$

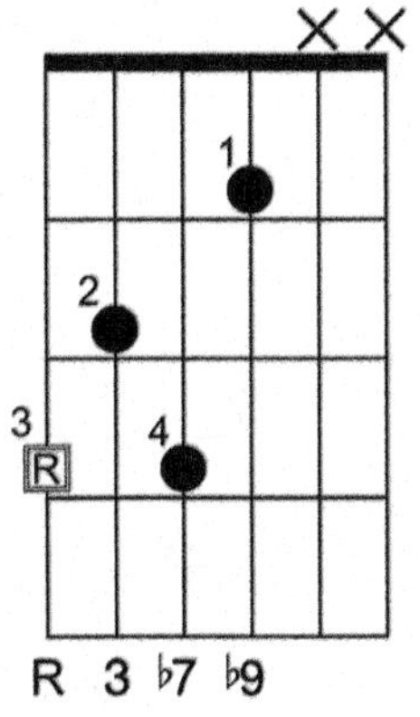

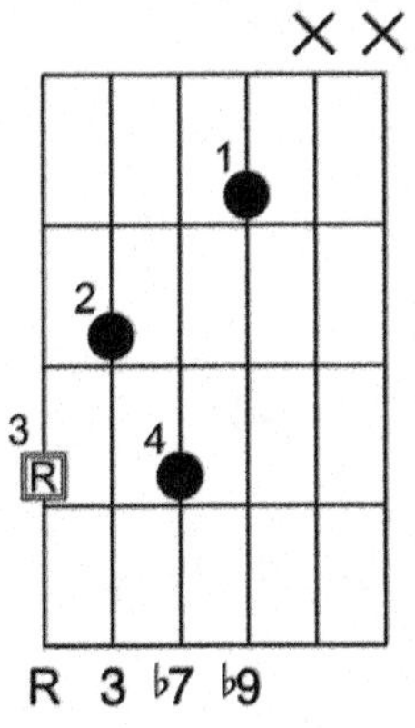

Pattern 4

E$^{7\flat 9}$

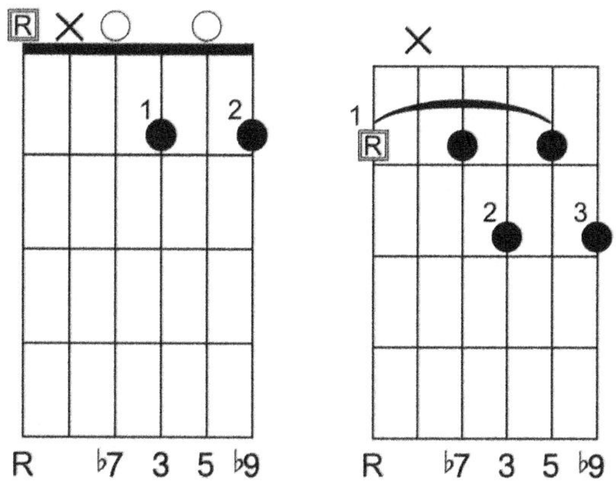

Pattern 4 (root on 4th)

E$^{7\flat 9}$

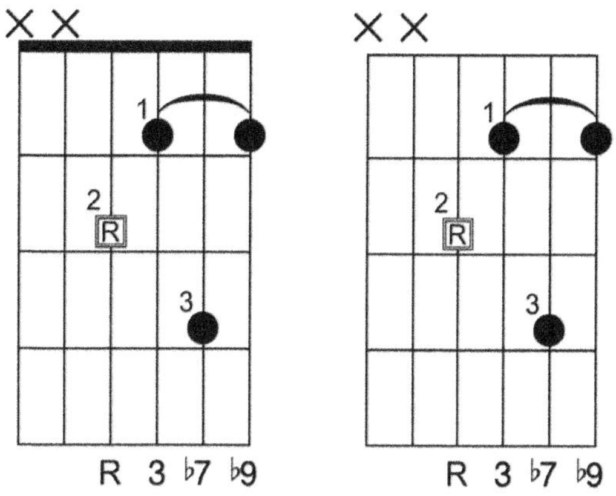

Minor 7th ♯5 (R ♭3 ♯5 ♭7)

Pattern 2

Am$^{7\sharp 5}$

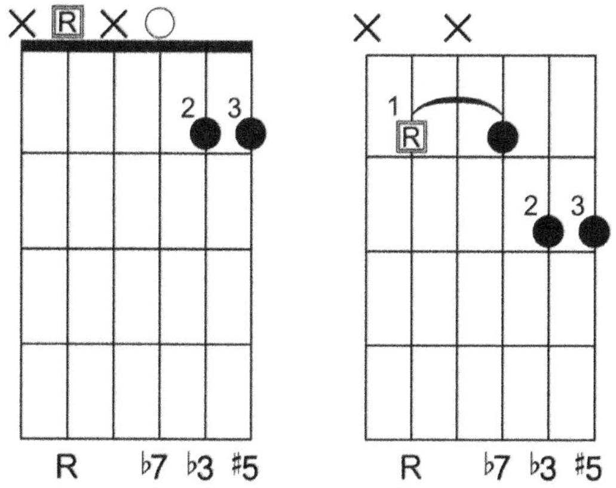

A different fingering for Pattern 2

Am$^{7\sharp 5}$

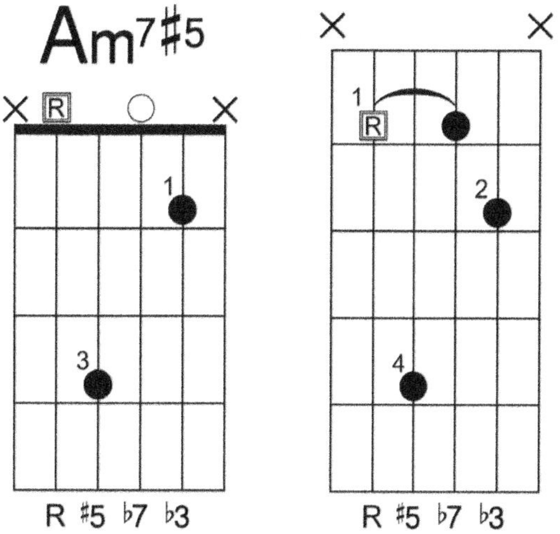

Pattern 4

Em7♯5

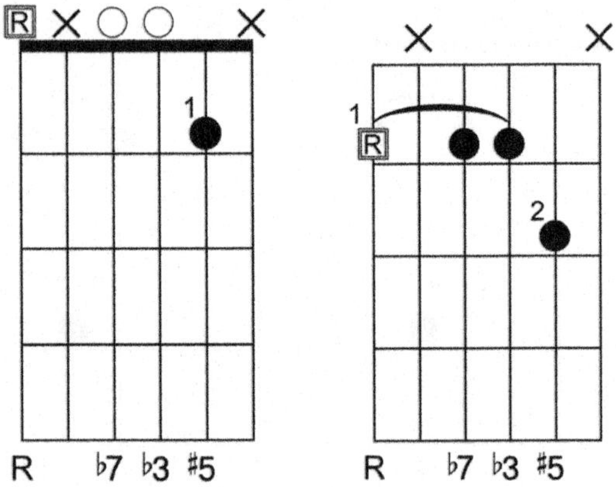

Q27) Can you work out / play G♭7♯5 pattern 4?

Q28) E7♭5 pattern 5?

Q29) A♭7♯9 pattern 1?

Q30) B7♭9 pattern 4 (root on 4th)?

Q31) Dm7♯5 pattern 2 (first version)?

Dominant 7th sus4 (R 4 5 ♭7)

Pattern 1

C7sus4

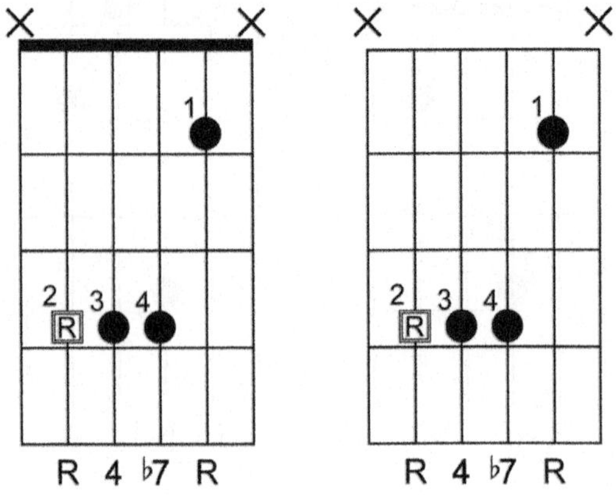

Pattern 2

A7sus4

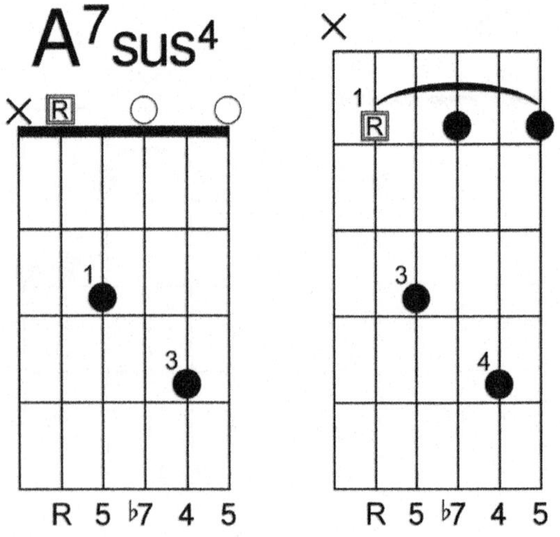

Pattern 4

E^7sus^4

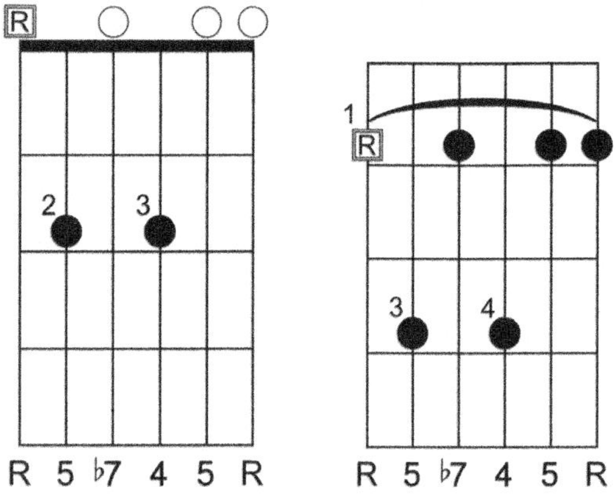

Pattern 5

D^7sus^4

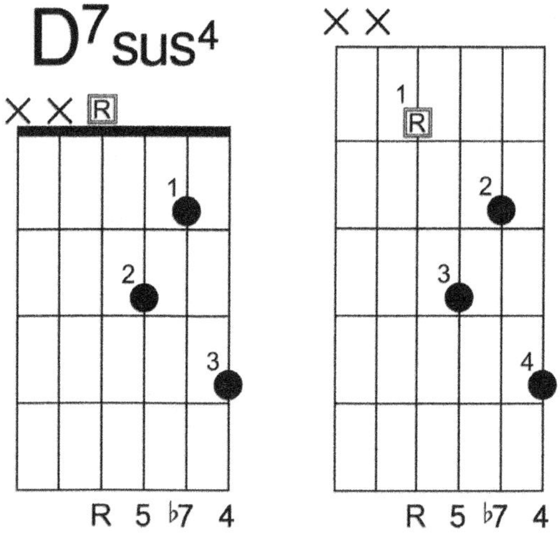

Diminished 7th (R ♭3 ♭5 ♭♭7)

Pattern 1

$Cdim^7$

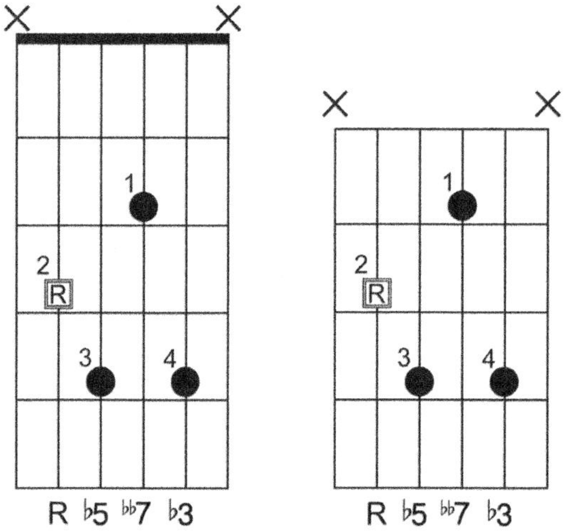

Pattern 3

$Gdim^7$

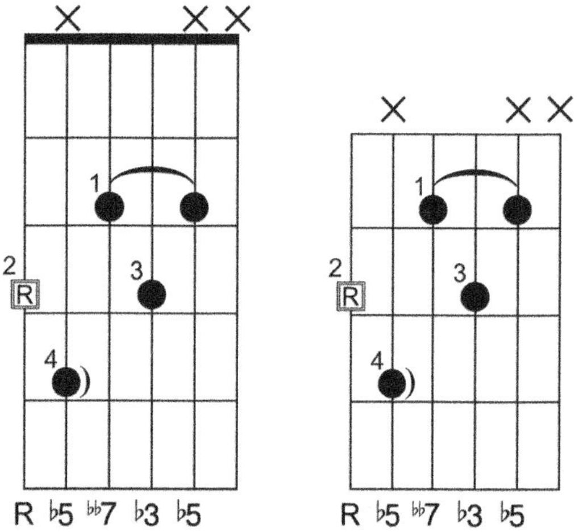

Pattern 4

Edim⁷

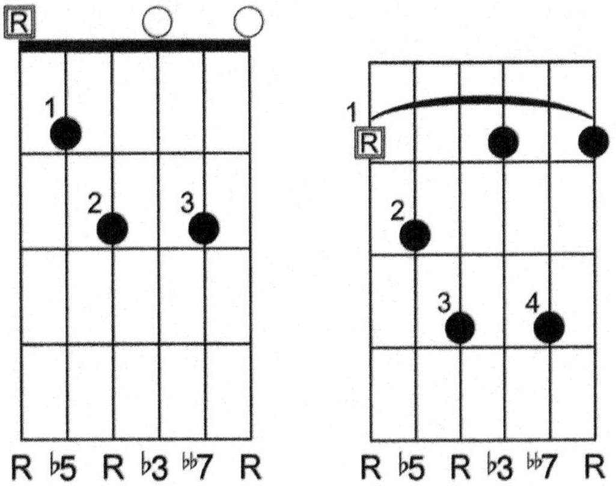

Pattern 5

Ddim⁷

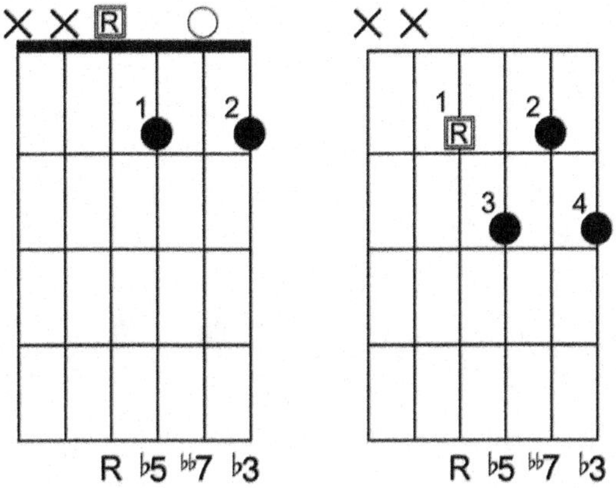

Minor, major 7th (R ♭3 5 7)

For pattern 2 you can play the 5th interval on *either* the 4th string or the 1st string, or both.

Pattern 1

Cm(maj⁷)

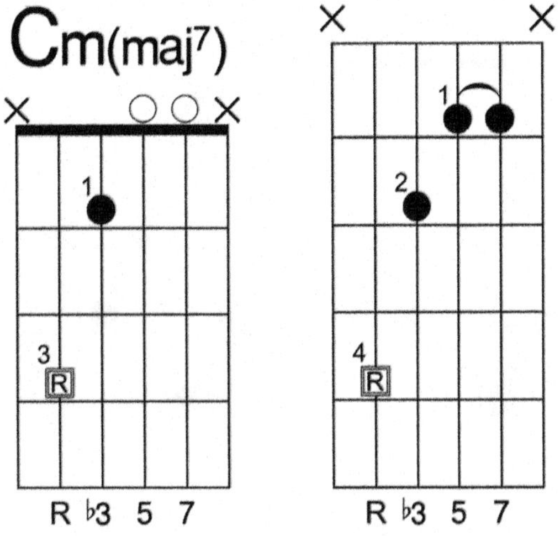

Pattern 2

Am(maj⁷)

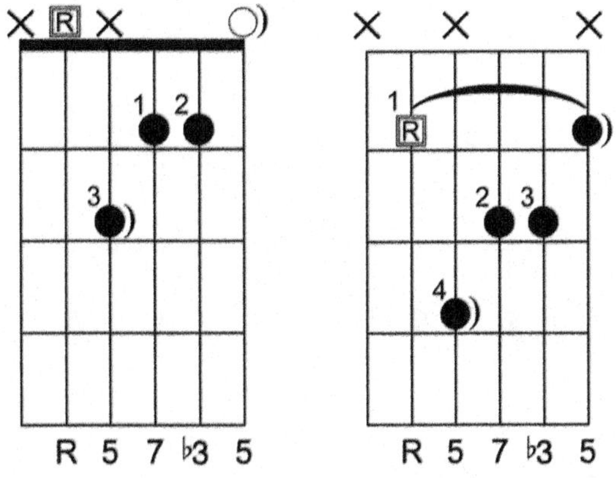

Pattern 3

Gm(maj7)

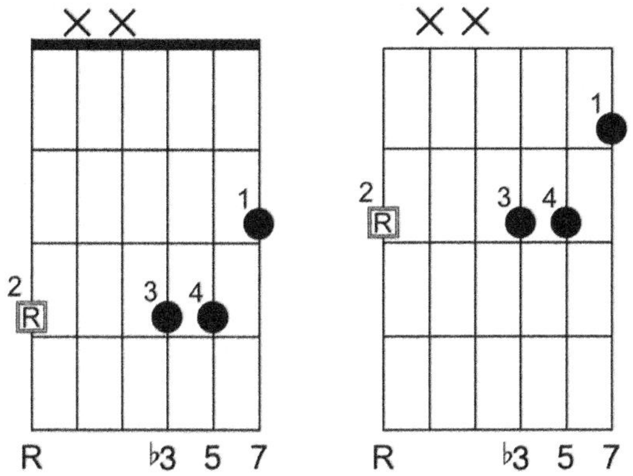

Pattern 4

Em(maj7)

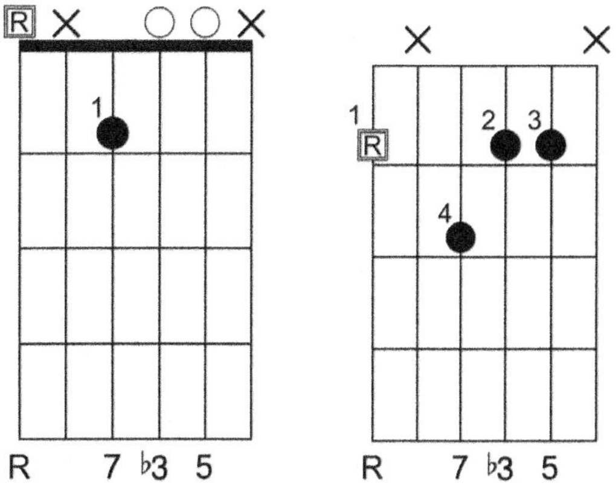

Pattern 4 transposable version can also be played with a barre, as shown below left.

Pattern 4

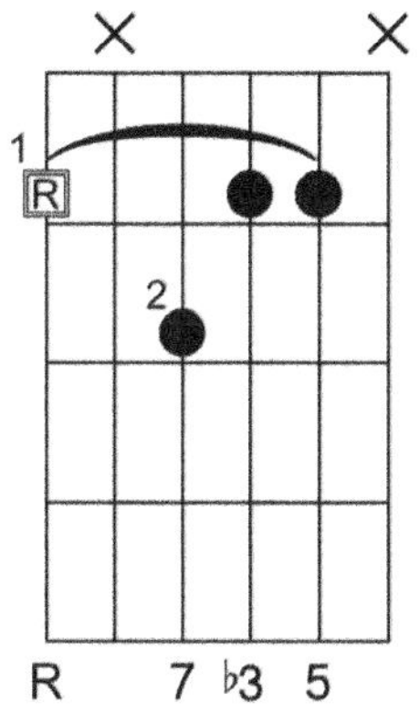

Pattern 5

Dm(maj7)

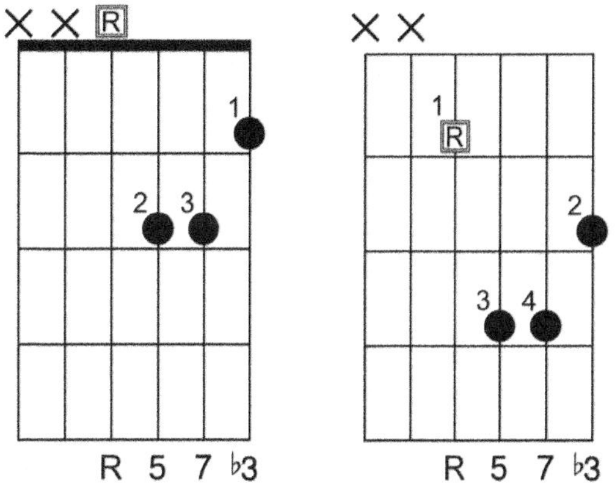

Major 6th (R 3 5 6)

Pattern 1

C6

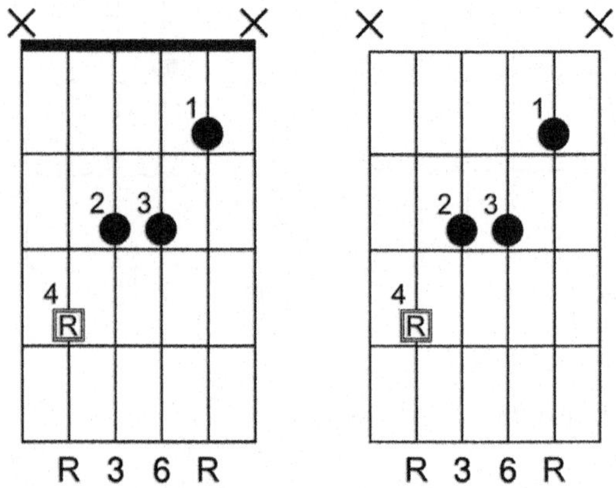

Pattern 2

A6

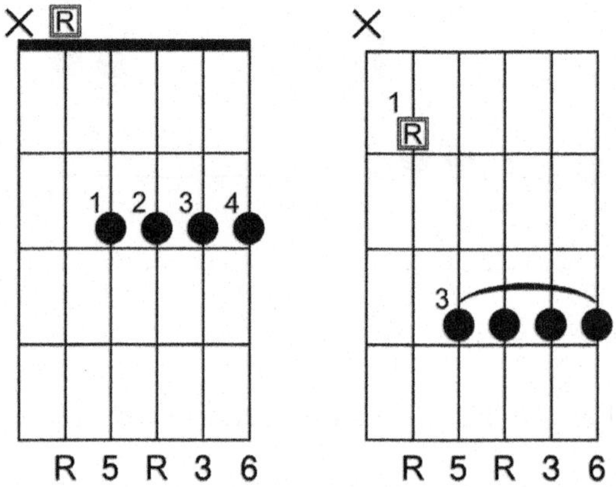

The A6 chord could also be played with a barre by using either the 1st, 2nd or 3rd finger across the 2nd fret of the fretted strings. Below are two different versions for Pattern 3.

Pattern 3

G6

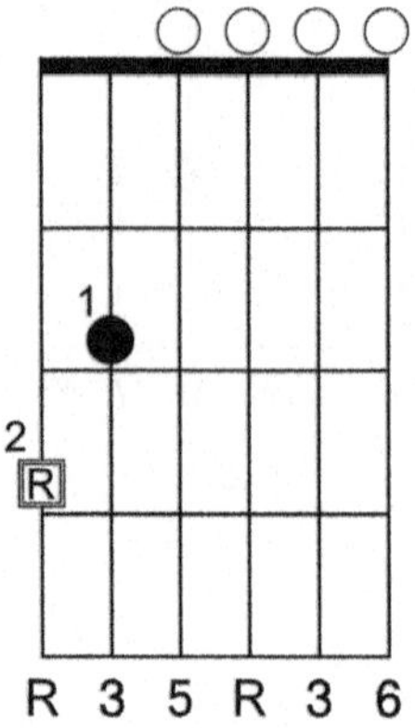

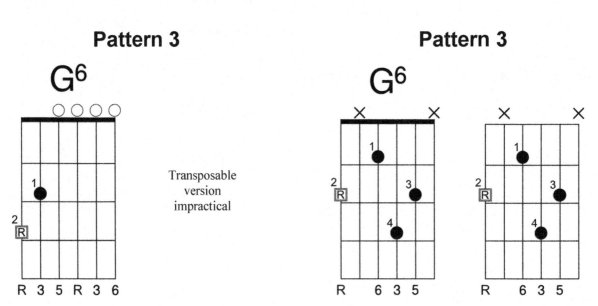

Transposable version impractical

Pattern 3

G6

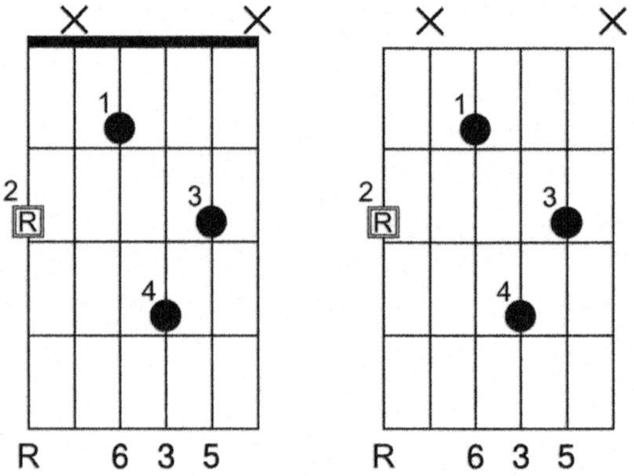

Pattern 4

E^6

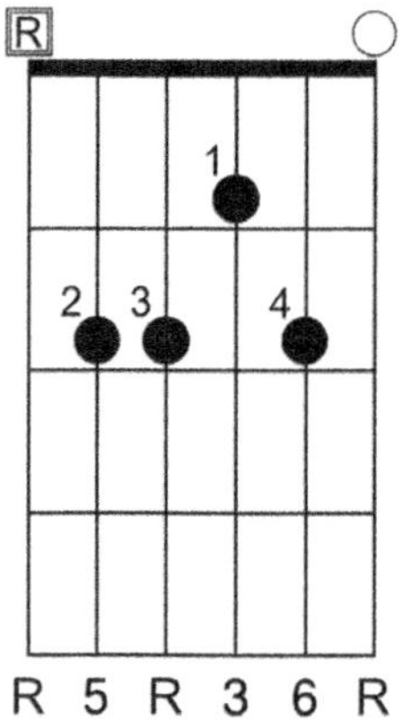

Transposable version impractical

Pattern 4 (root on 4th)

E^6

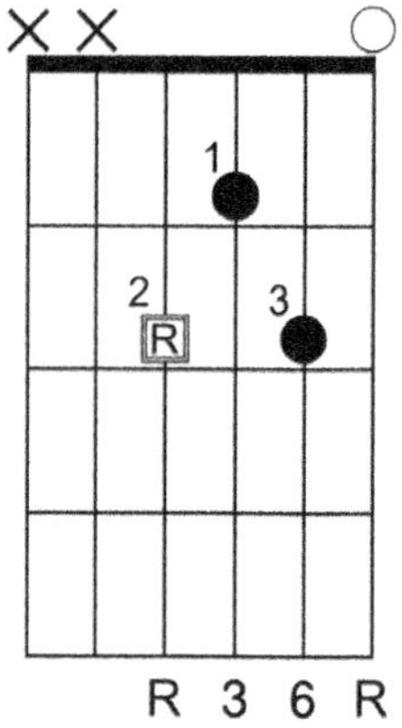

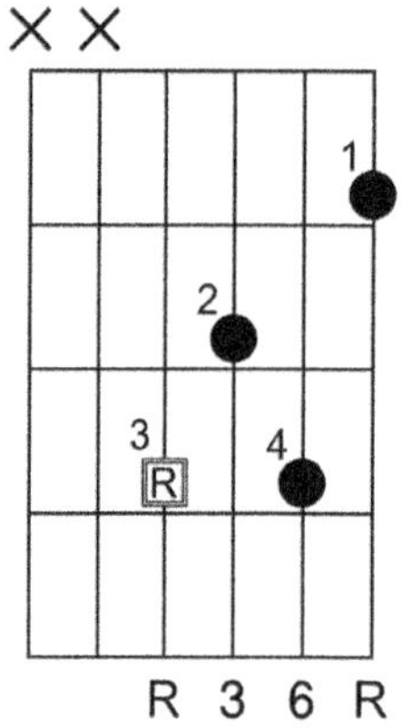

Pattern 5

D^6

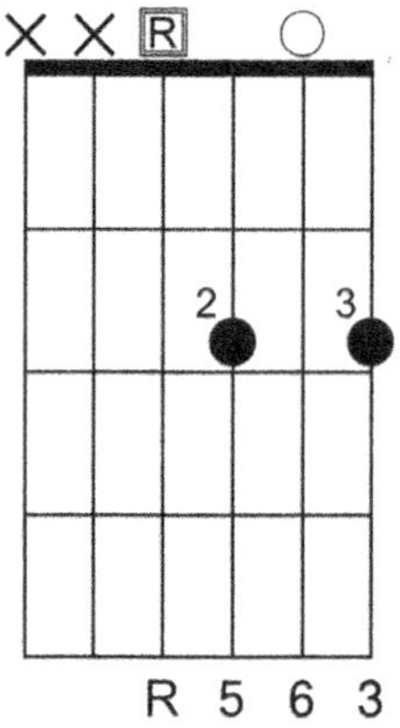

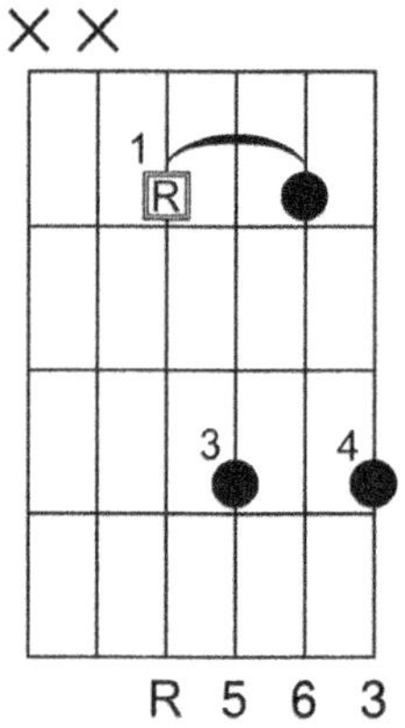

Q32) Can you work out / play F♯7sus4 pattern 4?

Q33) B♭dim7 pattern 1?

Q34) D♭m(maj7) pattern 3?

Q35) G6 pattern 5?

Minor 6th (R ♭3 5 6)

Pattern 1

Cm6

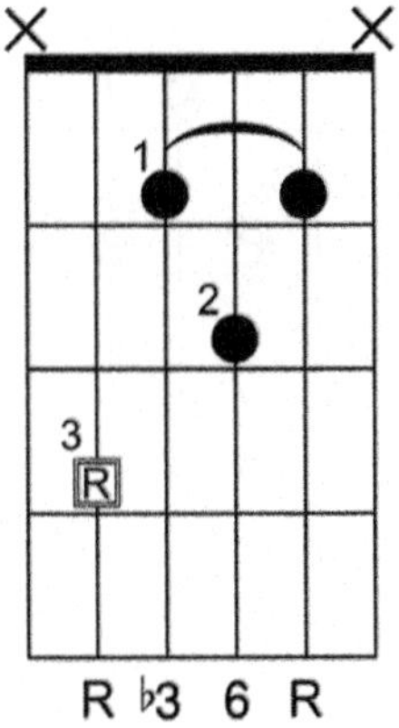

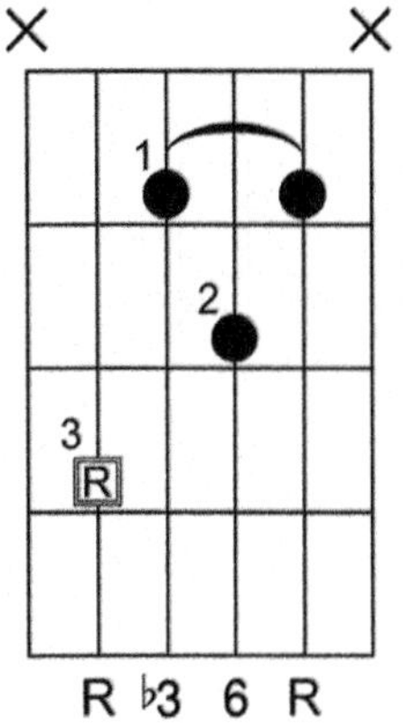

Pattern 2

No open chord version for A root

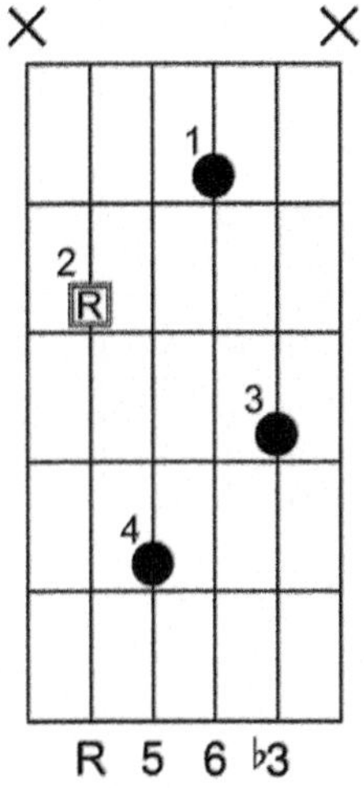

Pattern 3

Gm6

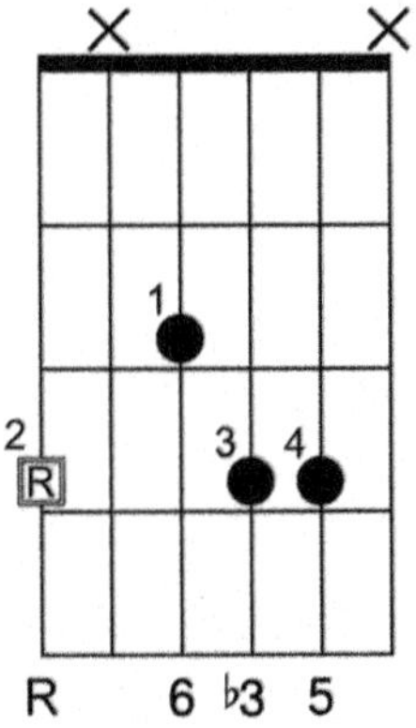

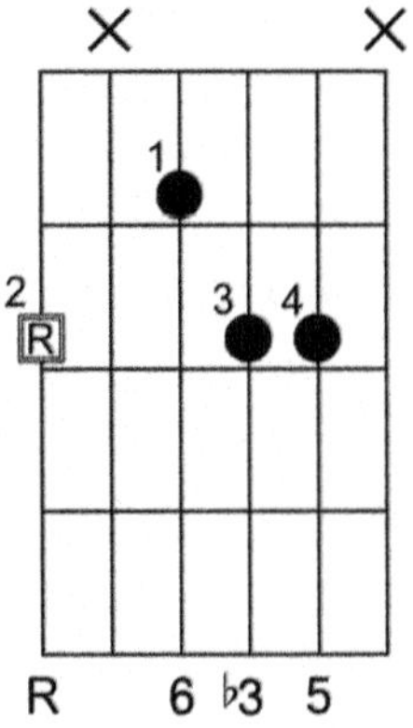

Pattern 4

Em6

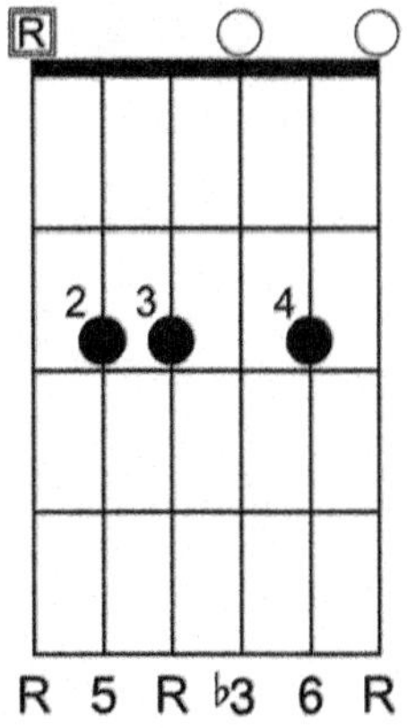

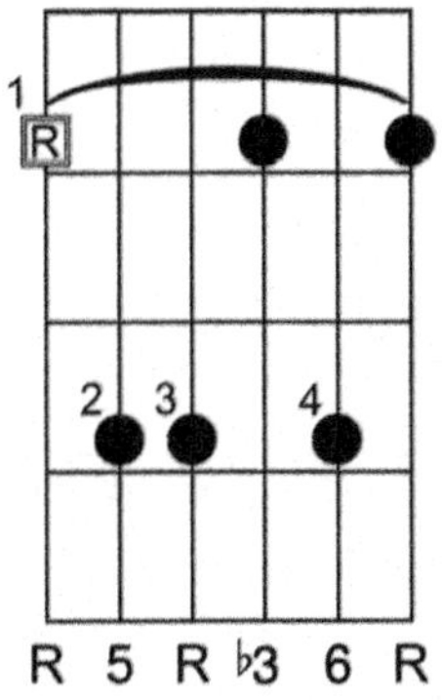

Pattern 4 (root on 4th)

Em6

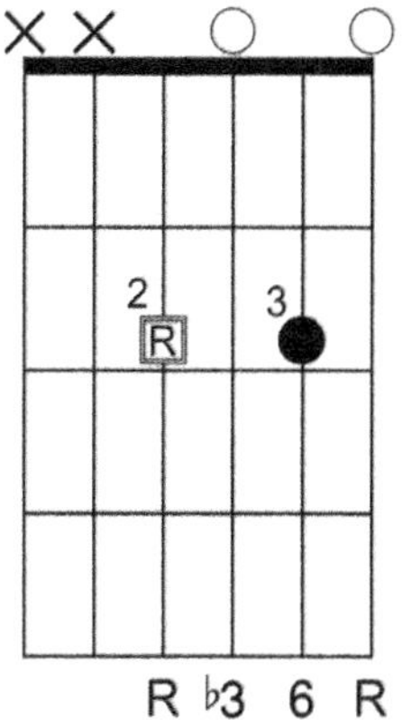

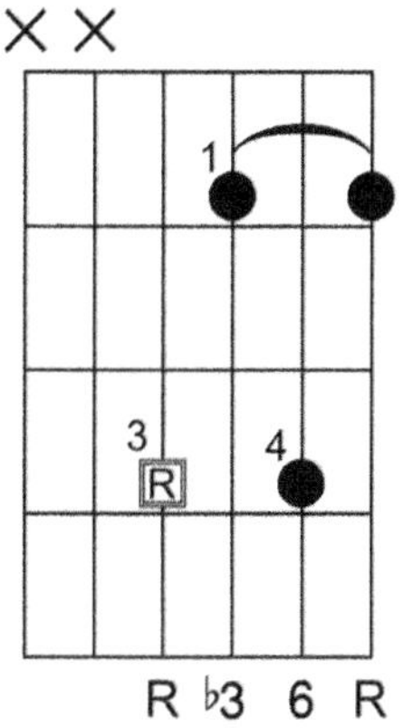

Pattern 5

Dm6

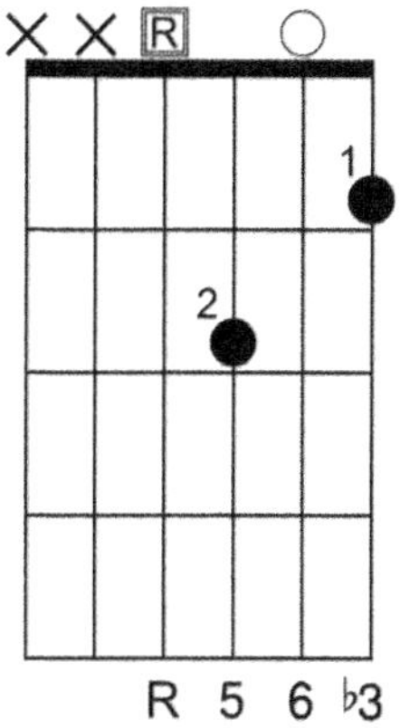

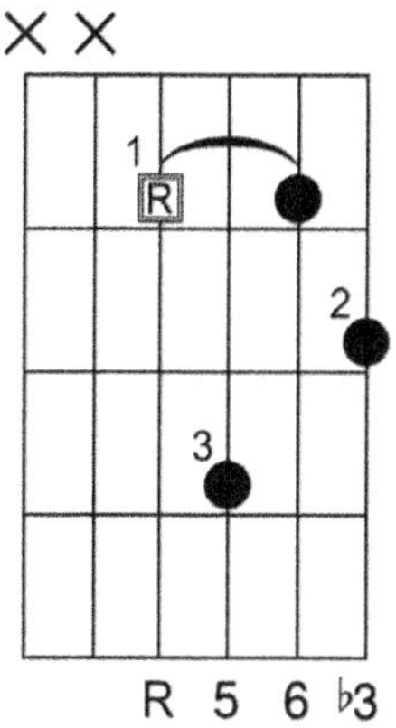

Added 9th (R 3 5 9)

Pattern 1

Cadd9

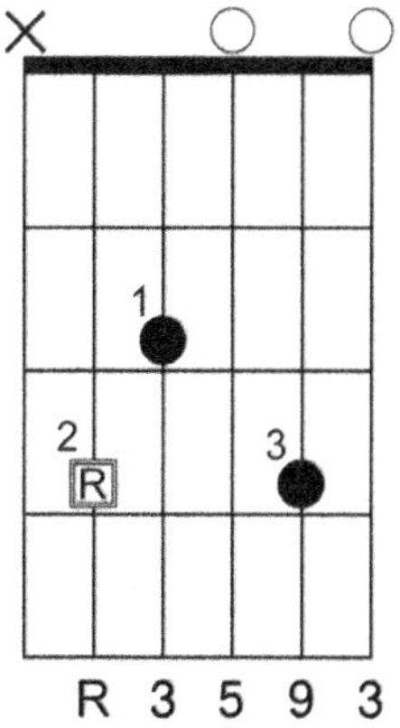

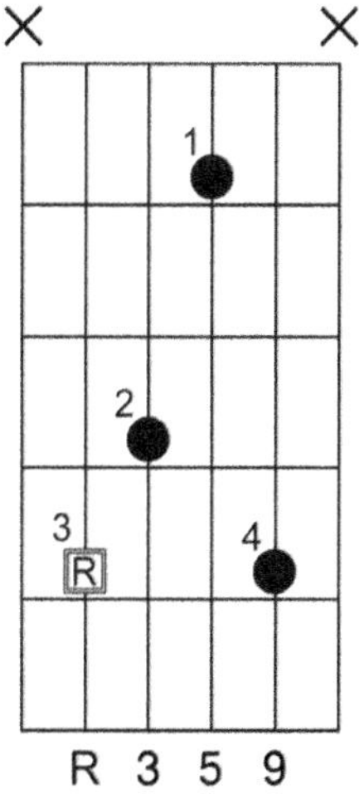

Pattern 2

Aadd9

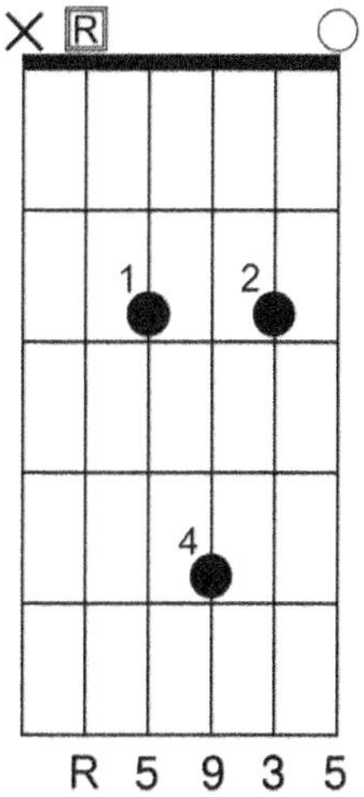

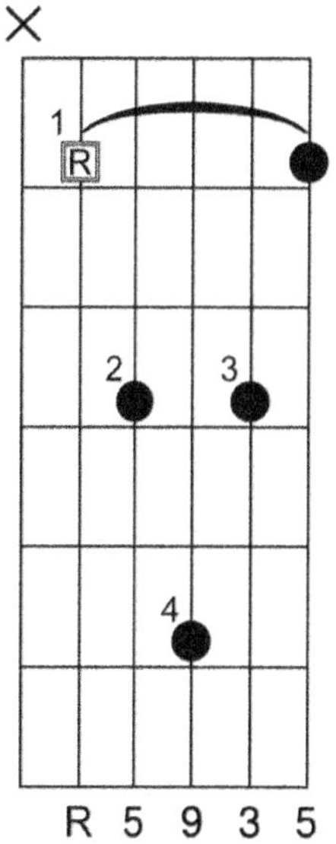

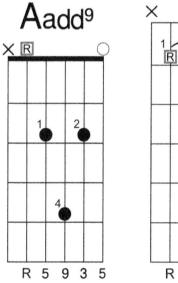

Below left is a version of Aadd9 using a partial-barre and omitting the 5th interval on the 1st string.

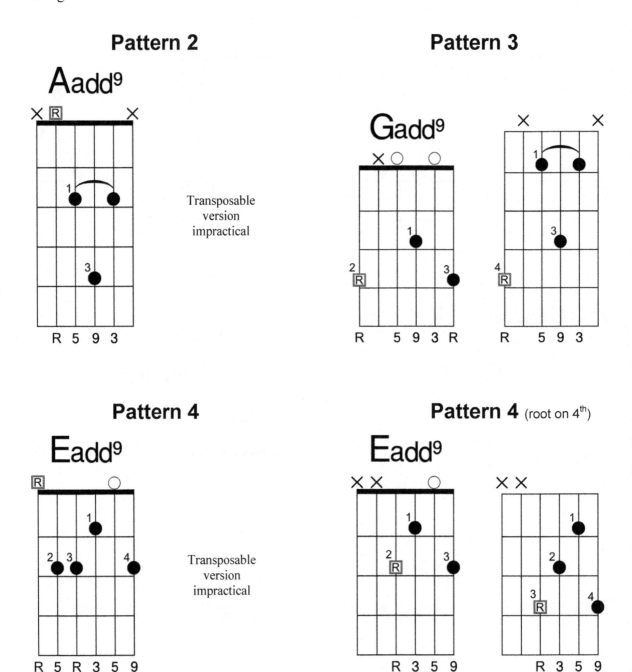

Pattern 2

Aadd9

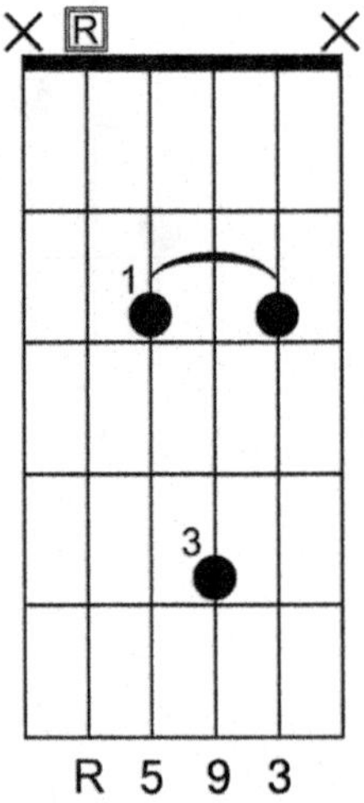

Transposable version impractical

Pattern 3

Gadd9

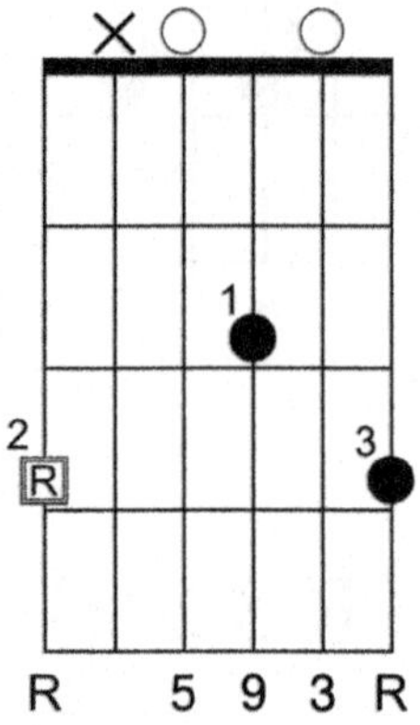

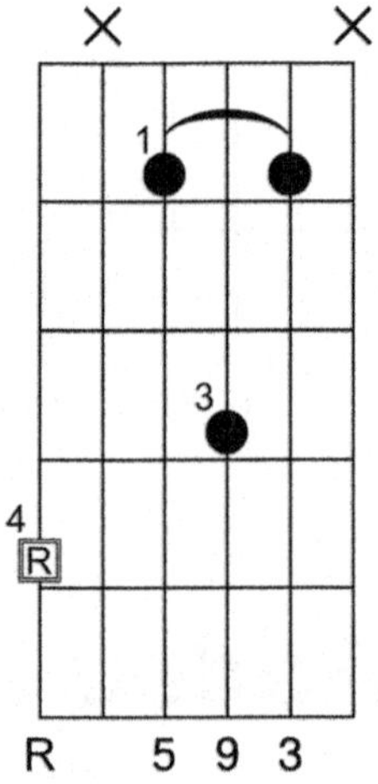

Pattern 4

Eadd9

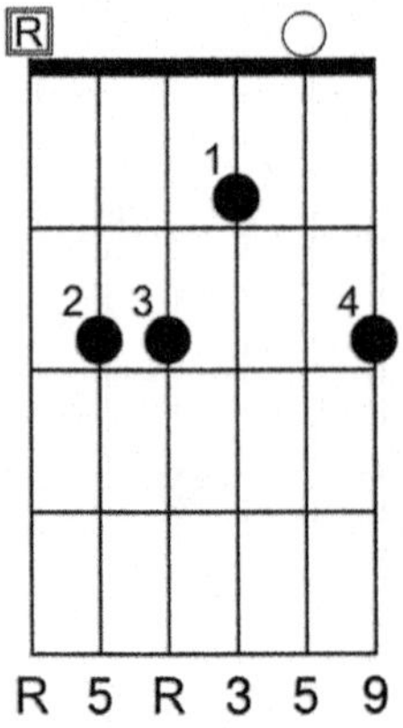

Transposable version impractical

Pattern 4 (root on 4th)

Eadd9

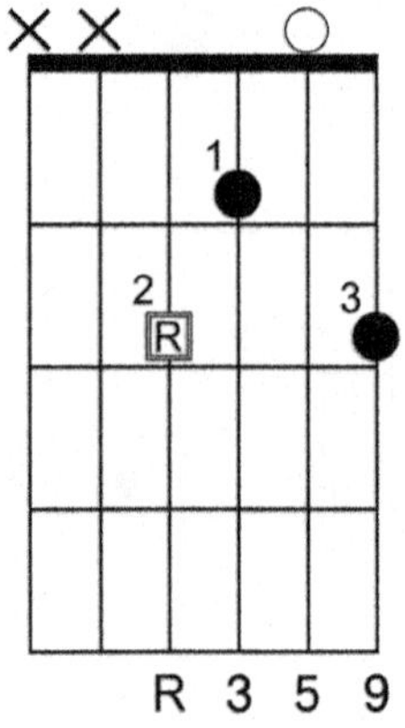

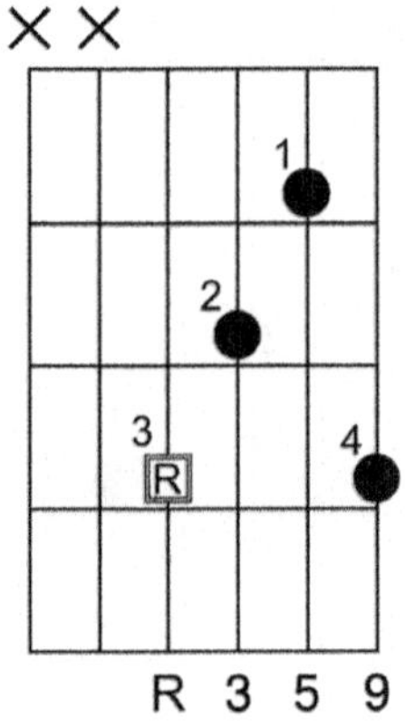

Minor added 9th (R ♭3 5 9)

Pattern 1

Cm(add9)

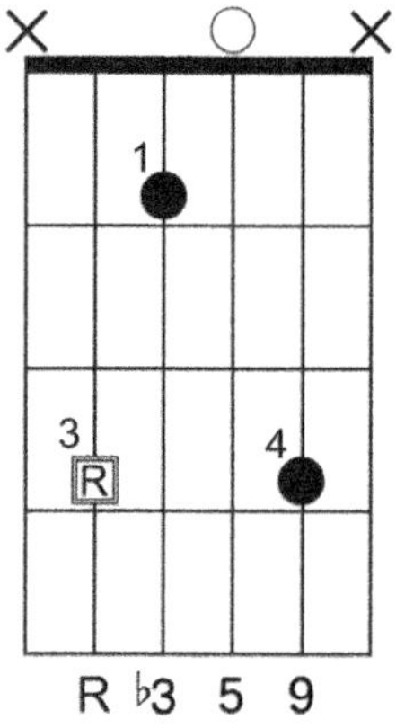

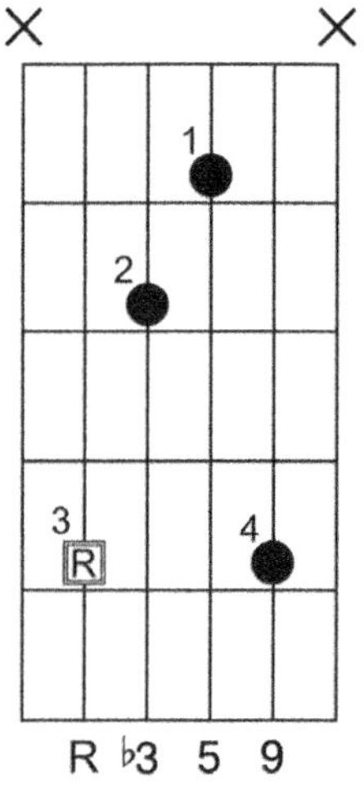

Pattern 2

Am(add9)

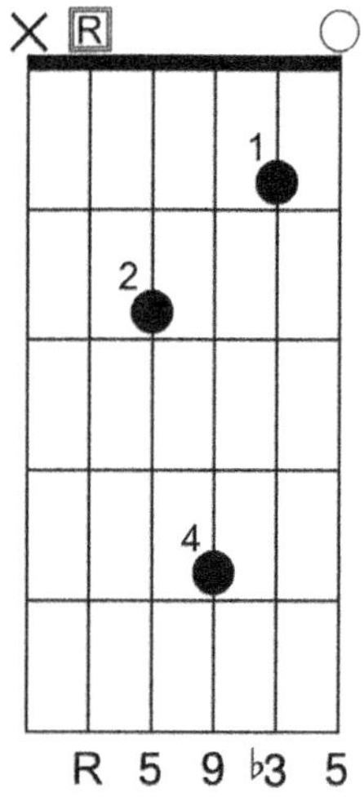

Transposable version impractical

Pattern 3

Gm(add9)

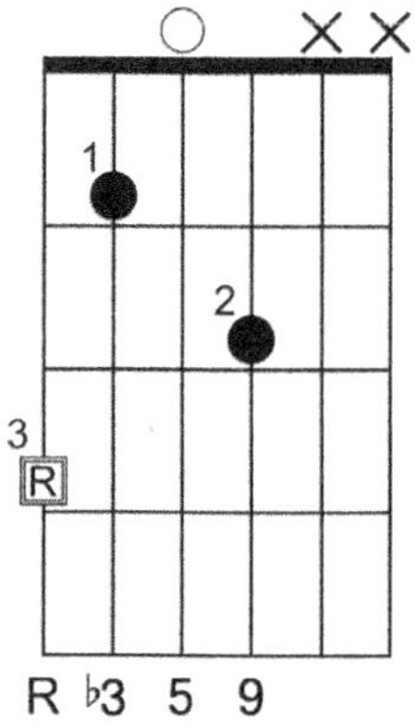

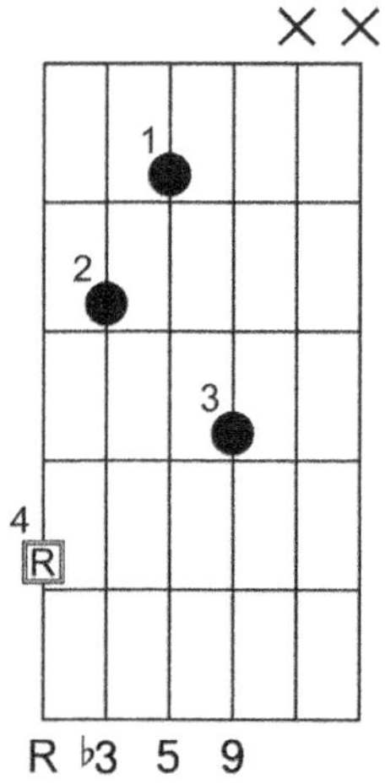

Pattern 4

Em(add9)

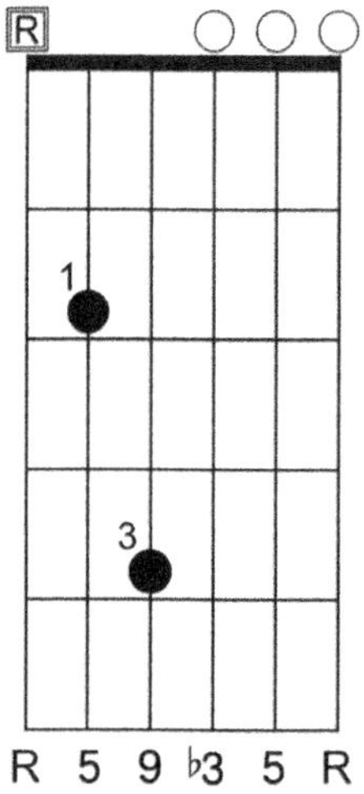

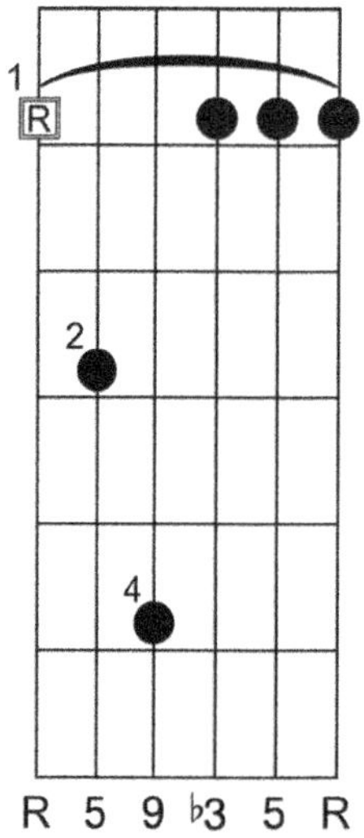

Pattern 4 (root on 4th)

Em(add9)

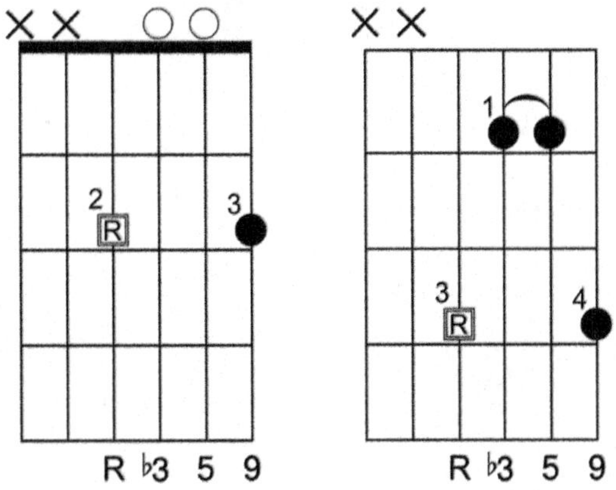

Q36) Can you work out / play Cm6 pattern 3?

Q37) C♯add9 pattern 4 (root on 4th)?

Q38) D♯m(add9) pattern 4?

Dominant 7th ♭5♭9 (R 3 ♭5 ♭7 ♭9)

Pattern 1

C7♭5(♭9)

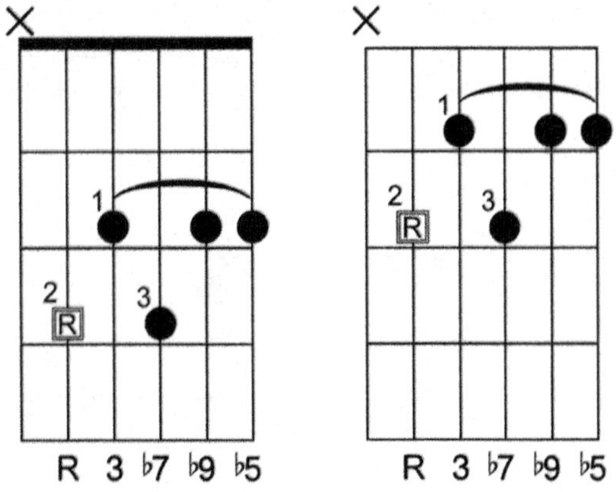

Pattern 3

G7♭5(♭9)

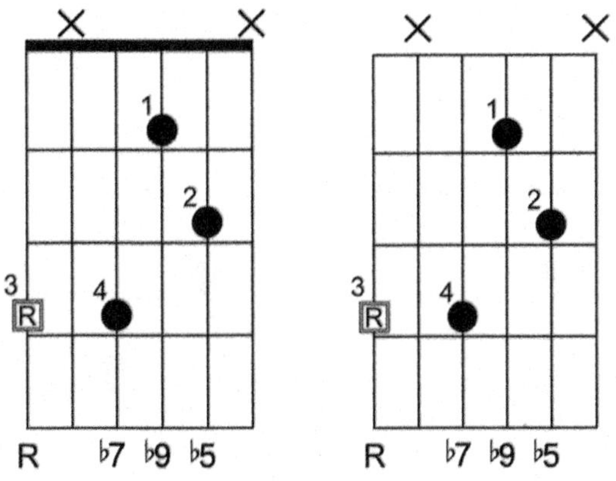

Dominant 7th #5#9 (R 3 #5 b7 #9)

Pattern 1

C7#5(#9)

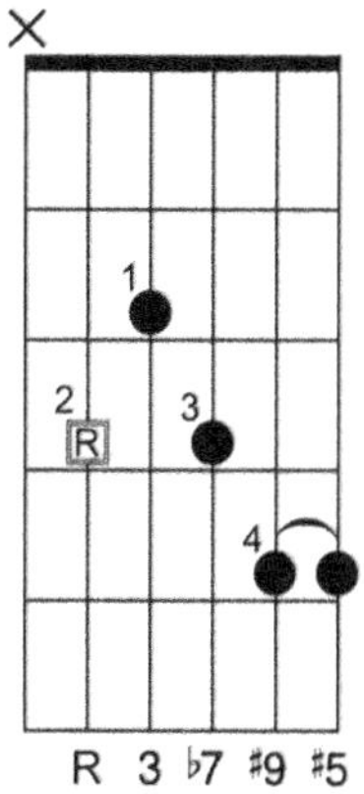

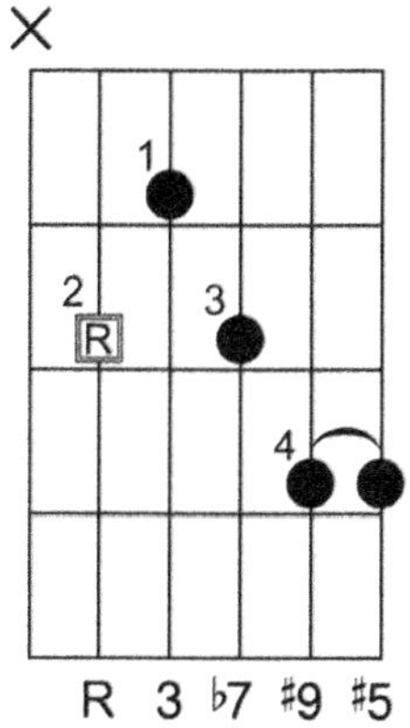

Pattern 4

E7#5(#9)

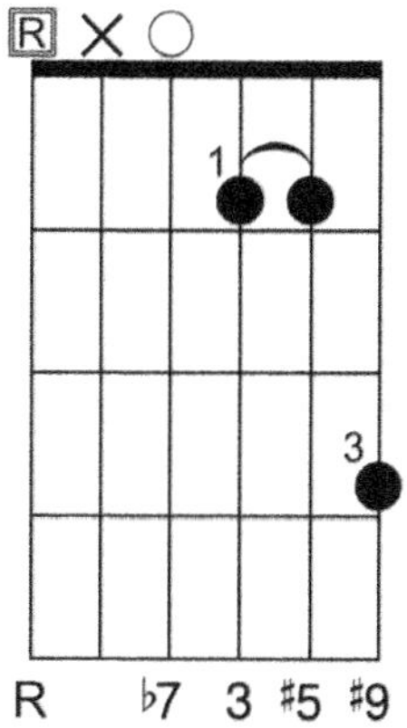

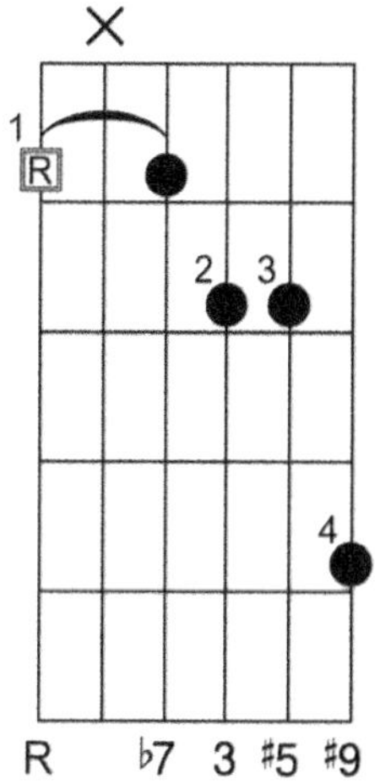

Dominant 7th b5#9 (R 3 b5 b7 #9)

Pattern 1

C7b5(#9)

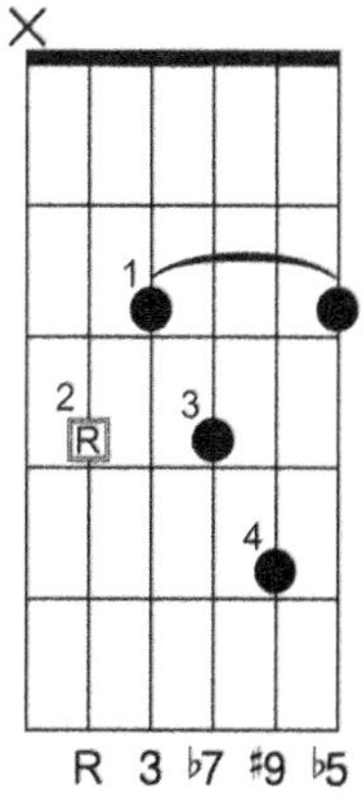

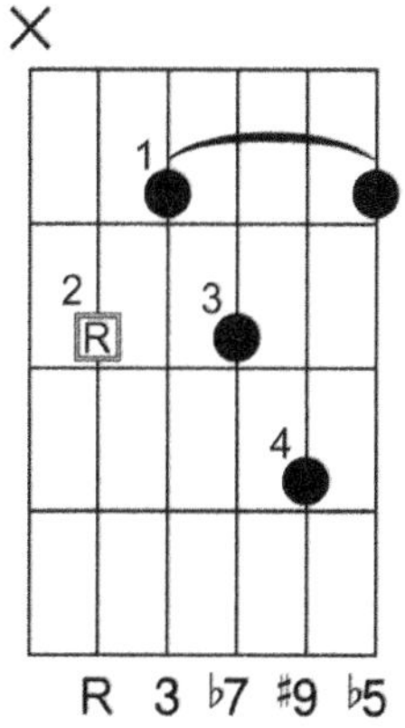

Pattern 3

G7b5(#9)

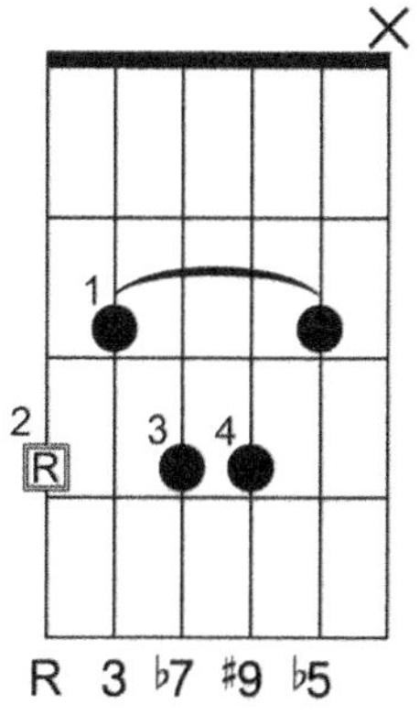

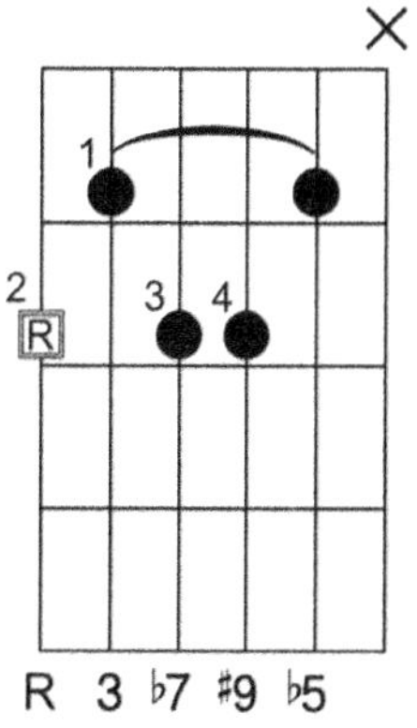

Dominant 7th ♯5♭9 (R 3 ♯5 ♭7 ♭9)

Pattern 1

C7♯5(♭9)

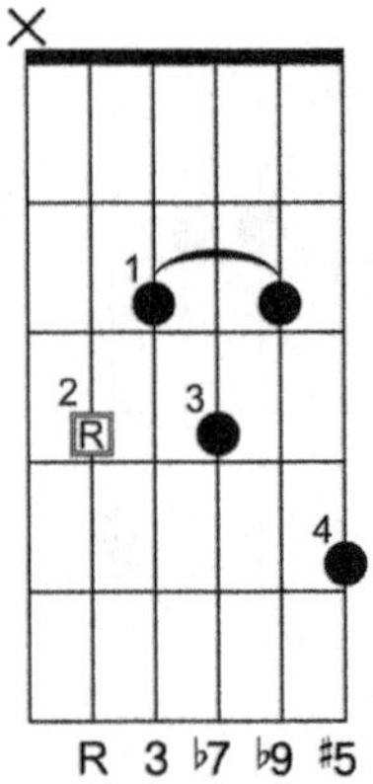

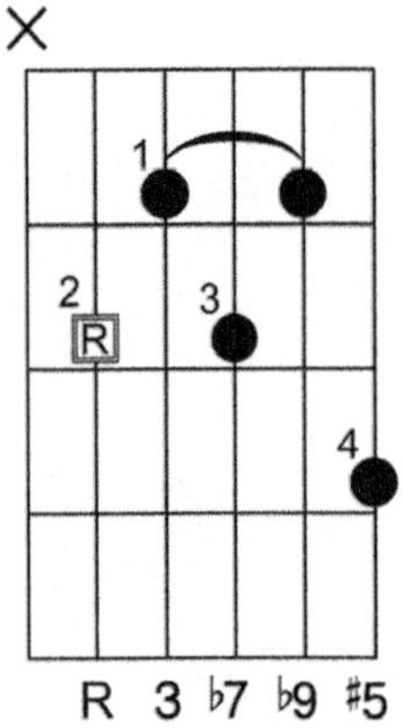

Pattern 4

E7♯5(♭9)

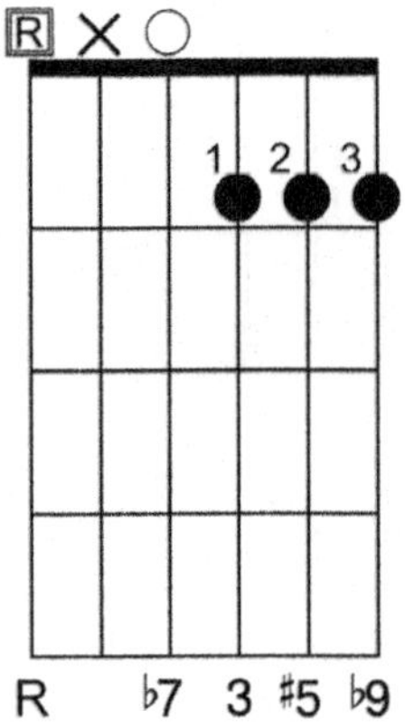

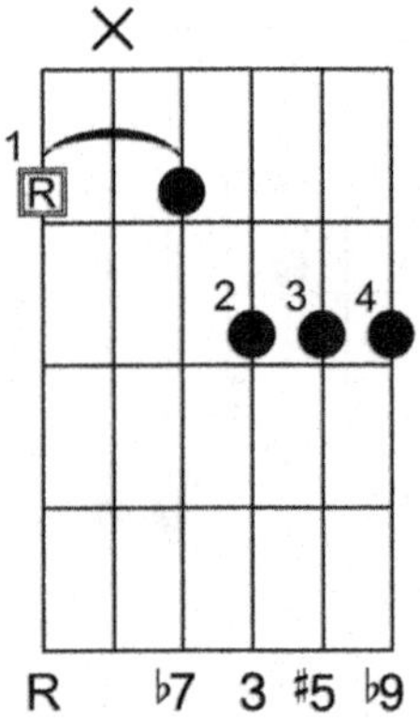

Major 9th ♯11 (R 3 5 7 9 ♯11)

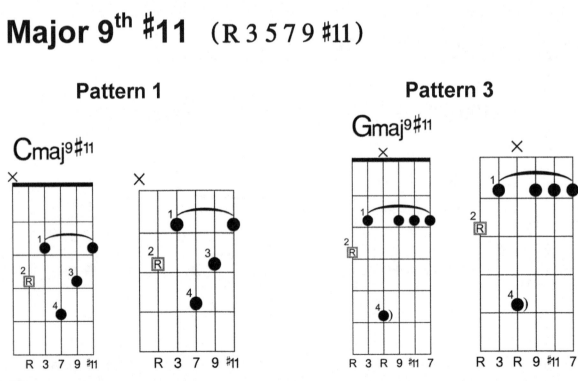

Pattern 1

Cmaj9♯11

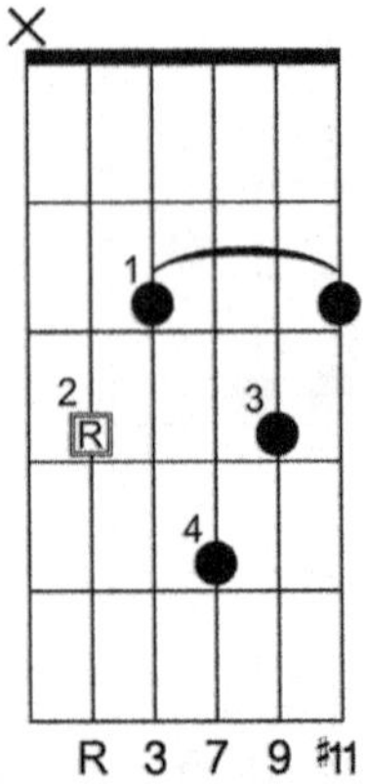

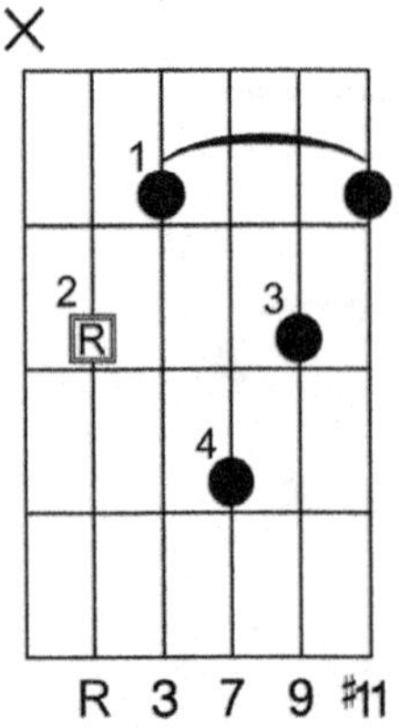

Pattern 3

Gmaj9♯11

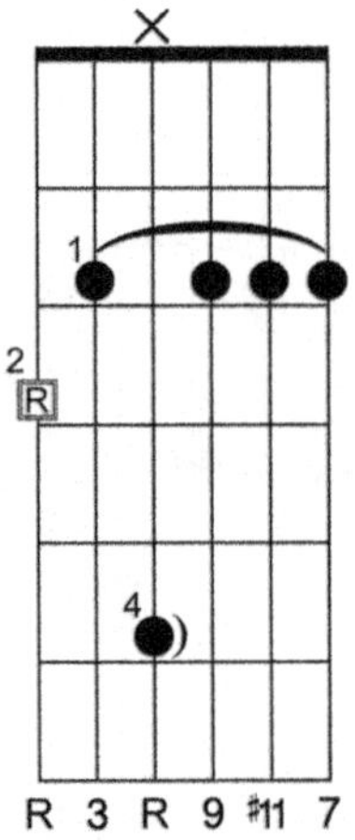

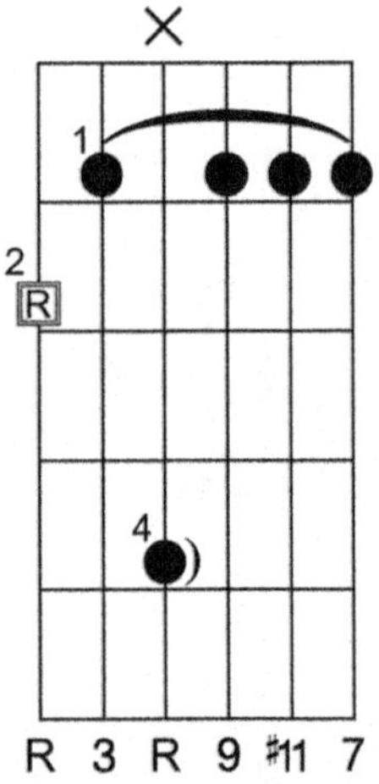

Dom 9♯11 (R 3 5 ♭7 9 ♯11) & Dom 9♭5 (R 3 ♭5 ♭7 9)

The difference between these two chords is that Dominant 9th ♯11 has a 5th whereas Dominant 9th ♭5 does not. Otherwise they are similar because the ♭5 and ♯11 can be played in each other's place.

The 5th can be omitted from the Dom9♯11 for easier fingering; doing so will make it identical to Dom9♭5. In such a case, whether the chord is a Dom9♯11 or a Dom9♭5 will depend on the musical piece in which it is being used and therefore what name it is given.

Therefore the following chords are named Dom9♭5 but could also be Dom9♯11 by regarding the ♭5 as ♯11.

Pattern 1

C9♭5

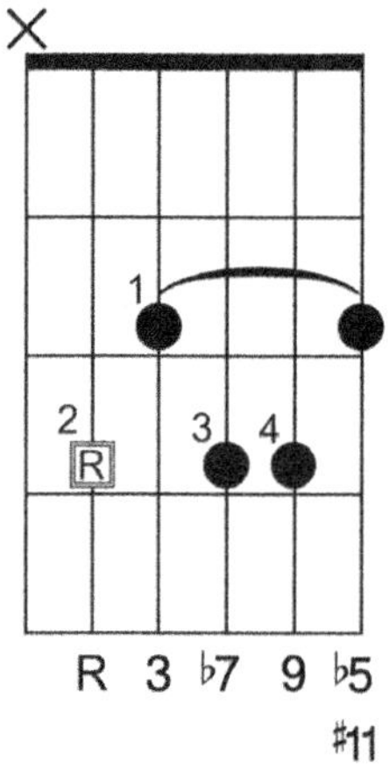

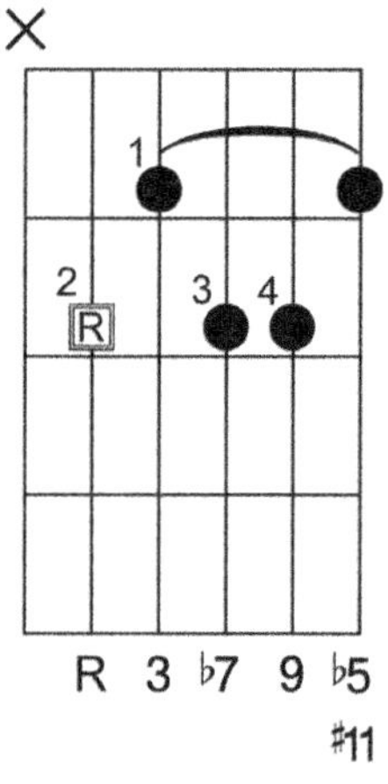

Pattern 3

G9♭5

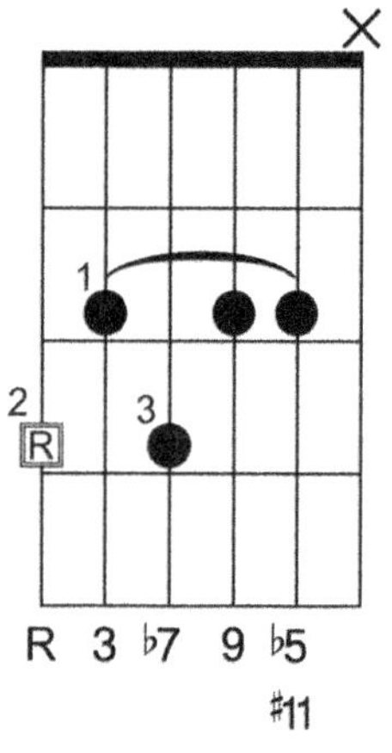

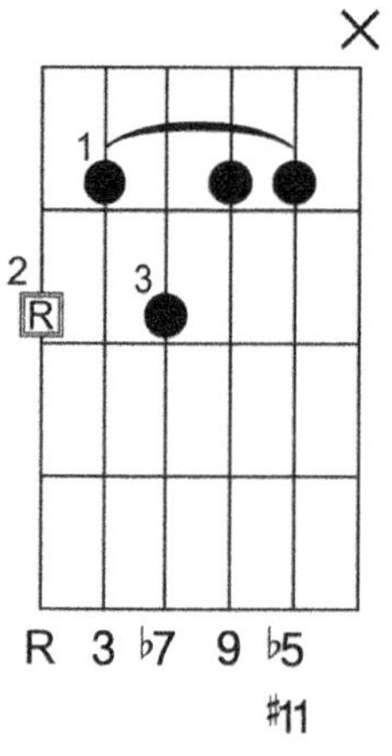

Dominant 9th ♯5 (R 3 ♯5 ♭7 9)

Pattern 1

C9♯5

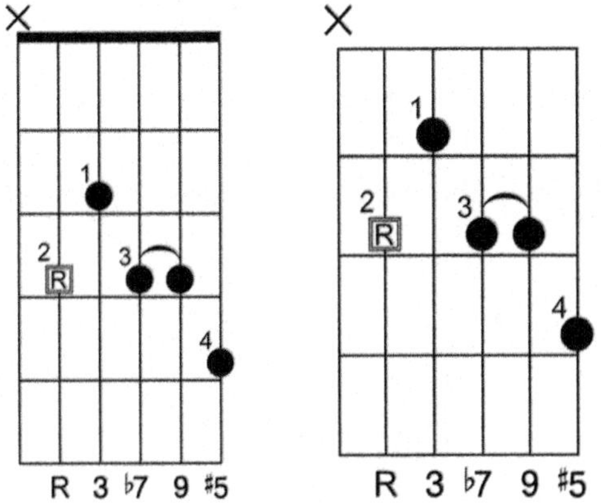

Pattern 4

E9♯5

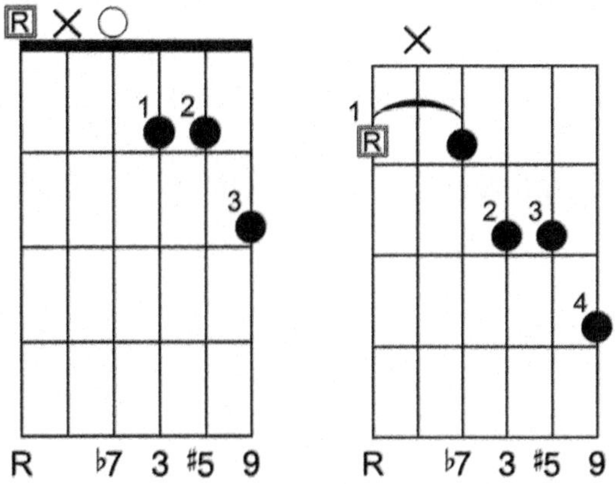

Dominant 9th sus4 (R 4 5 ♭7 9)

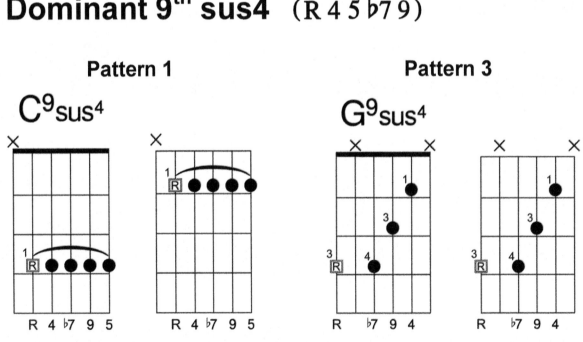

Pattern 1

C9sus4

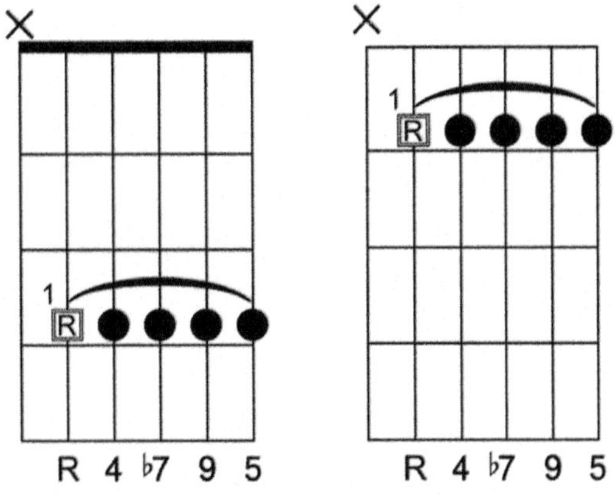

Pattern 3

G9sus4

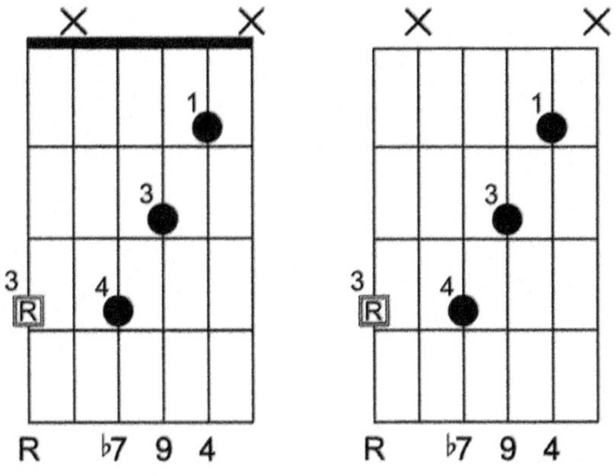

Pattern 5

D9sus4

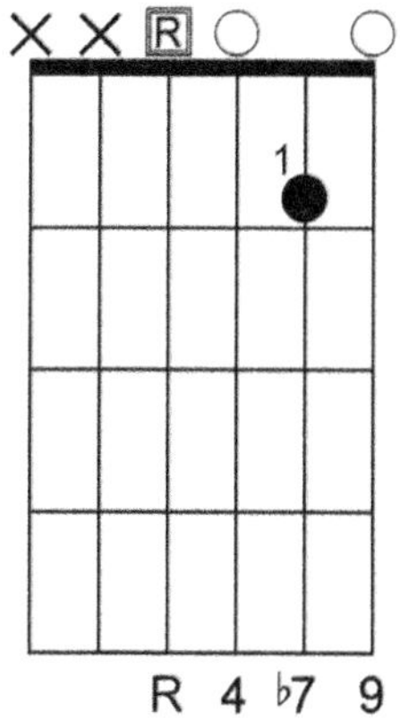

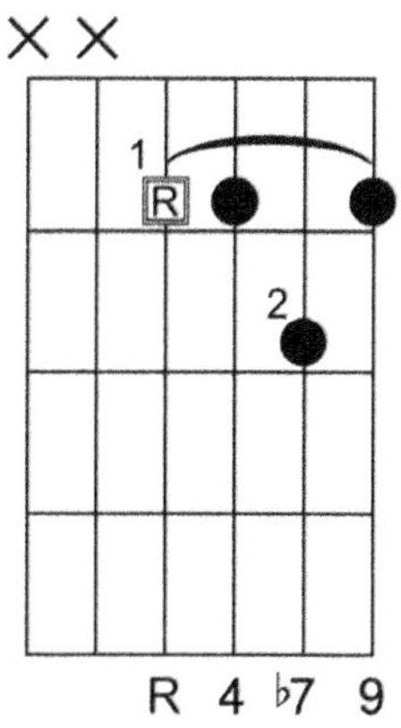

Q39) Can you work out / play A♭7♭5♭9 pattern 3?

Q40) E7♯5♯9 pattern 1?

Q41) G♯7♭5♯9 pattern 3?

Q42) F7♯5♭9 pattern 4?

Q43) E♭maj9♯11 pattern 1?

Sixth, added 9th (R 3 5 6 9)

Pattern 1

C6/9

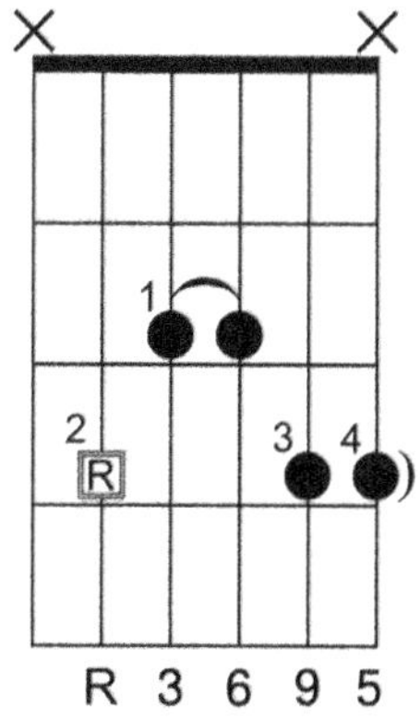

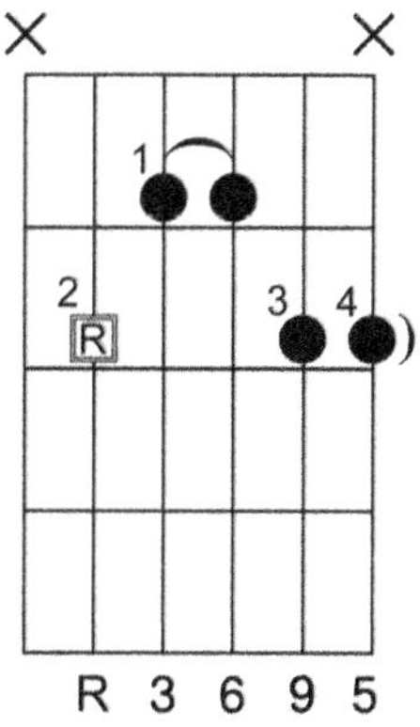

Pattern 3

G6/9

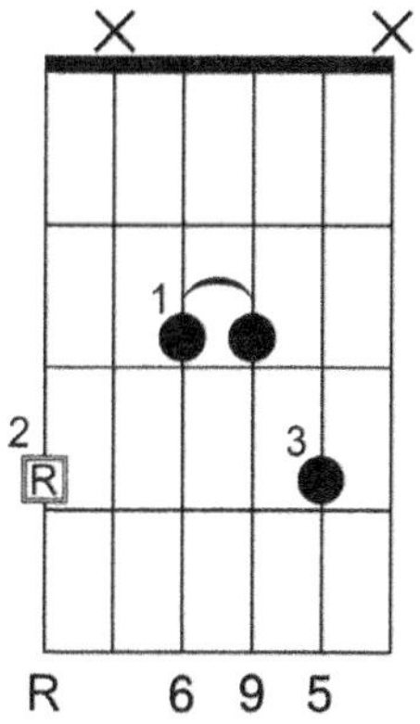

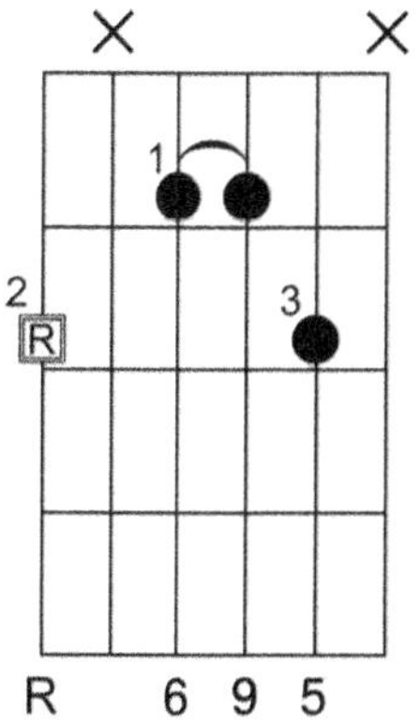

Pattern 4 (root on 4th)

E6/9

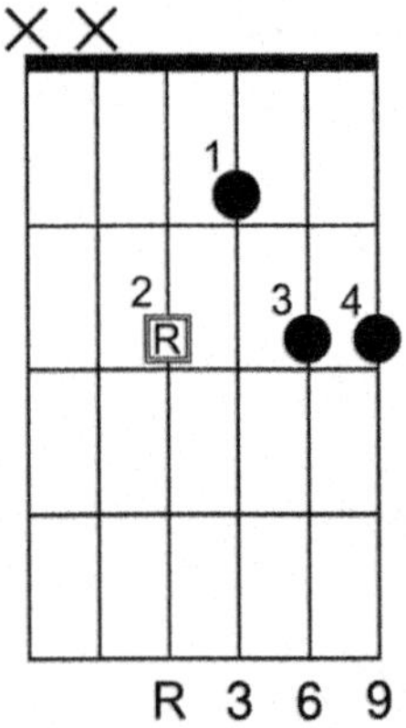

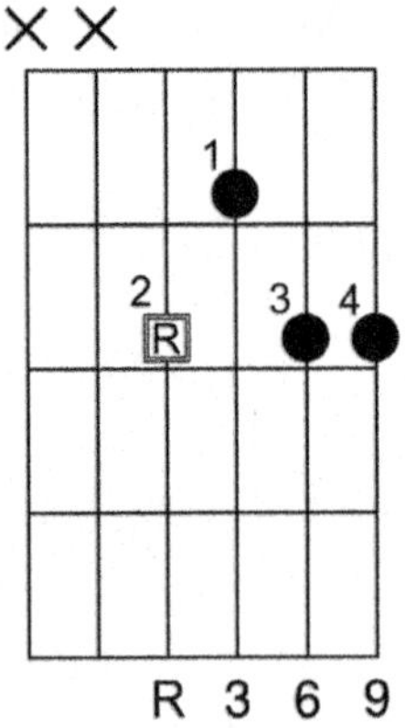

Q44) Can you work out / play A♯9♭5 pattern 1?

Q45) G9♯5 pattern 4?

Q46) F♯9sus4 pattern 5?

Q47) B♭6/9 pattern 4 (root on 4th)?

Minor ♭6th (R ♭3 5 ♭6)

Pattern 1

Cm♭6

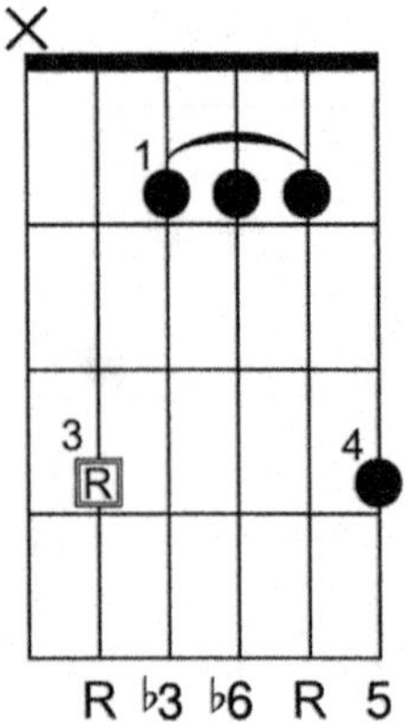

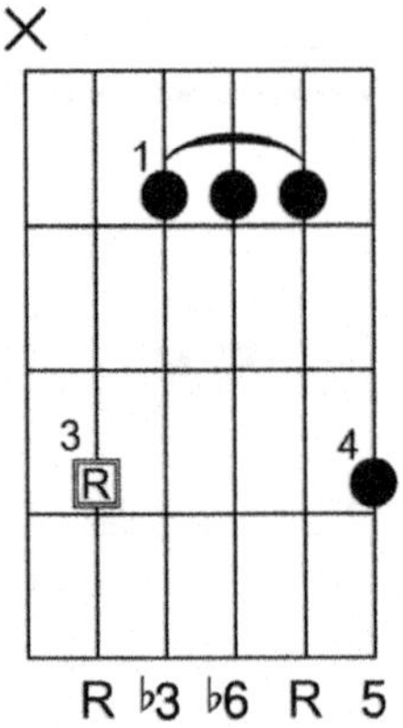

Pattern 2

Am♭6

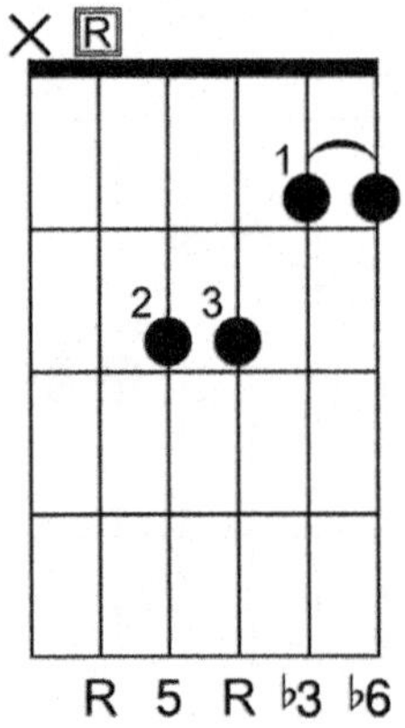

Transposable version impractical

Pattern 4

Em$^{\flat 6}$

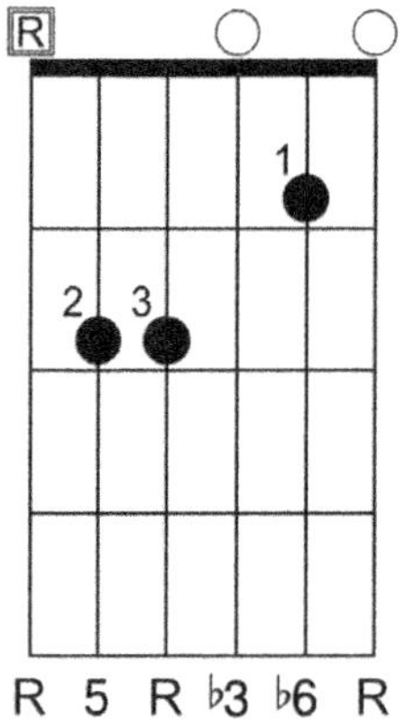

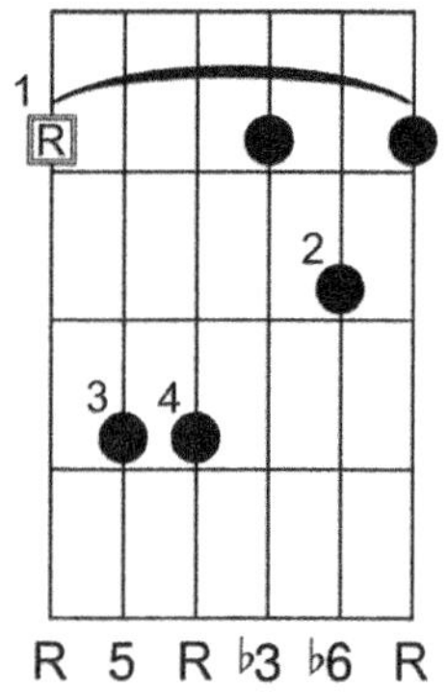

Q48) Can you work out / play Em$^{\flat}$6 pattern 1?

Minor 6th added 9 (R ♭3 5 6 9)

Pattern 1

Cm$^{6/9}$

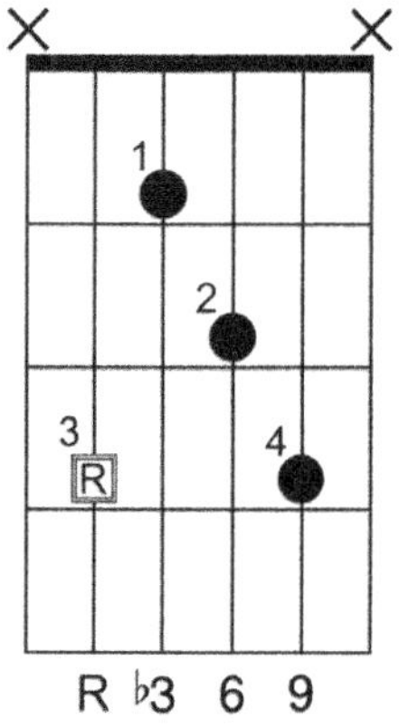

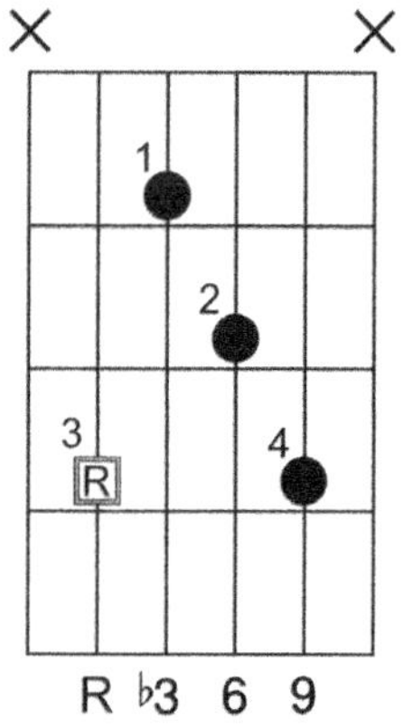

Pattern 4

Em$^{6/9}$

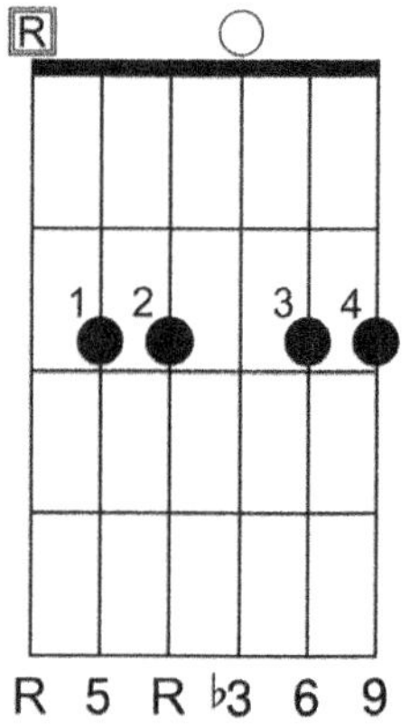

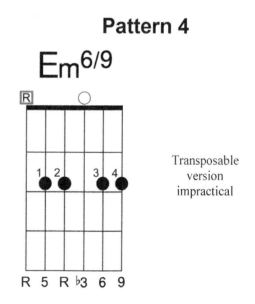

Transposable version impractical

Pattern 4 (root on 4th)

Em6/9

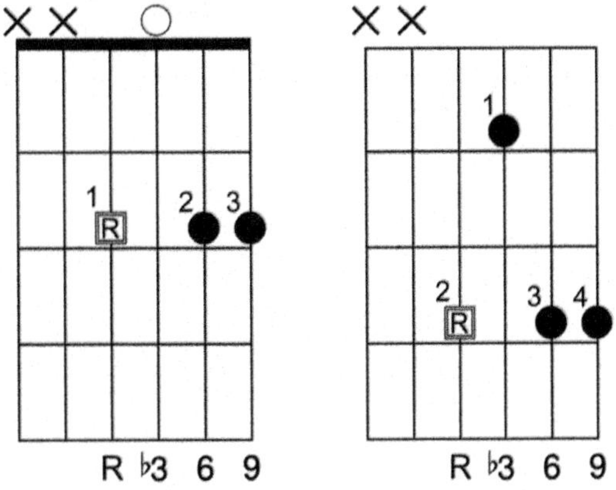

Q49) Can you work out / play Fm6/9 pattern 4 (root on 4th)?

Minor 9th ♯5 (R ♭3 ♯5 ♭7 9)

Pattern 4

Em9♯5

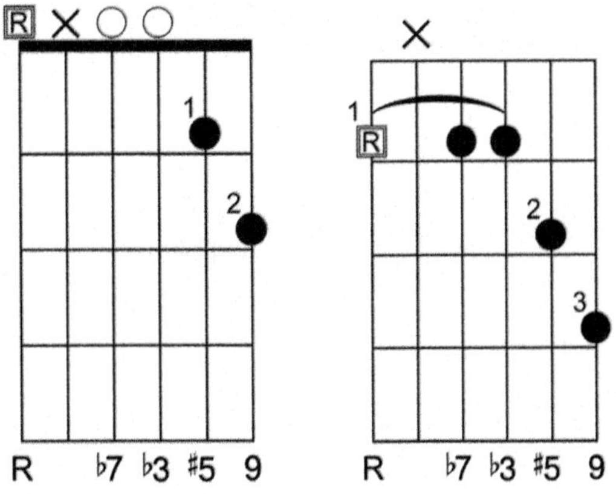

Q50) Can you work out / play Cm9♯5 pattern 4?

Minor 9th (major 7th) (R ♭3 5 7 9)

Pattern 1

Cm9(maj7)

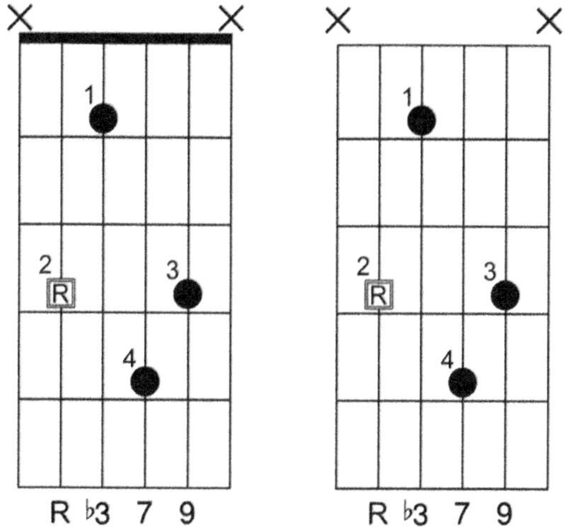

Pattern 3

Gm9(maj7)

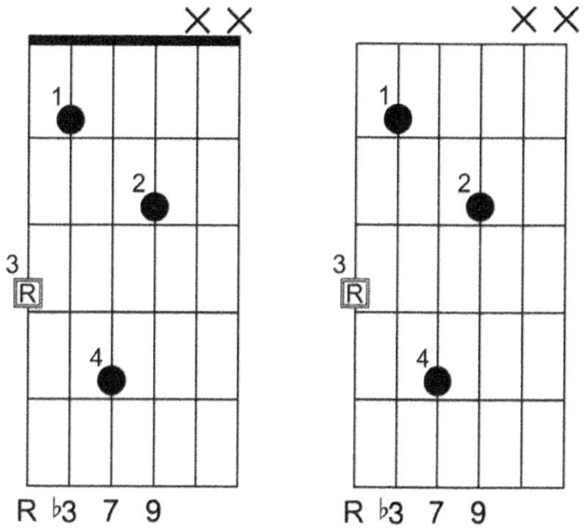

Pattern 4

Em9(maj7)

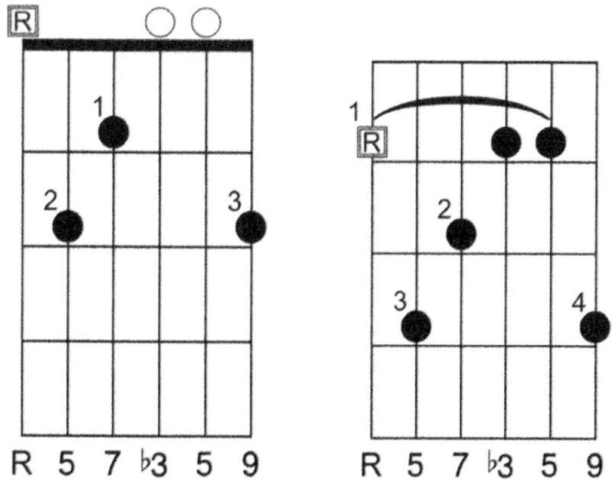

Q51) Can you work out / play Dm9(maj7) pattern 3?

Dominant 13th ♭9 (R 3 5 ♭7 ♭9 11 13)

Pattern 3

G13♭9

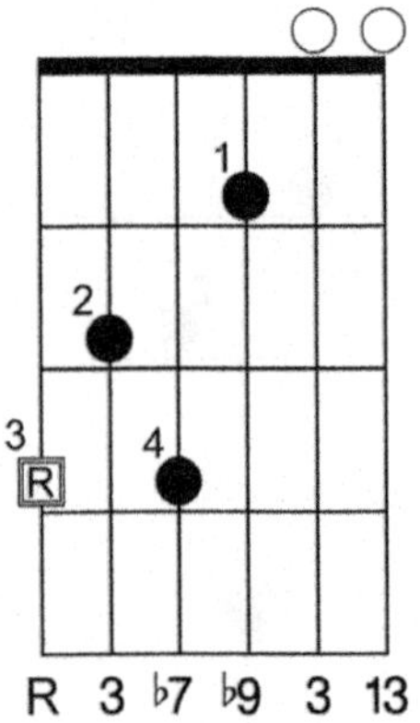

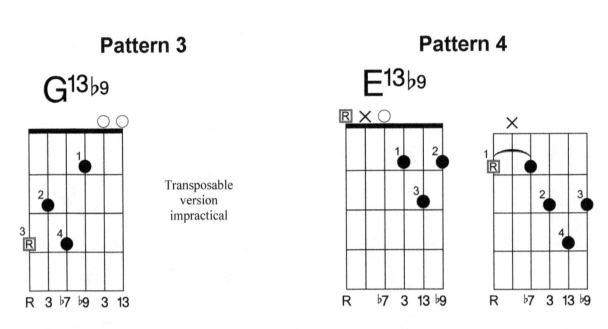

Transposable version impractical

Pattern 4

E13♭9

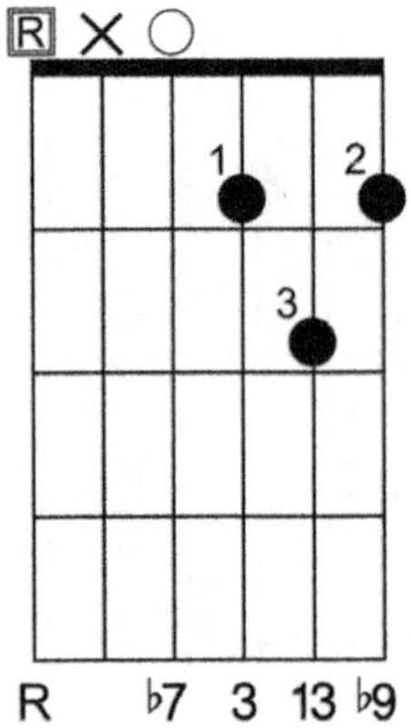

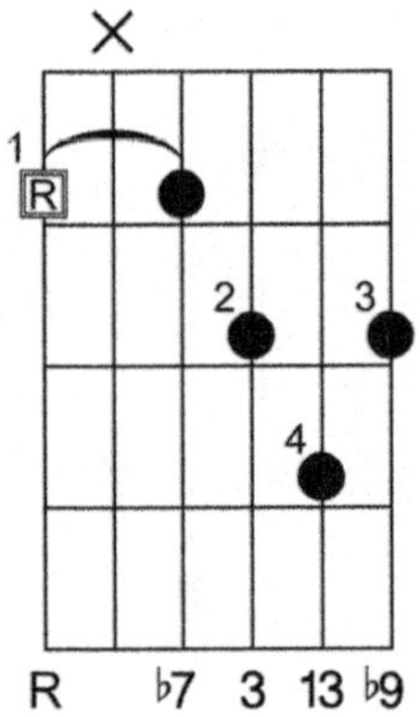

Dominant 13th ♯9 (R 3 5 ♭7 ♯9 11 13)

Pattern 1

C13♯9

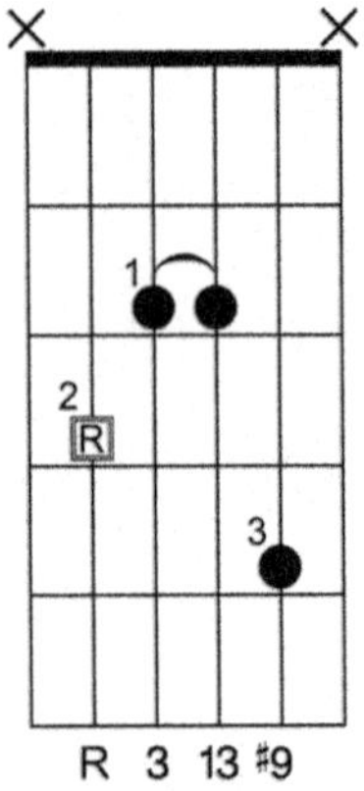

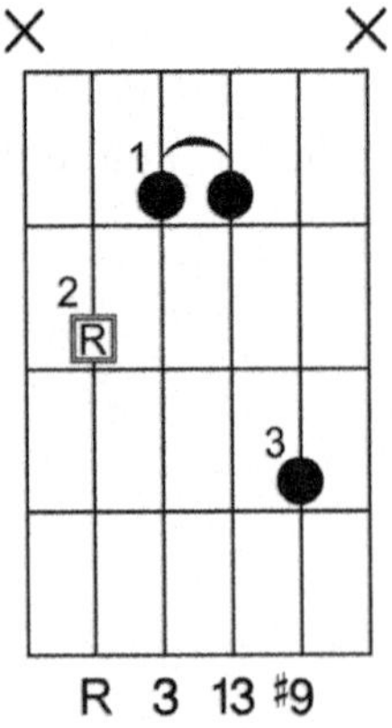

Pattern 4

E13♯9

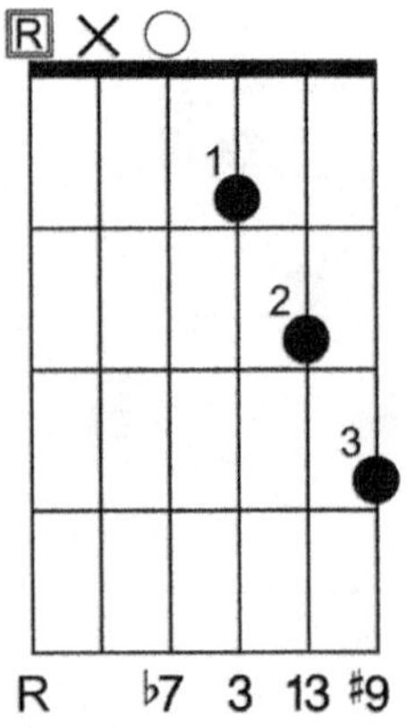

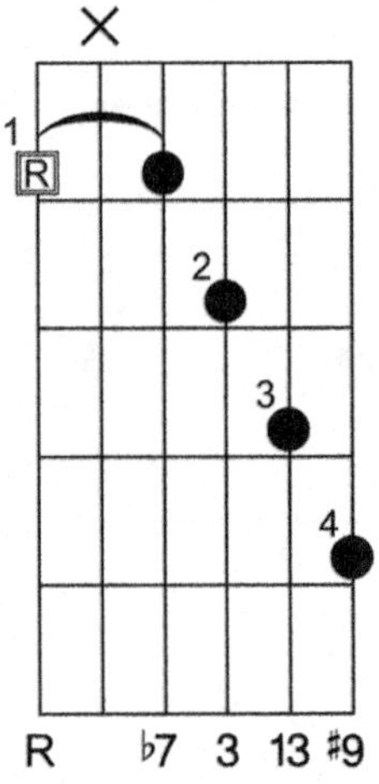

Dominant 13th #11 (R 3 5 ♭7 9 #11 13)

Pattern 1

C13#11

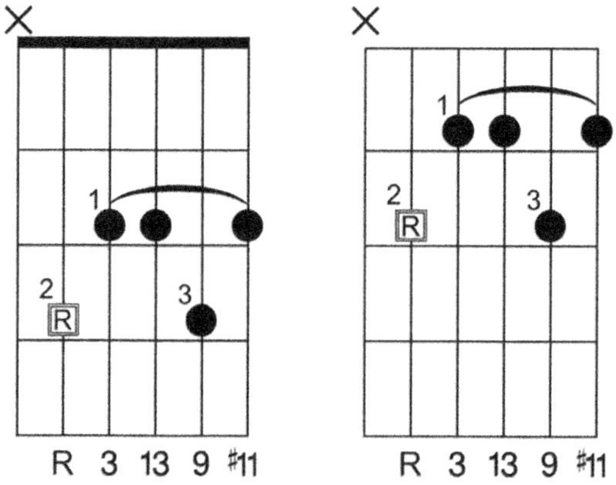

Q52) Can you work out / play B13♭9 pattern 4?

Q53) B13#9 pattern 1?

Q54) G♭13#11 pattern 1?

Dominant 13th sus4 (R 4 5 ♭7 9 13)

Pattern 2

A13sus4

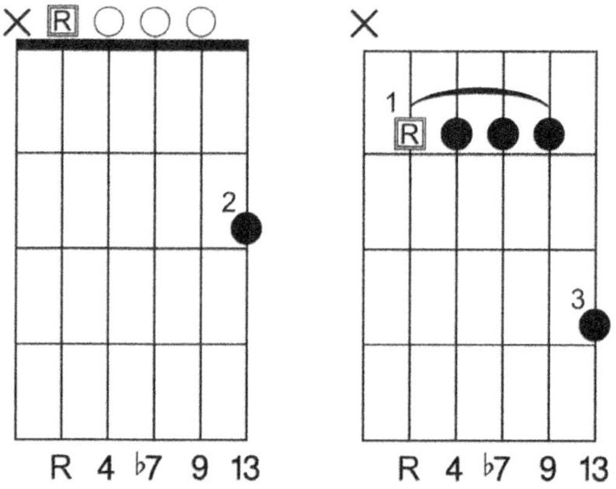

Pattern 4

E13sus4

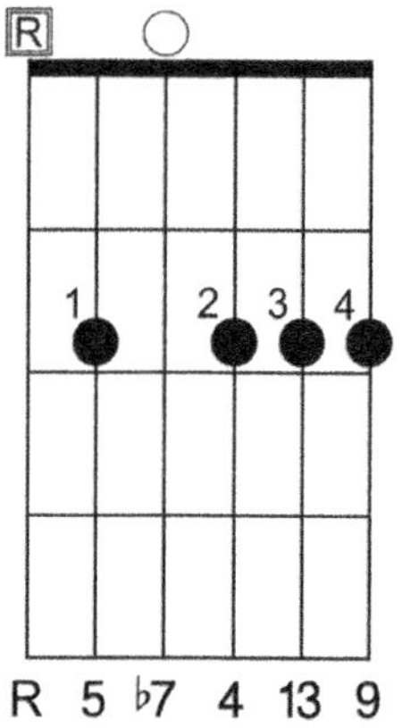

Transposable version impractical

Q55) Can you work out / play E13sus4 pattern 2?

Music Theory

The Major scale is the basis of music in the West. Everything else in Western music is defined in comparison to it.

The Major scale consists of seven notes, their distance from each other measured in tones (2 frets apart) and semitones (1 fret apart). This gives us numbers known as *intervals,* which relate to how far the notes are from the starting note (the root). As follows…

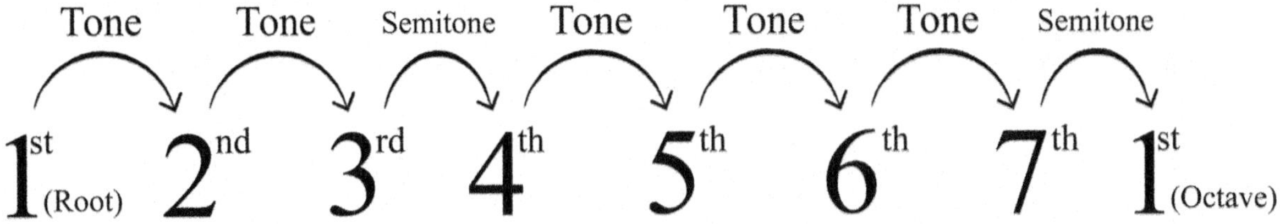

We will start by making a C major scale, as this scale contains no sharp or flat notes, which makes it simpler. The piano works well to show this due to the linear layout of its keys (similar to a single string of the guitar). On the piano a tone is two piano keys apart while a semitone is one piano key apart (black keys included when counting up or down). Here is a C major scale on the piano…

To create this scale on the guitar we will start with the 1st fret of the 2nd string (the B string) giving us the note of C. This will be the root note of our C major scale. From this root note move up the fret-board according to the formula TTSTTTS (T for tone and S for semitone) and we should end up with a completed C major scale, as shown on the next page.

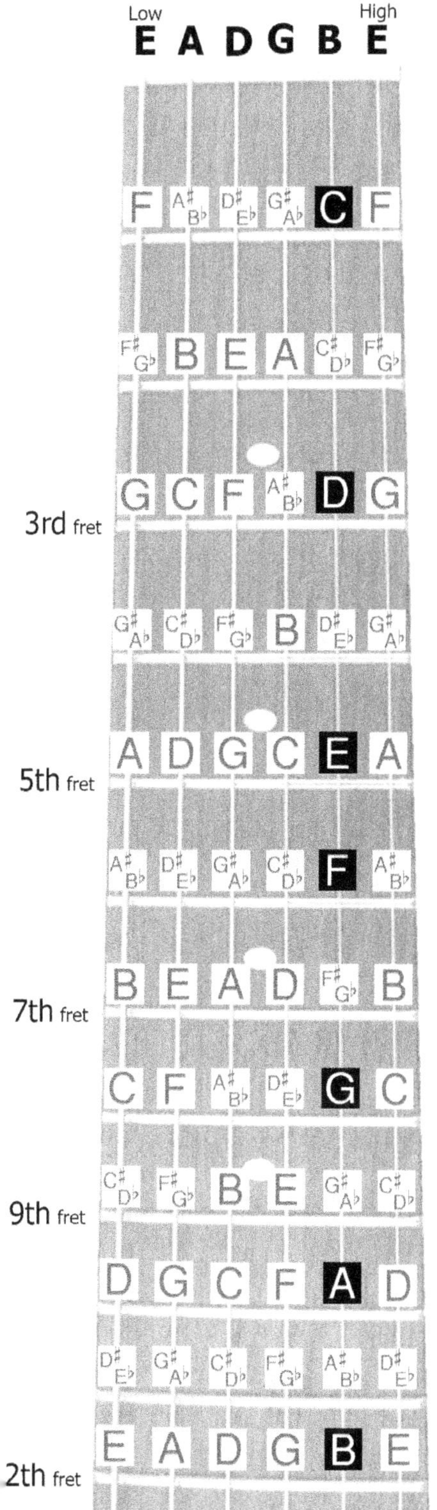

The last note of C major (C) is on the 13th fret of the B string.

On the guitar however, scales are usually played on multiple strings keeping the hand in the same area of the fret-board. Below is the scale played over multiple strings.

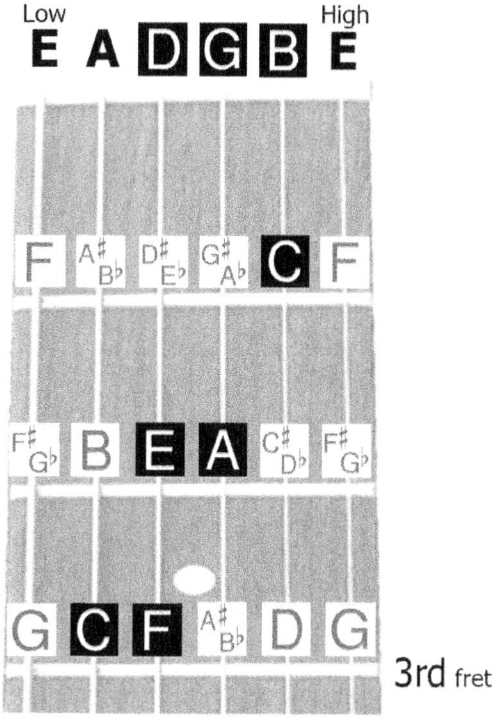

Here it is in tablature…

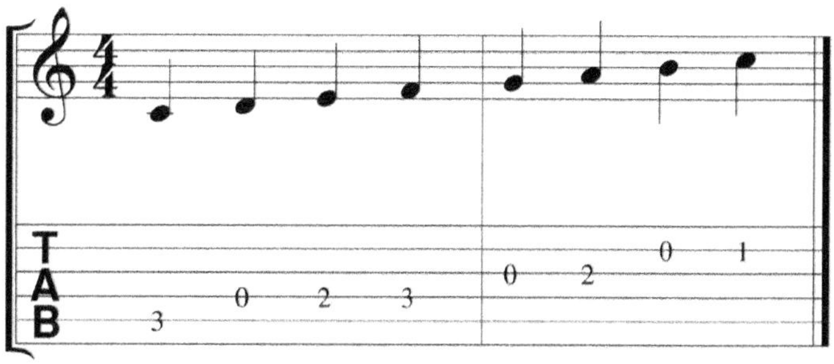

The first and most basic principle behind chords is that we take the odd-numbered intervals from the scale. For the major triad, we take the root (1st), major 3rd and the perfect 5th from the major scale as follows…

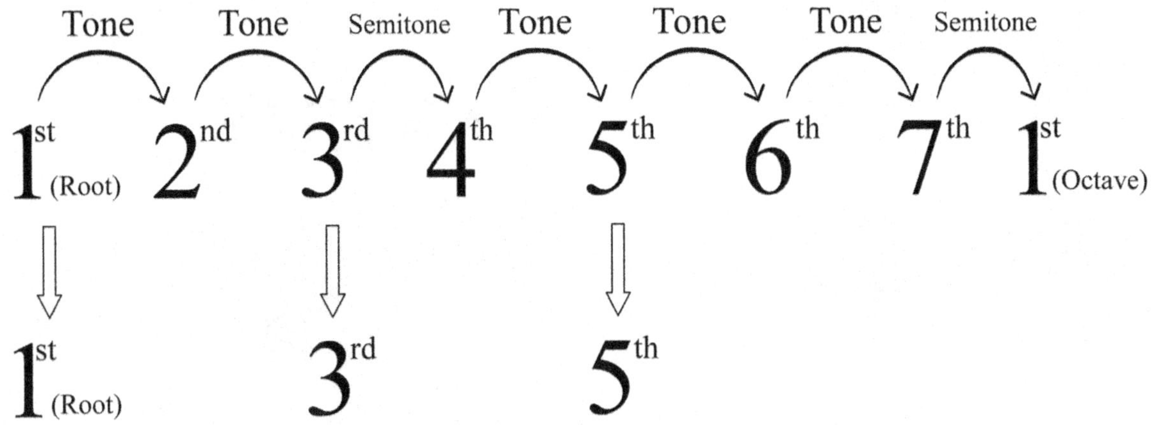

On the piano, for C major, it would look like this…

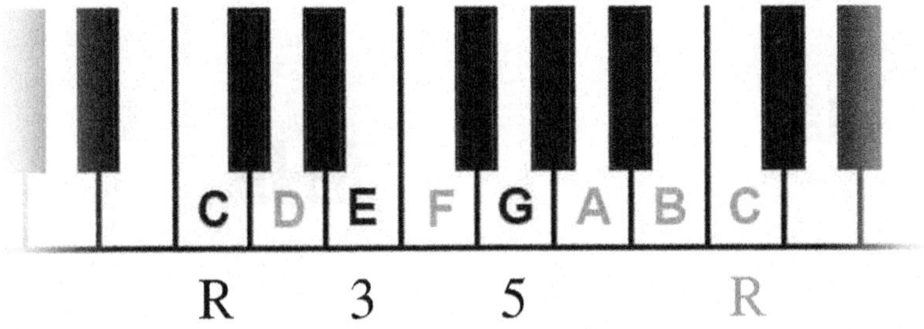

The fret-board diagram shows the C major scale (from the previous page) with the 3rd and 5th marked out in white circles, the roots in squares…

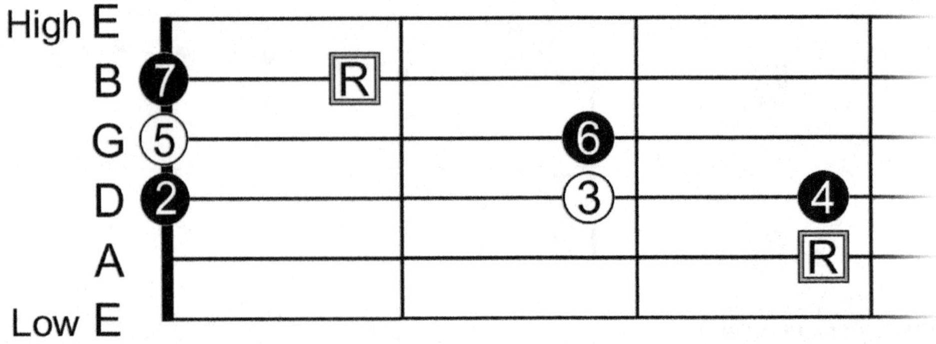

If we play these together we have a C major triad. In the photo the 3rd and 2nd fingers are used for the root (C) and 3rd (E) while the G string played open is the 5th interval. This major triad gives a clear major sound.

However if we play these intervals where they occur on other strings as well, then we get a fuller sounding chord. In the diagram to the right is the C major triad but with the root and 3rd (C and E) marked out again where they also occur in higher octaves on the top two strings...

Below is a C major chord on a conventional fret-board diagram…

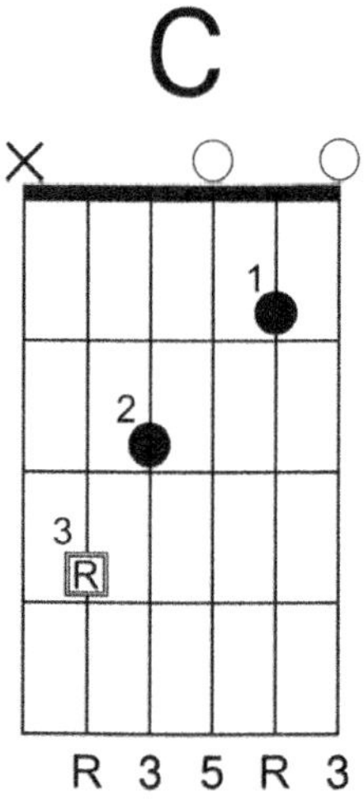

If we refer to the fret-board diagram on the previous page then we can find the 7th interval for a major 7th chord (which is constructed of the Root, 3rd, 5th and 7th), as shown to the right…

Note: The fundamental major scale, minor scale and intervallic structure of basic major and minor chords are also introduced in my other book: "Learn to Play Guitar" (pages 23-27, 30-35 and 37-42).

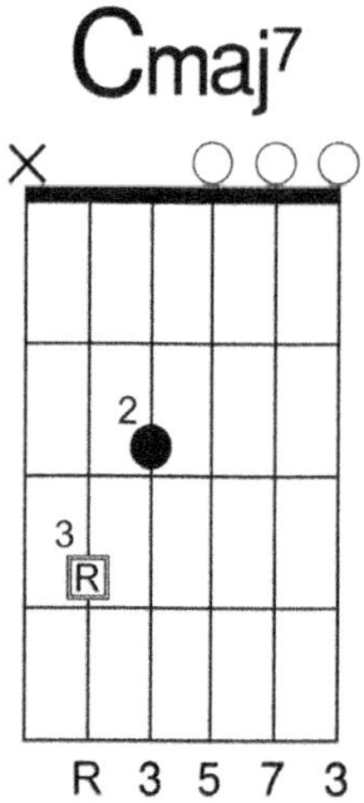

A chord's intervals don't have to be arranged in order, such as Root, 3rd, 5th etc. The other open chord shapes on page 6 are arranged differently, but they are still major chords.

There are, of course, many chord types other than major and major 7th and there are also more intervals than the ones from within the major scale. If we take the semitone increments between the notes of the major scale then we get more intervals (the major scale intervals are also known as *diatonic* intervals, so the ones in-between are *non-diatonic* intervals). Below is a list of the major scale intervals (R 2 3 4 5 6 7 R) with the intervals that are in-between them listed also (all abbreviations in brackets)…

Root (R) minor 2nd (♭2) Major 2nd (2) minor 3rd (♭3) Major 3rd (3) Perfect 4th (4)

Diminished 5th (♭5) Perfect 5th (5th) Augmented 5th (#5) minor 6th (♭6) Major 6th (6)

Double flat 7th (♭♭7) minor 7th (♭7) Major 7th (7) Octave of Root (R)

Note: As the names of the new intervals imply, these are regarded as lowered or raised versions of the major scale intervals. This semitone adjustment is indicated with the use of the flat ♭ or sharp # symbol, for instance ♭3 or #5. This is different from note names such as "G♭ or F#" so don't get them confused.

Here they are on the piano shown from the C major scale.

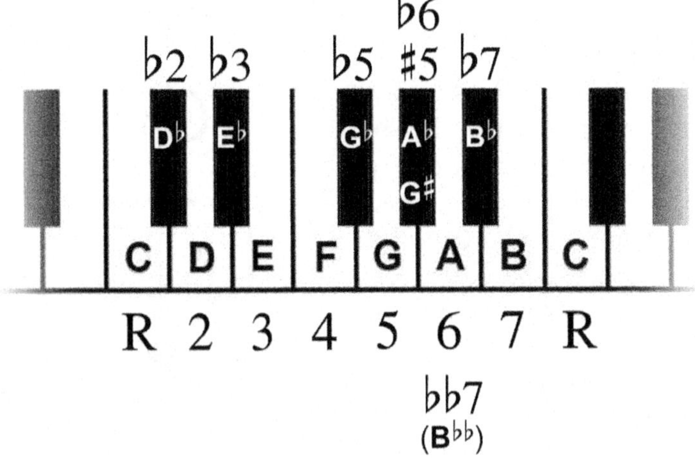

The ♭6 (A♭) and #5 (G#) are harmonic equivalents and so are the ♭♭7 (B♭♭) and 6th (A).

B♭♭ would be pronounced "B double flat".

These are known as *simple* intervals because they exist between the root note and the higher octave of the root note.

Intervals that go higher up are called compound intervals (the relevant dictionary definition of the word “compound” is “to add to or increase”). In relation to the original root note, these intervals are the simple ones, but in a higher octave. Here is an example using the notes from a C major scale…

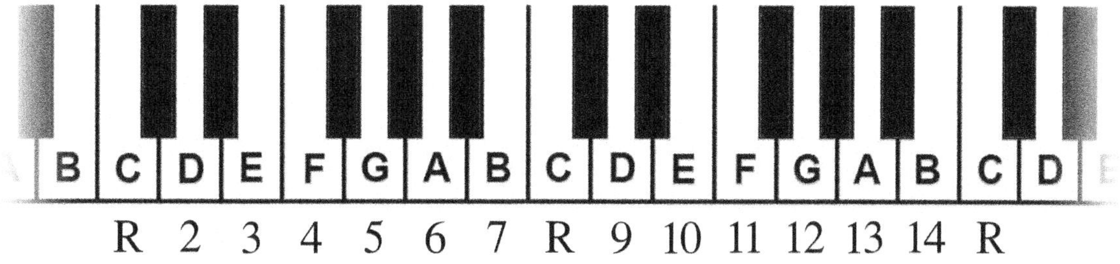

Starting on the left with the note of C it goes through the C major scale. When it reaches C again in a higher octave, the scale repeats again through a higher octave. The 9th is the higher octave of the 2nd, as is the 10th of the 3rd, the 11th of the 4th, the 12th of the 5th, the 13th of the 6th, and the 14th of the 7th.

In the same way that there are other intervals between those of the major scale there are also other compound intervals between the compound intervals of the major scale. Only a few compound intervals are actually used in chords however. As follows…

minor9th (♭9) Major9th (9) Sharp9th (♯9) Perfect11th (11) Sharp11th (♯11) Major13th (13)

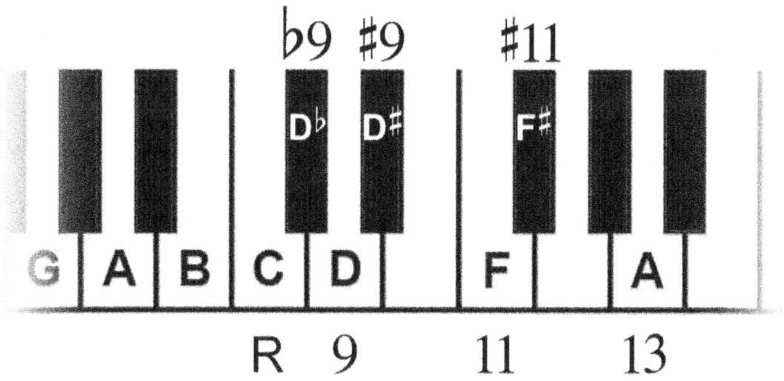

Chords that use the 9th, 11th or 13th are known as *extended chords*, such as major 9th (page 23) or Dominant 13th (page 29). Chords that use the ♭9th, ♯9th or ♯11th (as well as ♭5th or ♯5th) are known as *altered chords*, such as Dominant 7th♯5 (page 35) or Dominant 7th♭9 (page 38).

Following are all of the intervals we have just looked at, shown as shapes on the fret-board. These make up the chords within this book. Simple intervals and their compound equivalents are included on the same diagrams, and each interval appears in more than one place. * As $\flat 2^{nd}$ is never used within chords, only the $\flat 9^{th}$ is shown between the Root (R) and the 2nd / 9th.

From Root Note on 6th string

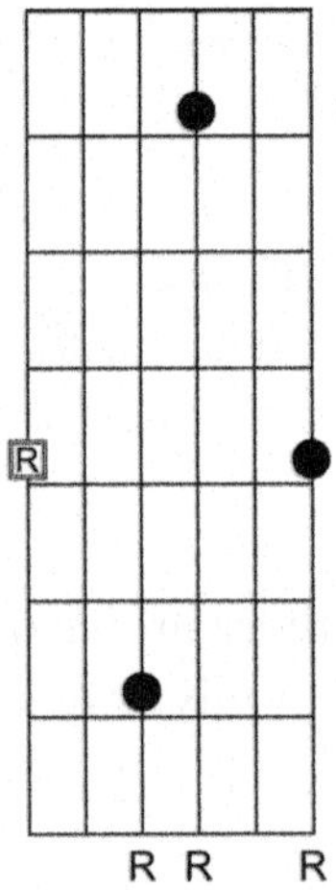

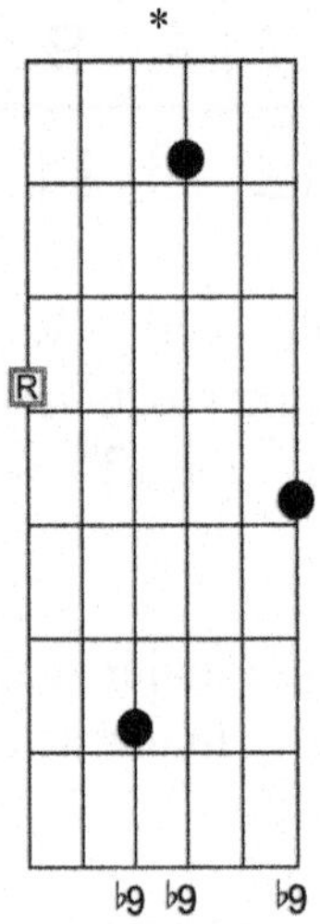

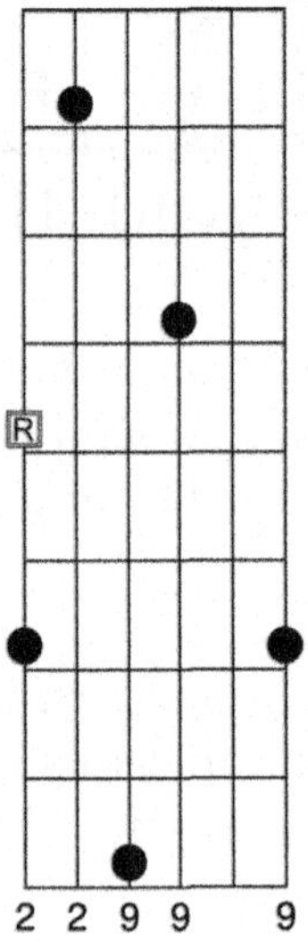

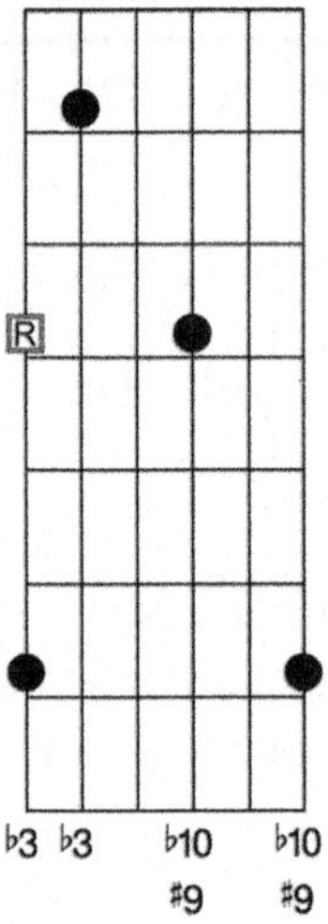

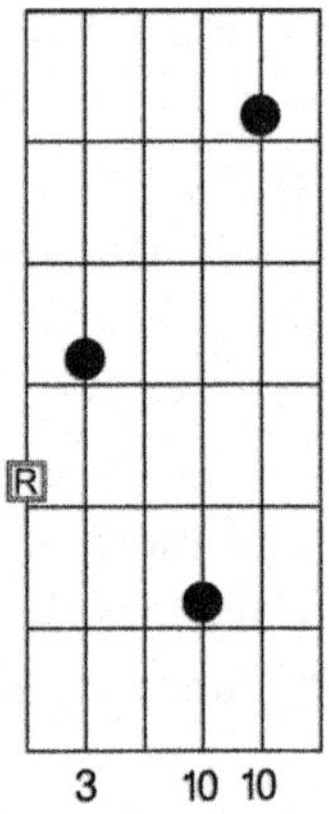

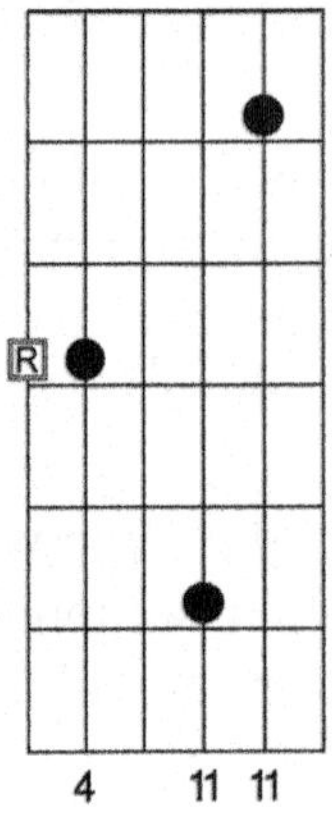

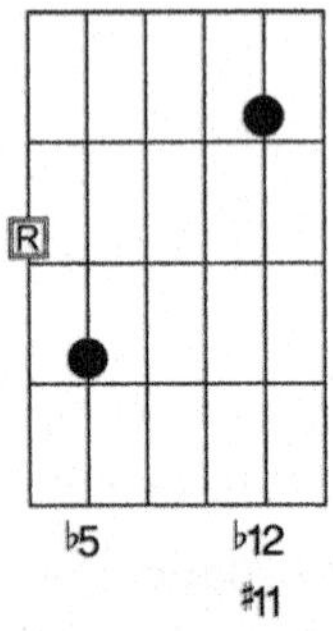

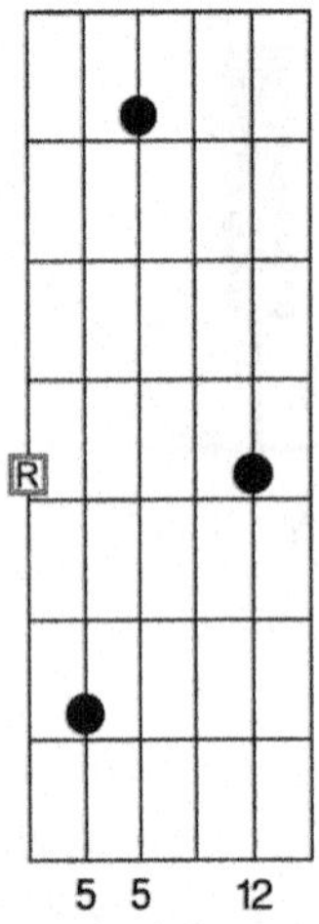

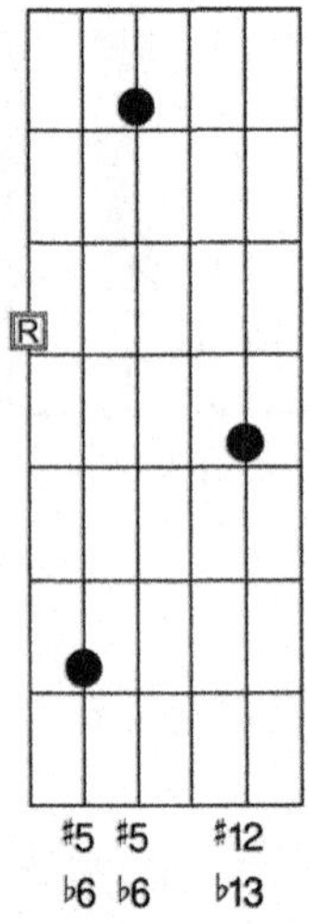

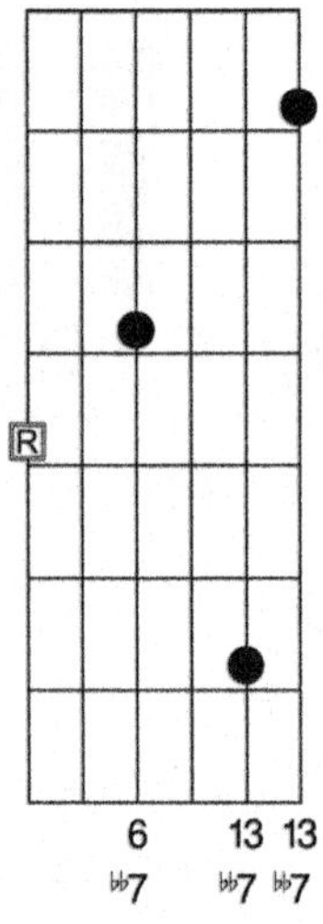

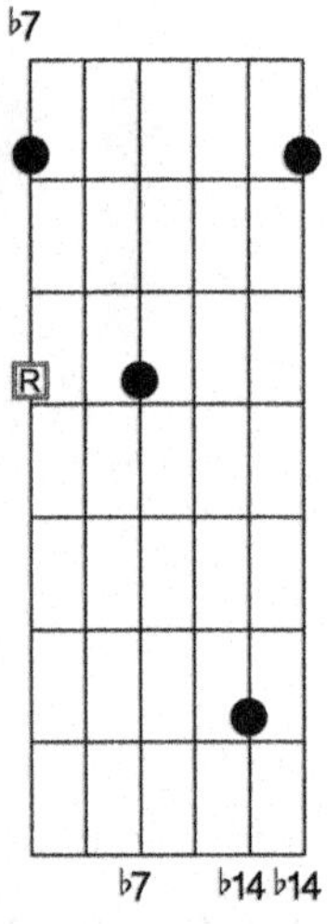

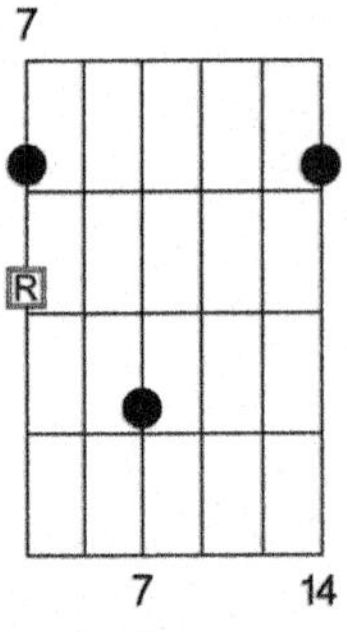

From Root Note on 5th string

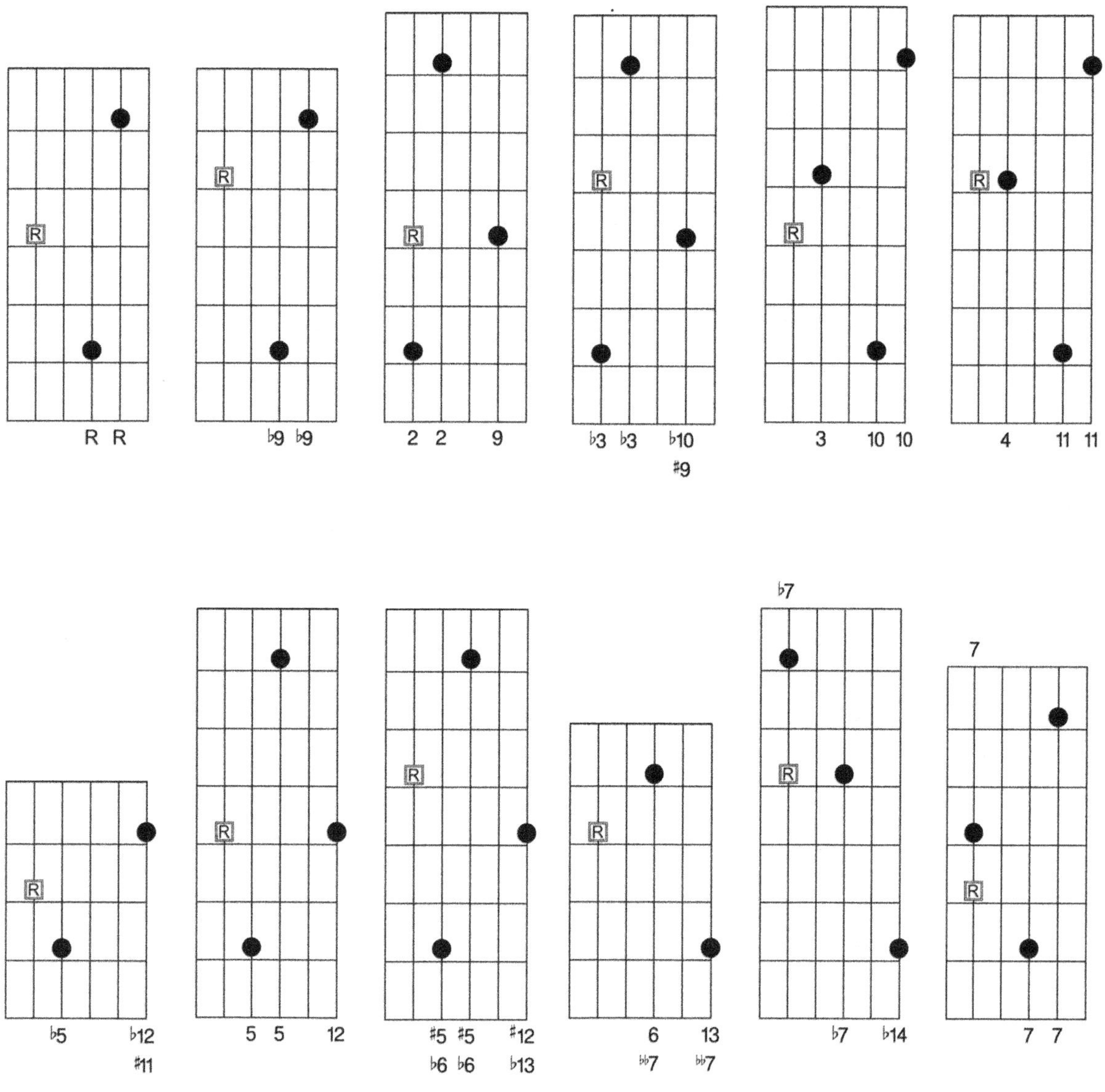

From Root Note on 4th string

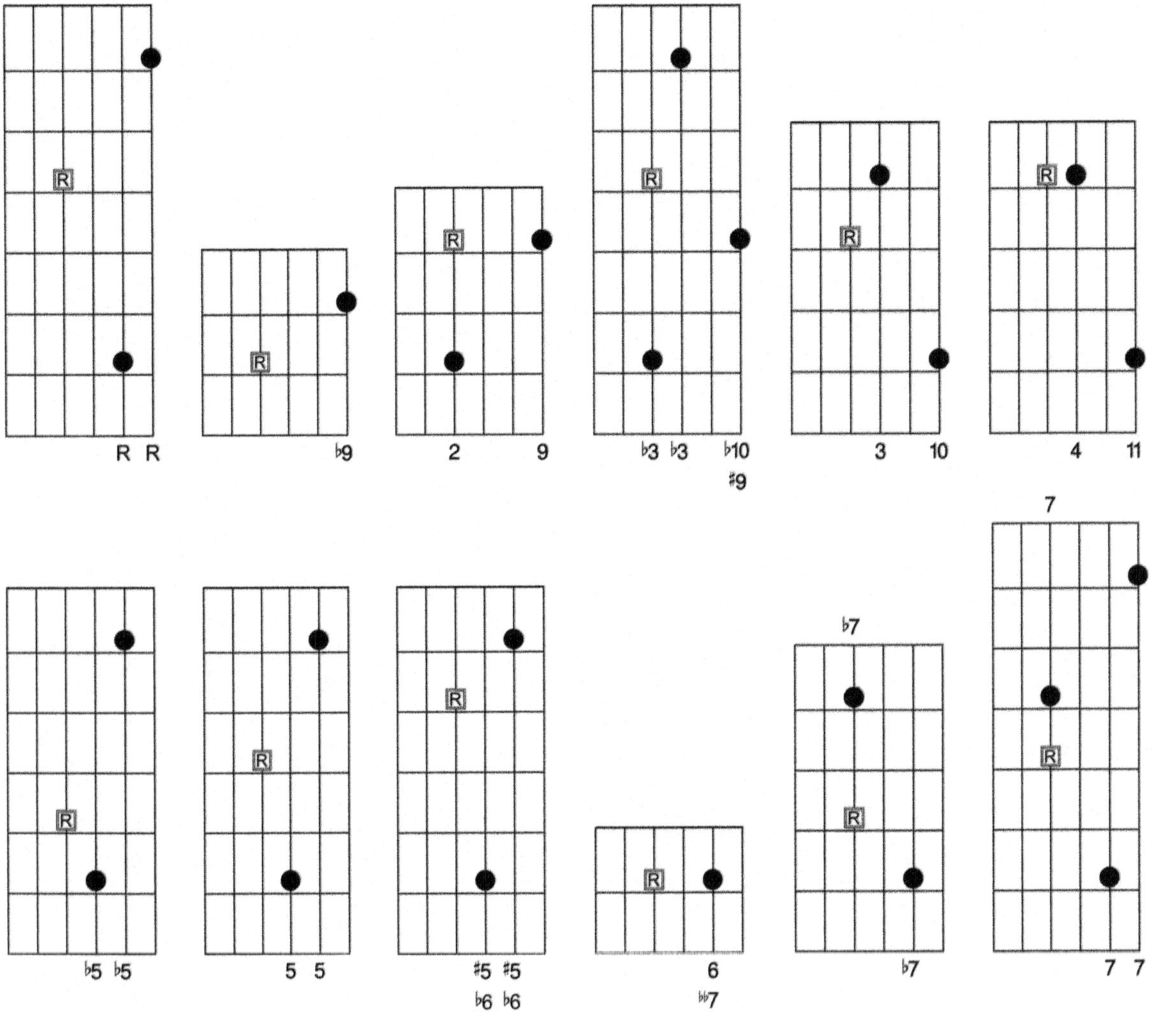

All of the above intervals are shown on frets but the same shapes apply when the Root or interval is on an open string, for example the 5th on the open 2nd string, or the Root of the 13th on the open 5th string, as shown to the right…

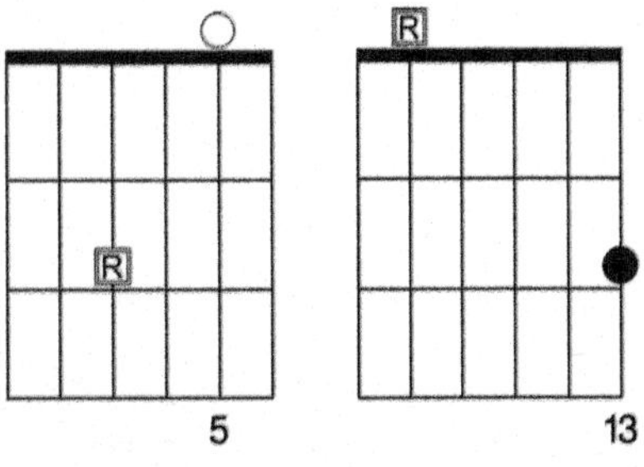

So how come only certain compound intervals are used in chords? Chords are usually constructed from the odd numbered intervals, such as the major (R, 3, 5) or major 7th (R, 3, 5, 7) chords. The compound intervals of the Root, 3rd, 5th and 7th (8th, 10th, 12th and 14th) are not worth noting as such because essentially they are the same (all be it in a higher octave), therefore would not make any significant change to a chord's structure or sound. This is why for instance, the C major chord explained on page 65 would not be called "C major 10th"; even though the note of E on the open 1st string is the 10th interval, it is the higher octave of the 3rd, which is already in the chord.

Compound intervals 9th, 11th and 13th do change the structure and sound of the chord. For example a Cadd9 chord would consist of Root, 3rd, 5th and 9th (the 9th being the compound interval of the 2nd). Here is a Cadd9 chord on the piano to show it simply in a line and then a Cadd9 chord on the fret-board to its right.

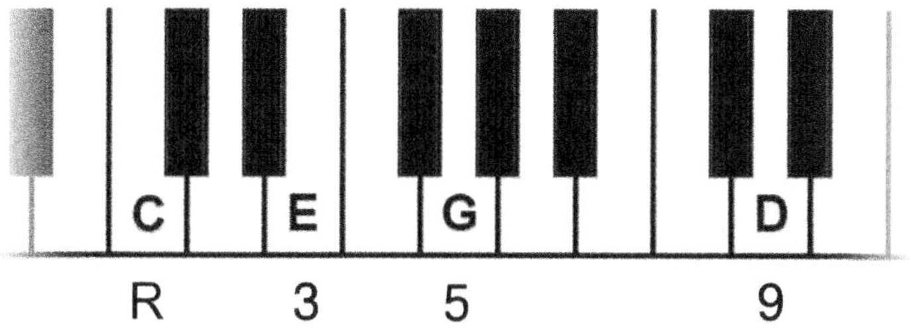

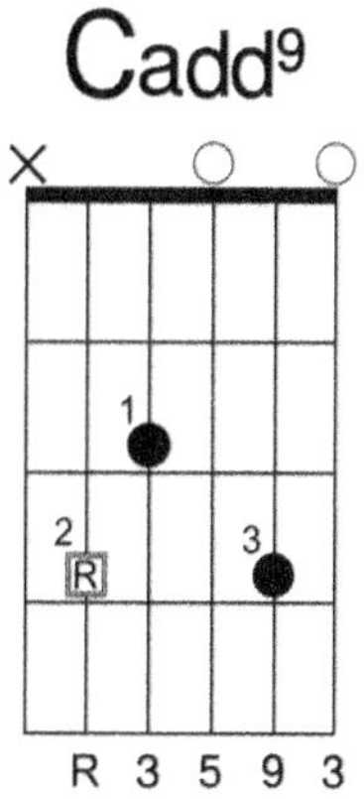

Because the guitar has a limit of six notes at the same time on its six strings there is a relatively limited number of ways to finger chords and without making them impossible to play. On a piano, potentially there is a maximum of ten different notes that can be played (for all fingers and thumbs). The major 13th chord contains 7 intervals, on the piano a Gmaj13 chord for instance might look like this…

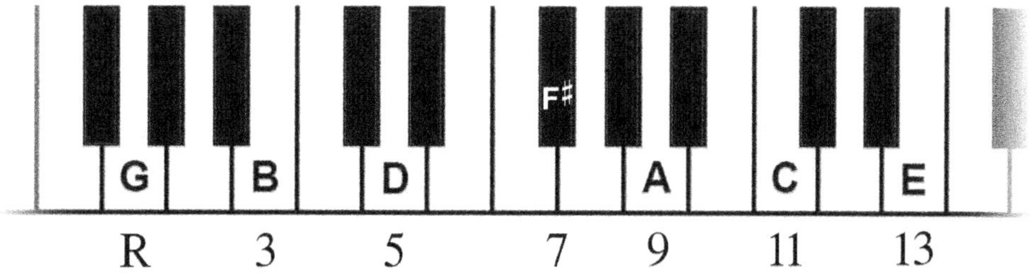

On the guitar not all of a chord's intervals are always played. Ones that don't affect the function of the chord can be left out, particularly for more complex chord types with more intervals. In the Gmaj13 chord below there is no 11th. To its right a Dominant 11th chord (made up of R, 3, 5, ♭7, 9, 11) but for the A11 there is no 9th.

This comes down to practicality; it would have been near impossible to finger either of those chords if playing all intervals (the first instance of this within the book is page 20; the Dominant 7th pattern 1 chord has no 5th).

For the same reason the location of the compound interval can be played *closer* to the root note within the 1st octave where its simple interval counterpart would normally be. For the Gmaj13 chord, the 13th is played where the 6th would be. For the A11 chord the 11th is played where the 4th would be.

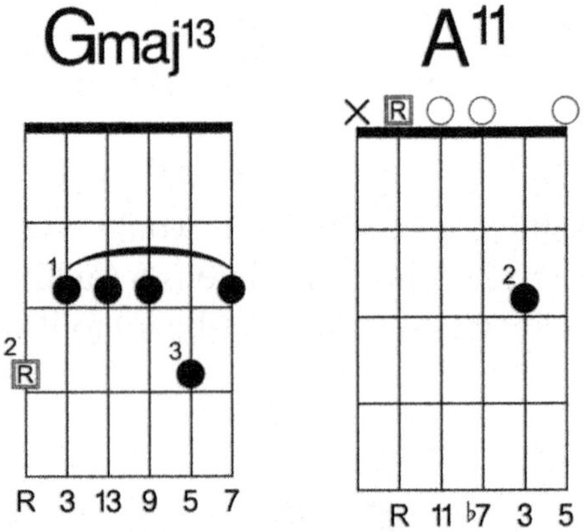

Simple intervals other than the Root, 3rd, 5th and 7th can also be used in chords, such as the 2nd in the sus2 chord or the 6th in the major 6th chord. Similarly to the above, because of the relative limitations of the fret-board, in some instances the location of the simple interval is played *further* from the root note and above the 1st octave where its compound interval counterpart would be.

For the Asus2 chord the 2nd is played where the 9th would normally be. For the A6 chord the 6th is played where the 13th would normally be.

Again this comes down to practicality; it would have been near impossible to finger either of those chords if playing the simple intervals in their normal locations.

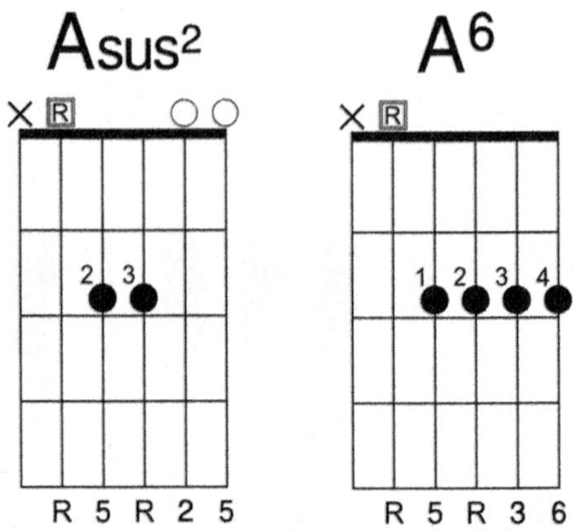

So to conclude: If it's an odd numbered interval (3rd ♭3rd, ♭5th, 5th, ♯5th, ♭♭7th, ♭7th or 7th) none of these, when compounds, are indicated as such because they won't change the structure or sound of the chord. In other words you will never see a chord indicated with the intervals ♭10th, 10th, ♭12th, 12th, ♯12th, ♭♭14th, ♭14th or 14th.

and…

Certain intervals can be left out to make chords more practical to play, and for the same reason simple and compound intervals can substitute each other's location on the fret-board.

A final note regarding the theory and fret-board knowledge side of things; knowing as many chord shapes as you need for whatever you are playing can be very useful, however aiming to know *all* chords and their shapes like this is not a worthwhile pursuit in the long run.

…*if* you aim for such a thing then it is better to understand the individual intervals on the fret-board and to be able to construct and identify chords from their intervallic structure (for instance being able to make a sus4 chord from its structure of Root, 4th and 5th) . This way you have the knowledge to construct new chords when you come across them (rather than starting from scratch learning new chord shapes). Granted that both methods will take time and may not be easy, the latter is the easier of the two for such a purpose. This is *if* you aim for such a thing, so don't be put off, this book is primarily a reference book of transposable chord shapes.

On the next page is a full list of the chords within this book. The left column is the chord type and the middle column shows the various symbols used for it, separated by commas and shown in C. The same symbols apply whatever the chord; for example B+ is for B augmented, or G♯+ is for G sharp augmented. This could also be useful if you see a chord symbol elsewhere and want to know what it is. On the right column is the formula for each chord type.

Chord Type	Symbol	Formula
Major	C	1 3 5
minor	Cm, C-	1 ♭3 5
Augmented	Caug, C+	1 3 ♯5
Diminished	Cdim, C°	1 ♭3 ♭5
Suspended	Csus4, Csus	1 4 5
Suspended 2nd	Csus2	1 2 5
Power Chords	C5	1 5
Major 7th	Cmaj7, CM7, C△7	1 3 5 7
Dominant 7th	C7, Cdom7	1 3 5 ♭7
minor 7th	Cm7, Cmin7, C-7	1 ♭3 5 ♭7
minor 7th ♭5	Cm7♭5, C-7♭5, Cø7	1 ♭3 ♭5 ♭7
Major 9th	Cmaj9, CM9, C△9	1 3 5 7 9
Dominant 9th	C9, Cdom9	1 3 5 ♭7 9
minor 9th	Cm9, Cmin9, C-9	1 ♭3 5 ♭7 9
Dominant 11th	C11, Cdom11	1 3 5 ♭7 9 11
minor 11th	Cm11, Cmin11, C-11	1 ♭3 5 ♭7 9 11
Major 13th	Cmaj13, CM13, C△13	1 3 5 7 9 11 13
Dominant 13th	C13, Cdom13	1 3 5 ♭7 9 11 13
minor 13th	Cm13, Cmin13, C-13	1 ♭3 5 ♭7 9 11 13
Major 7th ♯5	Cmaj7♯5, CM7♯5, C△7♯5	1 3 ♯5 7
Major 7th ♯11	Cmaj7♯11, CM7♯11, C△7♯11	1 3 5 7 ♯11
Major 7th ♭5	Cmaj7♭5, CM7♭5, C△7♭5	1 3 ♭5 7
Dominant 7th ♯5	C7♯5, C+7, Caug7	1 3 ♯5 ♭7
Dominant 7th ♭5	C7♭5, C7(-5)	1 3 ♭5 ♭7
Dominant 7th ♯11	C7♯11, C7(+11)	1 3 5 ♭7 ♯11
Dominant 7th ♯9	C7♯9, C7(+9)	1 3 5 ♭7 ♯9

Dominant 7th ♭9	C7♭9, C7(-9)	1 3 5 ♭7 ♭9
minor 7th ♯5	Cm7♯5, C-7♯5	1 ♭3 ♯5 ♭7
Dominant 7th sus4	C7sus4, C7sus	1 4 5 ♭7
Diminished 7th	Cdim7, C°7	1 ♭3 ♭5 ♭♭7
minor, major7th	Cm(maj7), C-(maj7)	1 ♭3 5 7
Major 6th	C6, Cmaj6	1 3 5 6
minor 6th	Cm6, Cmin6, C-6	1 ♭3 5 6
added 9th	Cadd9, C(add9)	1 3 5 9
minor added 9th	Cm(add9), C-(add9)	1 ♭3 5 9
Dominant 7th ♭5 ♭9	C7♭5(♭9), C7♭5♭9	1 3 ♭5 ♭7 ♭9
Domininant 7th ♯5 ♯9	C7♯5(♯9), C+7(♯9)	1 3 ♯5 ♭7 ♯9
Dominant 7th ♭5 ♯9	C7♭5(♯9), C7♭5♯9	1 3 ♭5 ♭7 ♯9
Dominant 7th ♯5 ♭9	C7♯5(♭9), C+7(♭9)	1 3 ♯5 ♭7 ♭9
Major 9th ♯11	Cmaj9♯11, CM9♯11, C△9♯11	1 3 5 7 9 ♯11
Dominant 9th ♭5	C9♭5, C9(-5)	1 3 ♭5 ♭7 9
Dominant 9th ♯11	C9♯11, C9(+11)	1 3 5 ♭7 9 ♯11
Dominant 9th ♯5	C9♯5, C+9, C9(+5)	1 3 ♯5 ♭7 9
Dominant 9th sus4	C9sus4, C9sus	1 4 5 ♭7 9
Sixth, added 9	C6/9	1 3 5 6 9
minor ♭6th	Cm♭6, Cmin♭6, C-♭6	1 ♭3 5 ♭6
minor 6th, added 9	Cm6/9, Cmin6/9, C-6/9	1 ♭3 5 6 9
minor 9th ♯5	Cm9♯5, Cmin9♯5, C-9♯5	1 ♭3 ♯5 ♭7 9
minor 9th (major 7th)	Cm9(maj7), C-9(maj7)	1 ♭3 5 7 9
Dominant 13th ♭9	C13♭9, C13(-9)	1 3 5 ♭7 ♭9 11 13
Dominant 13th ♯9	C13♯9, C13(+9)	1 3 5 ♭7 ♯9 11 13
Dominant 13th ♯11	C13♯11, C13(+11)	1 3 5 ♭7 9 ♯11 13
Dominant 13th sus4	C13sus4, C13sus	1 4 5 ♭7 9 13

Inverted Chords

So far in this book we have dealt with chords in which the lowest note (the bass note) is the Root note. An inverted chord is when a note from within the chord *other* than the Root is used for the bass note. An inverted chord appears as a normal chord symbol followed by a slash and another note, for instance "Em/B" which would be pronounced "E minor over B". The note after the slash is the bass note for the chord, so Em/B would be an E minor chord with the note of B for its bass note. An initial confusion behind slash chords can be when a major chord is used (and these are quite common), because the symbol for a major chord is the root note alone, so a D major chord with an A for the bass note would look like "D/A".

Major, 1st inversion (R 3 5) with 3rd as Bass

The major chord is made up of the Root, 3rd and 5th. When the 3rd is used for the bass note this is known as a 1st inversion. The following shapes are based on the CAGED patterns; they are the same but with the interval of the 3rd as the lowest bass note. In some cases the original root note within a small square is no longer present, so if locating a chord by this root note we can look at where it *would* be. In such cases the R within a square has been left for you to refer to but is faint with a diagonal line through it indicating *not* to play it.

Pattern 1

C/E

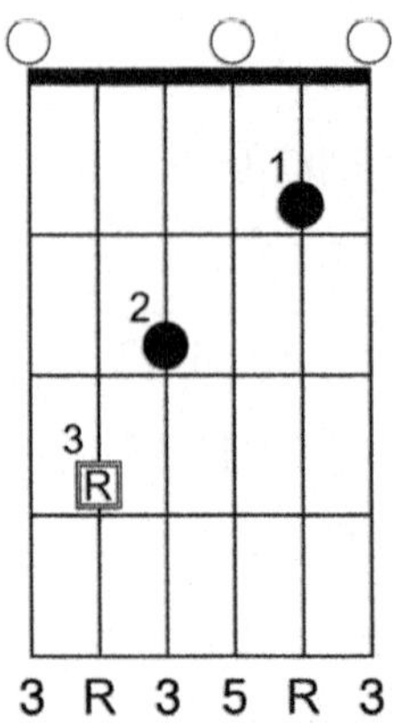

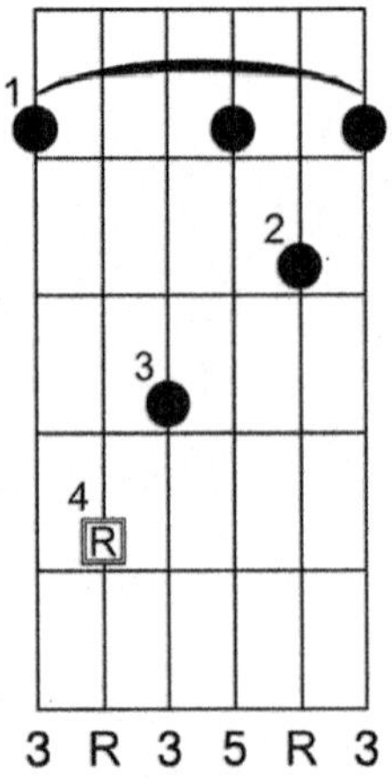

Pattern 2

A/C♯

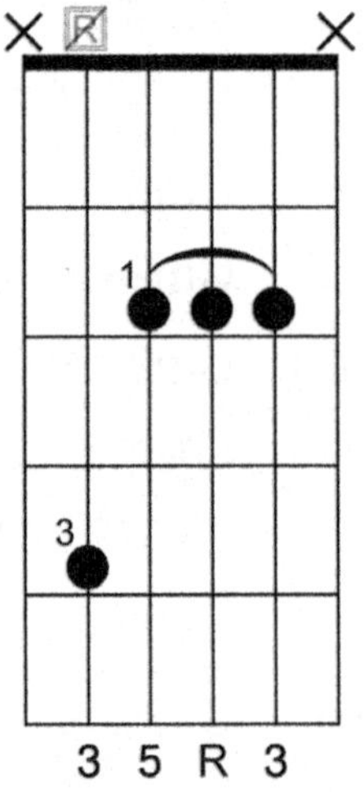

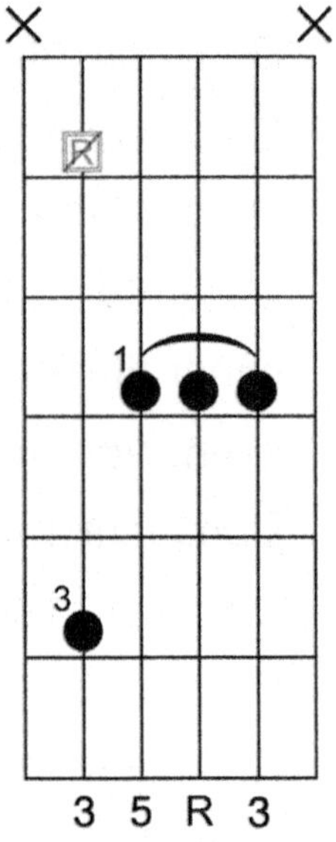

Pattern 3

G/B

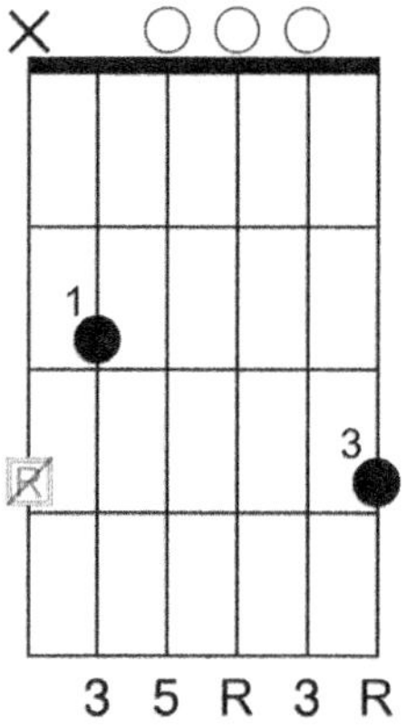

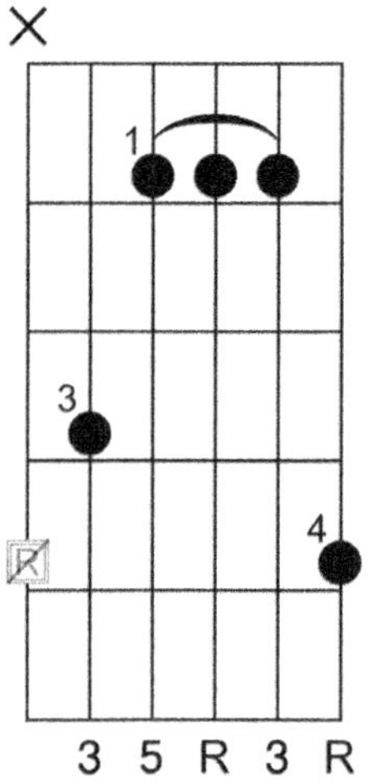

Pattern 4 (root on 4th)

No open chord version for G♯ 3rd

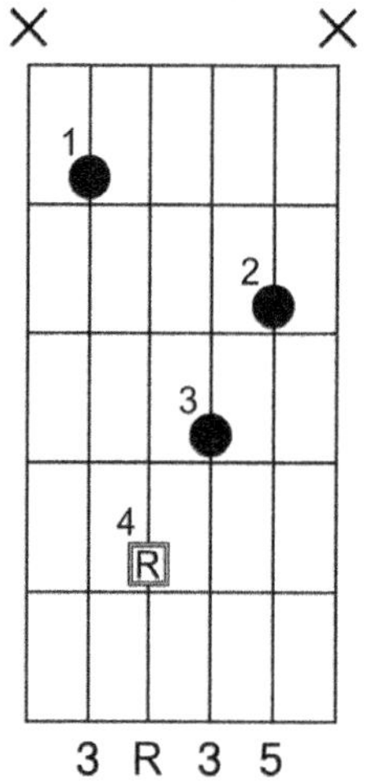

Pattern 5

D/F♯

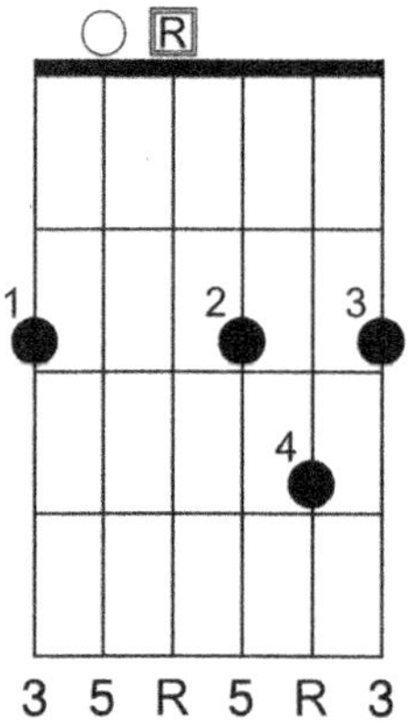

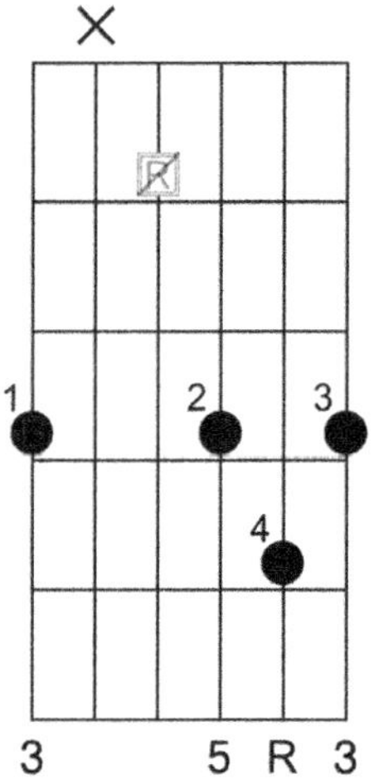

The answers to the following questions are based on where the root note is, or would be, from the original CAGED shape (i.e. the "R" in a small square).

Q56) C major 1st inversion (C/E) pattern 2?

Major, 2nd inversion (R 3 5) with 5th as Bass

When the 5th is used for the bass note this is known as a 2nd inversion.

Pattern 1

C/G

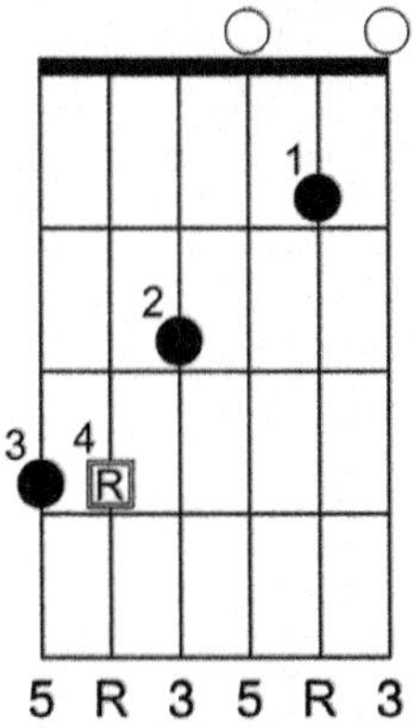

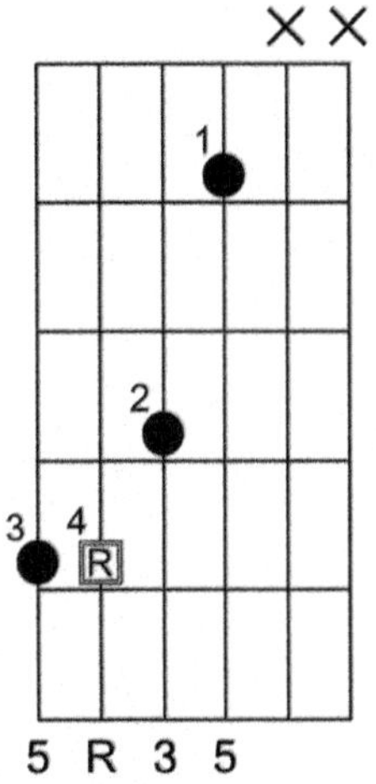

Pattern 2

A/E

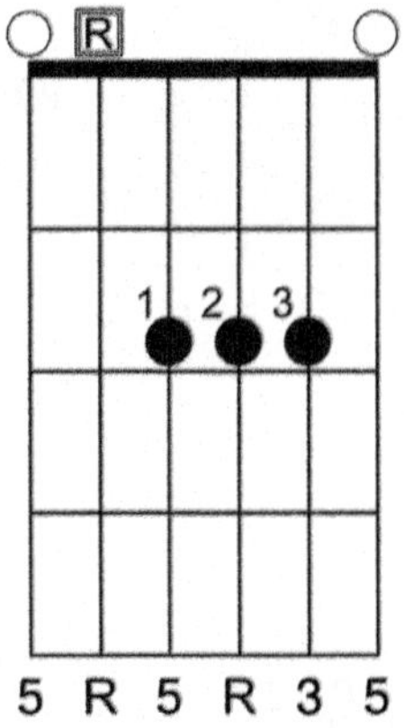

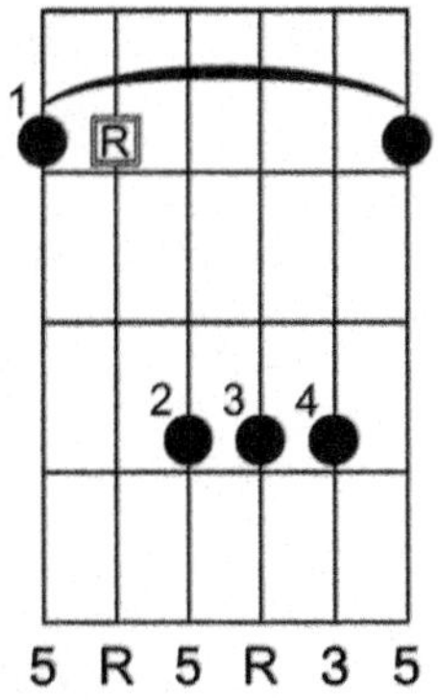

Pattern 3

G/D

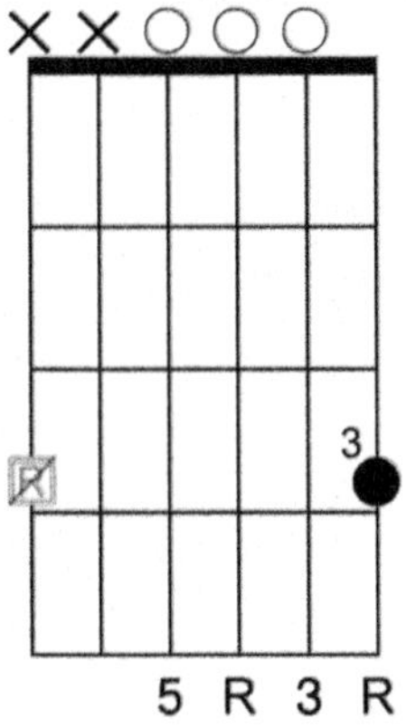

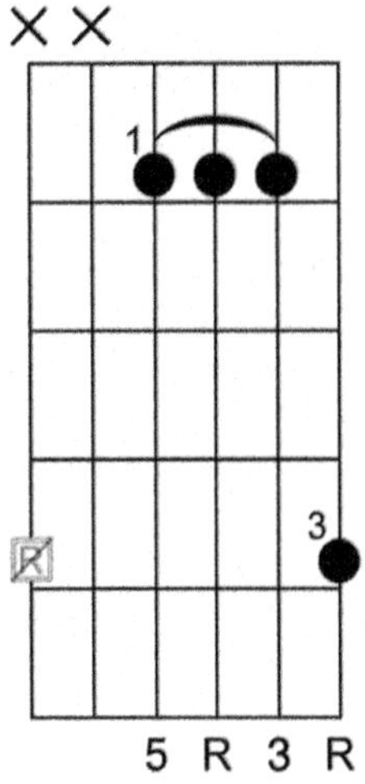

Pattern 4 (root on 4th)

E/B

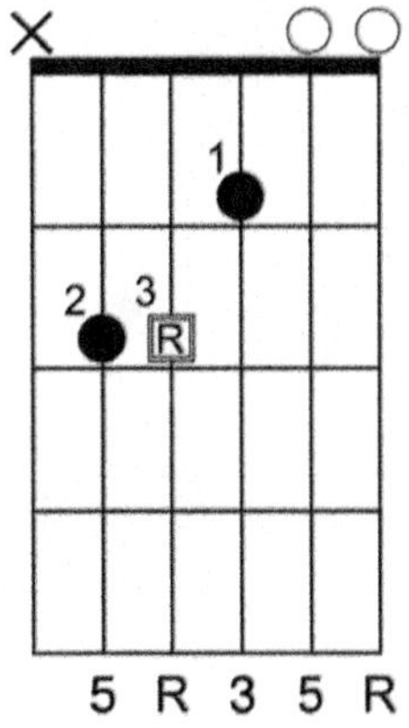

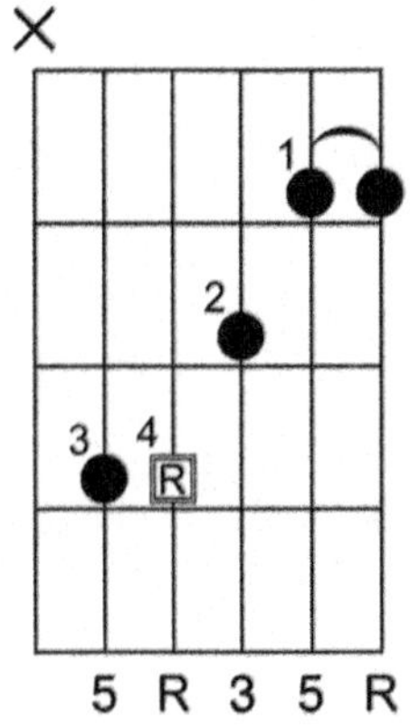

Pattern 5

D/A

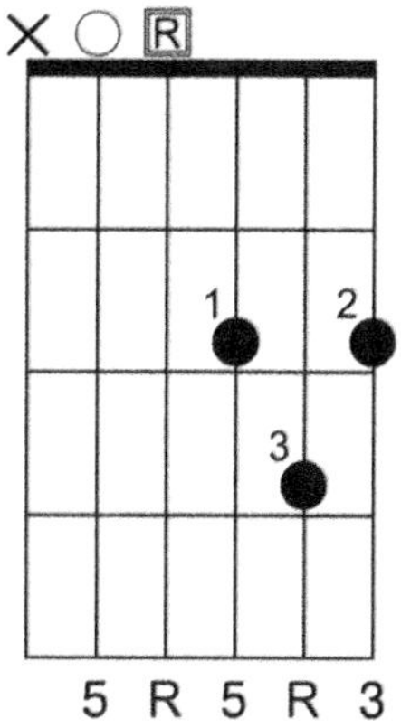

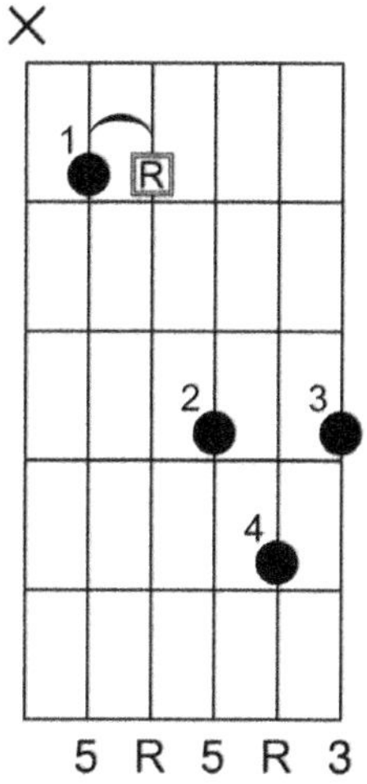

Q57) B major 2nd inversion (B/F♯) pattern 4 (root on 4th)?

Minor, 1st inversion (R ♭3 5) with ♭3rd as Bass

For minor type chords, when the ♭3rd is used for the bass note this is a 1st inversion.

Pattern 2

Am/C

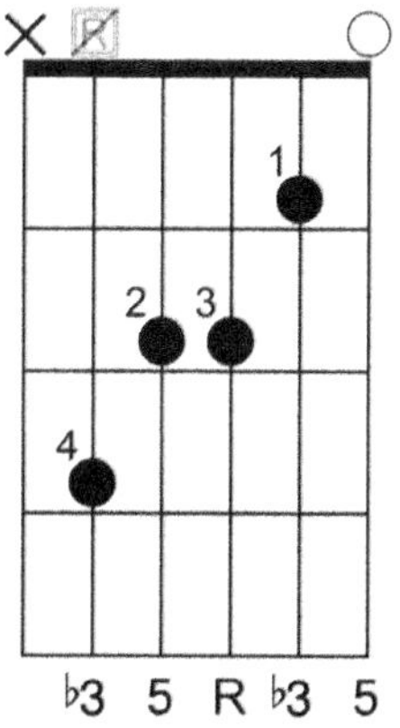

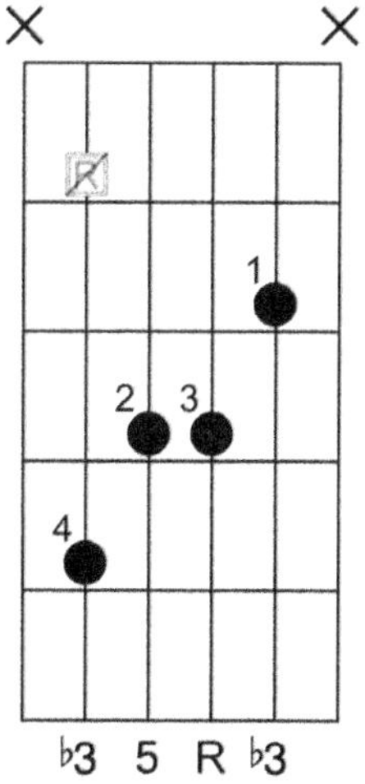

Pattern 3

Gm/B♭

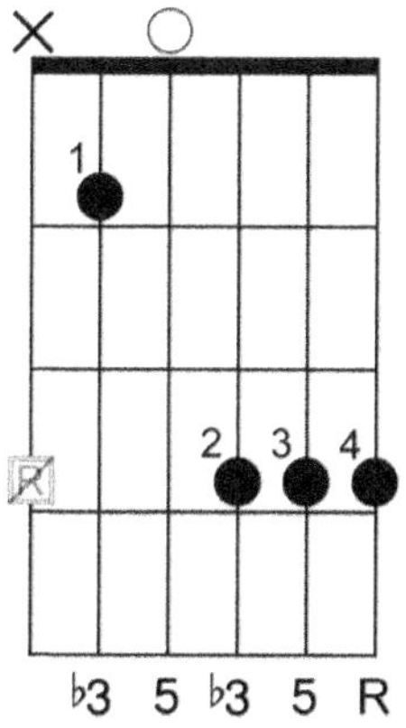

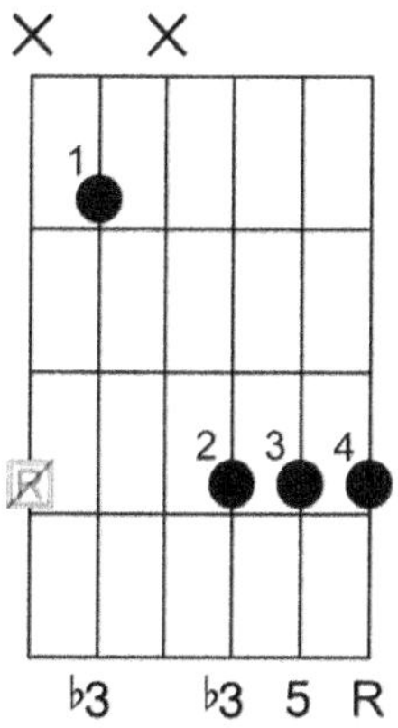

Pattern 4

Em/G

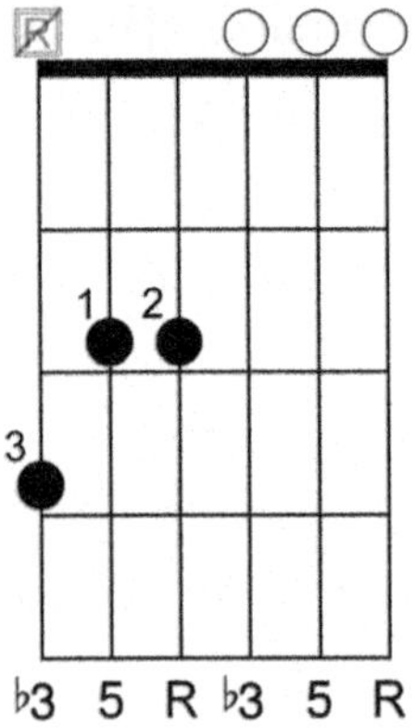

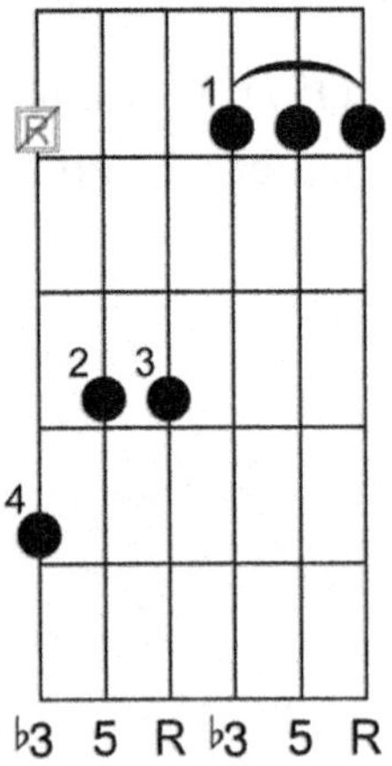

Pattern 5

Dm/F

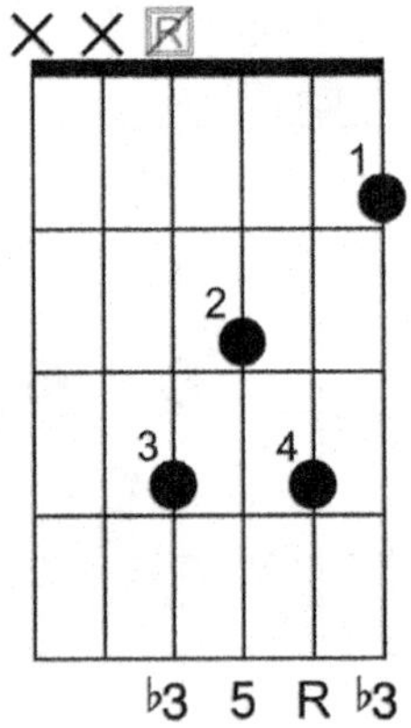

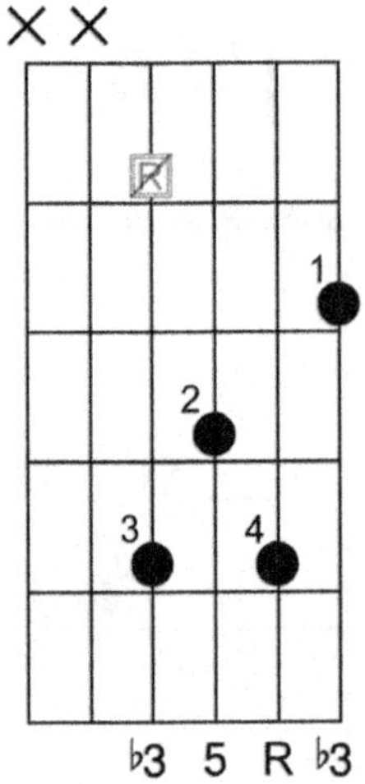

Pattern 2 above, is actually the same shape as major 6th pattern 1 (page 44) and pattern 5 is the same shape as major 6th pattern 4 (root on 4th) (page 45). In answer to anyone's question of "how many chords are there?" well, quite a few, but it is finite because eventually they start looking like each other.

Pattern 5

Dm/F

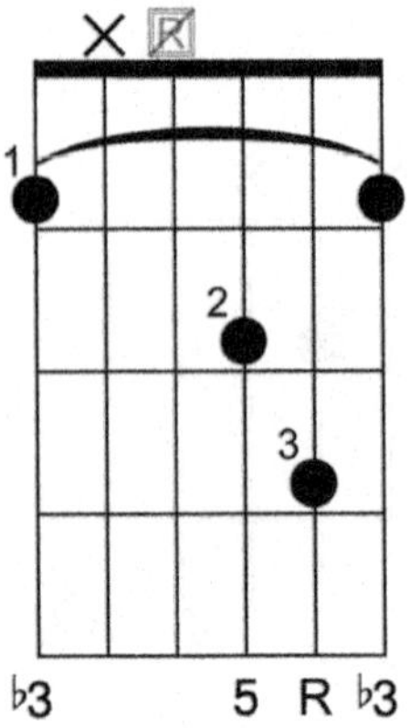

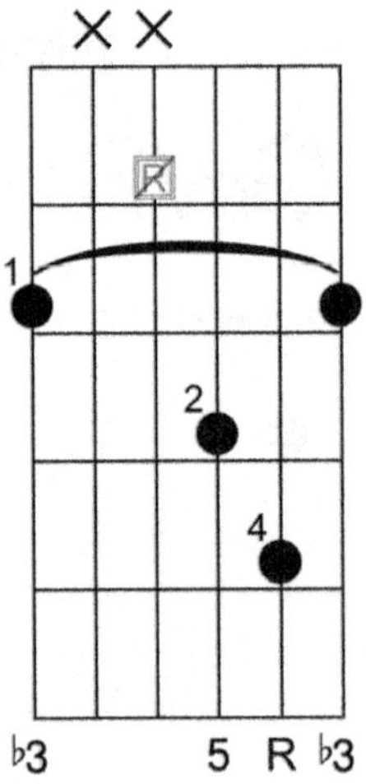

Q58) Fm 1st inversion (Fm/A♭) pattern 2?

Minor, 2nd inversion (R ♭3 5) with 5th as Bass

For minor type chords, when the 5th is used for the bass note this is a 2nd inversion.

Pattern 1

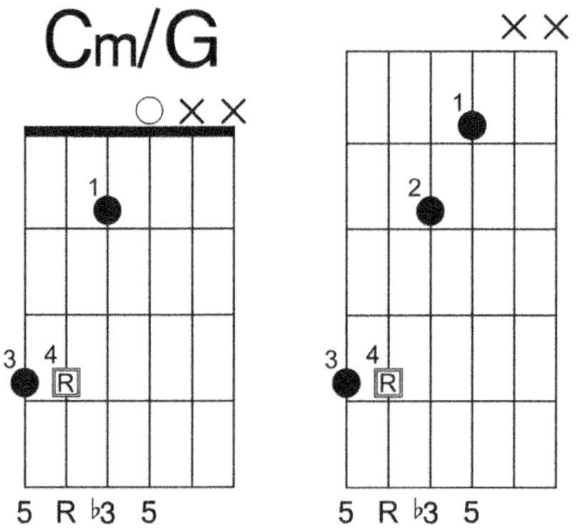

Pattern 2

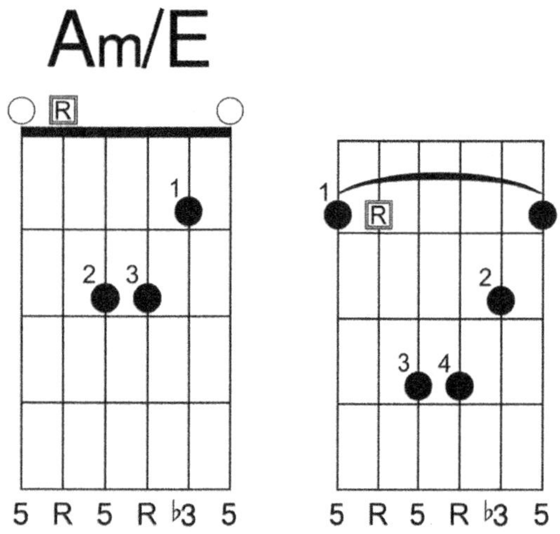

Pattern 3

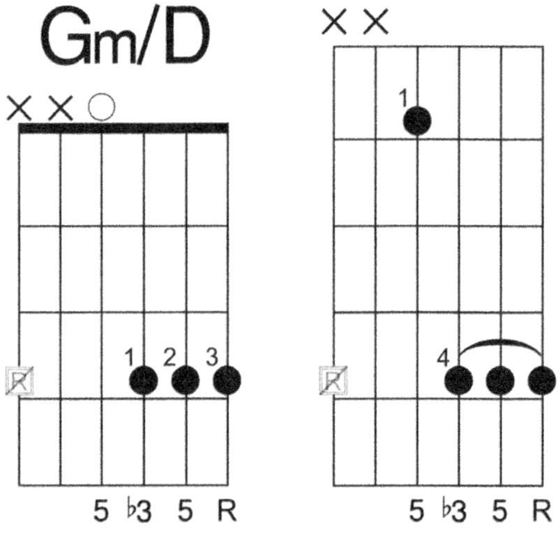

Pattern 4 (root on 4th)

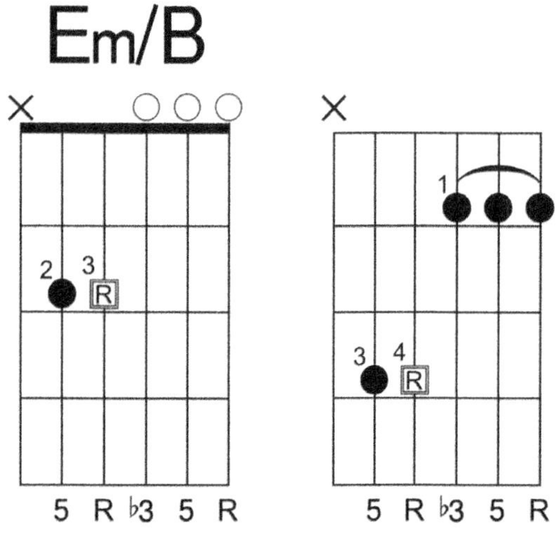

Pattern 5

Dm/A

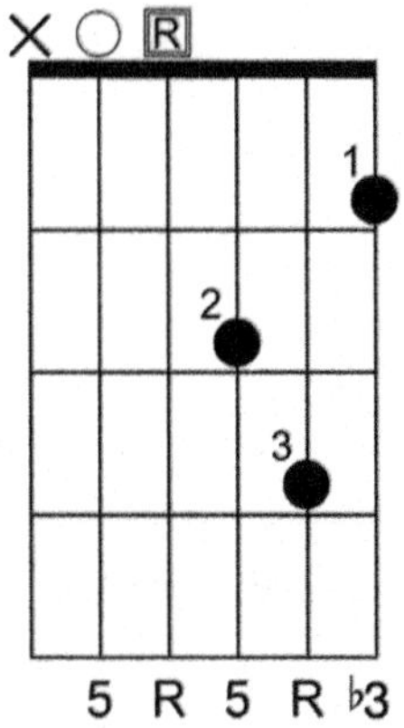

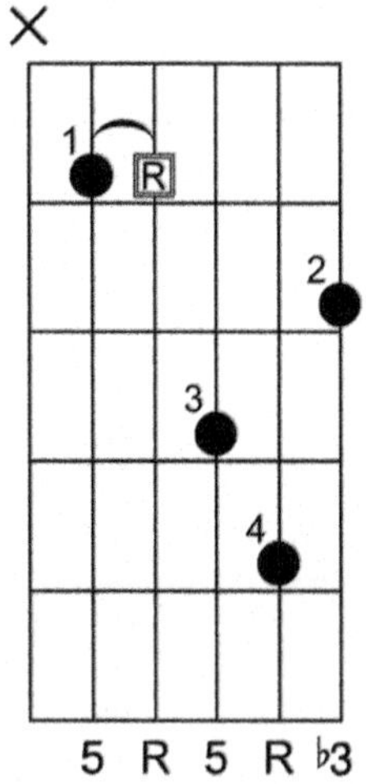

Q59) E♭m 2nd inversion (E♭m/B♭) pattern 3?

7th type chords such as major 7th, Dominant 7th and minor 7th can also be inverted. The same 1st and 2nd inversions will apply by using the 3rd or 5th interval as the bass note. With a 7th interval there is also the option to use the 7th interval as the bass note for a 3rd inversion.

In the next section a few examples are given for the more commonly used 7th chord inversions…

Inverted 7th Chords

Dominant 7th, 1st inversion

(R 3 5 ♭7) with 3rd as Bass

Pattern 1

C7/E

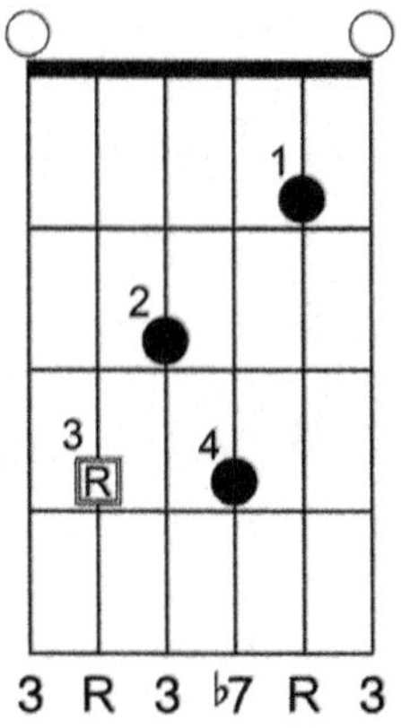

Transposable version impractical

Minor 7th, 2nd inversion

(R ♭3 5 ♭7) with 5th as Bass

Pattern 2

Am7/E

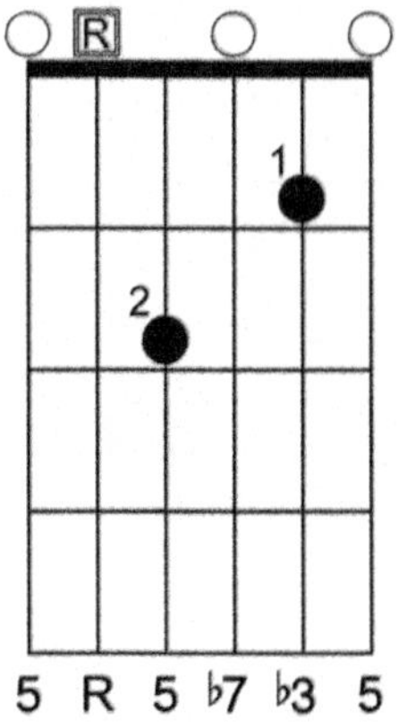

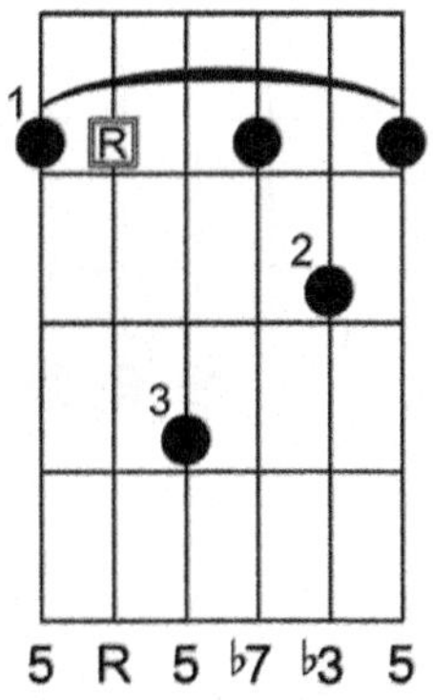

Dominant 7th, 2nd inversion
(R 3 5 ♭7) with 5th as Bass

Pattern 1

C7/G

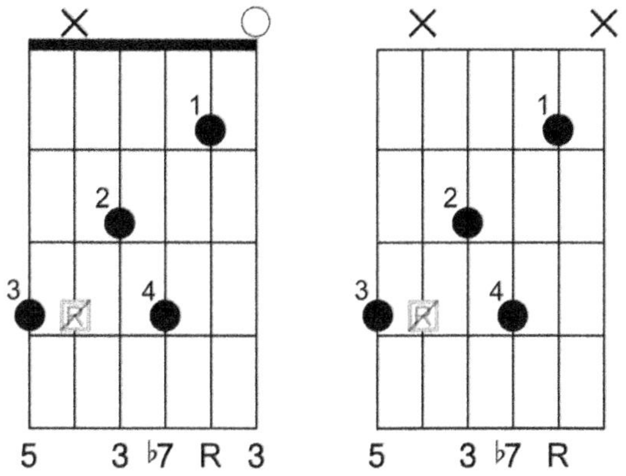

Dominant 7th, 3rd inversion
(R 3 5 ♭7) with ♭7th as Bass

Pattern 1

C7/B♭

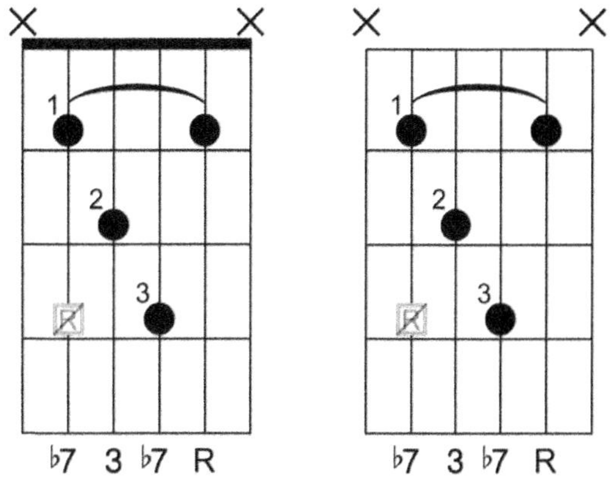

When the bass note is *not* from within the chord, this is simply known as a "Slash chord".

Minor 7th, 4th as Bass
(R ♭3 5 ♭7) with 4th as Bass

Pattern 1

Cm7/F

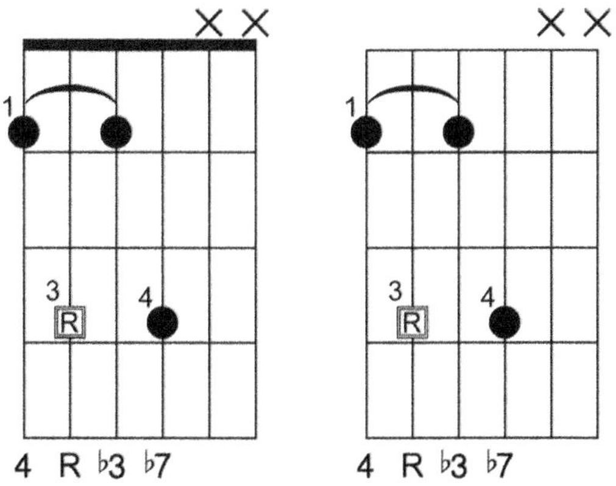

Pattern 4 (root on 4th string)

Em7/A

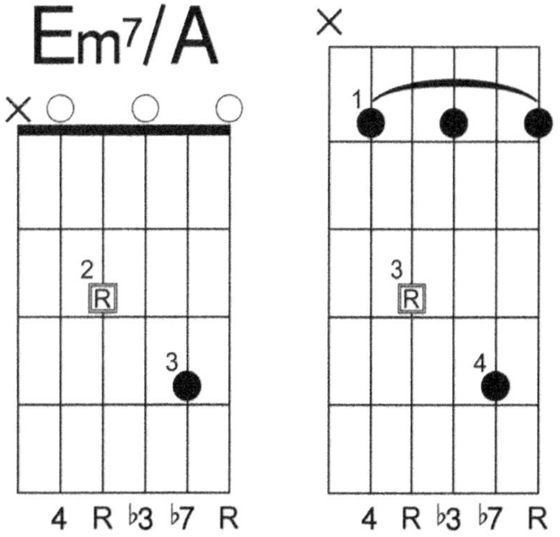

Cm7 over F Pattern 1 (Cm7/F) is similar in shape to Dominant 7th sus4 pattern 4 (page 41).

Major, 2nd as Bass

(R 3 5) with 2nd as Bass

Pattern 2

A/B

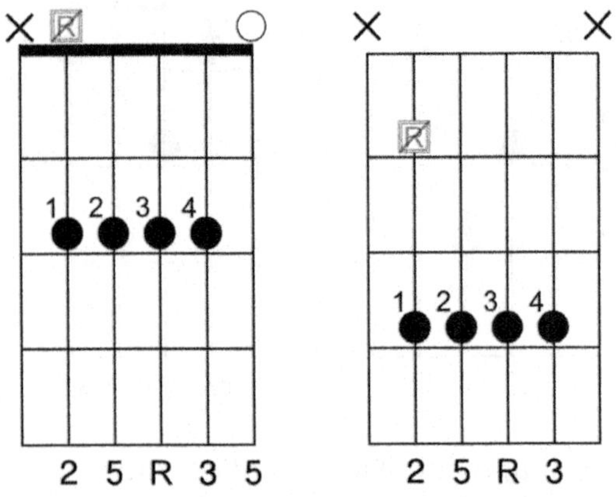

Pattern 5

D/E

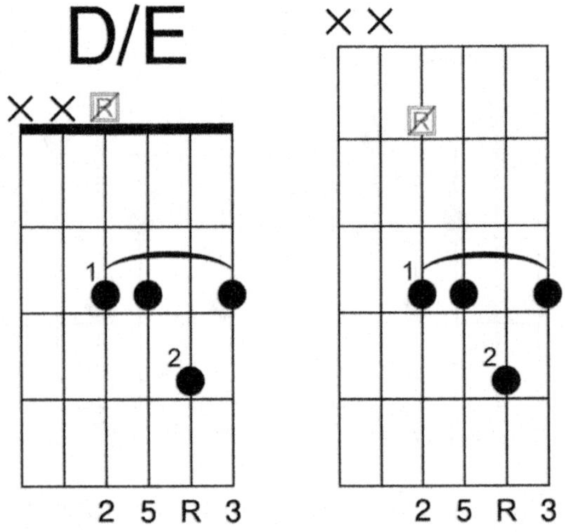

Minor, 6th as Bass

(R ♭3 5) with 6th as Bass

Pattern 2

Am/F♯

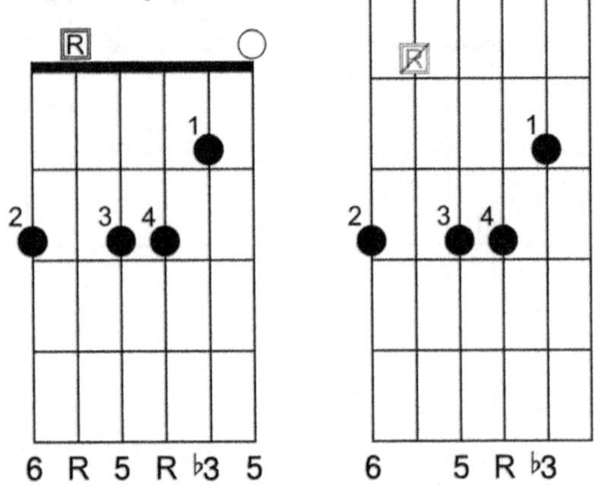

D/E pattern 5 and the transposable version are the same shape as Dominant 9th sus4 pattern 5 (page 55).

The transposable version of Am/F♯ is the same shape as the minor 7th ♭5 pattern 3 (page 22).

Q60) G7 3rd inversion (G7/F) pattern 1?

Q61) E major 2nd as bass (E/F♯) pattern 2?

In the case of a minor chord in which there is a ♭7 as the bass note, we could call this a Slash chord, or the 3rd inversion of a minor 7th. Below it is shown as slash chord Dm over C.

Minor, ♭7th as Bass

(R ♭3 5) with ♭7th as Bass

Pattern 5

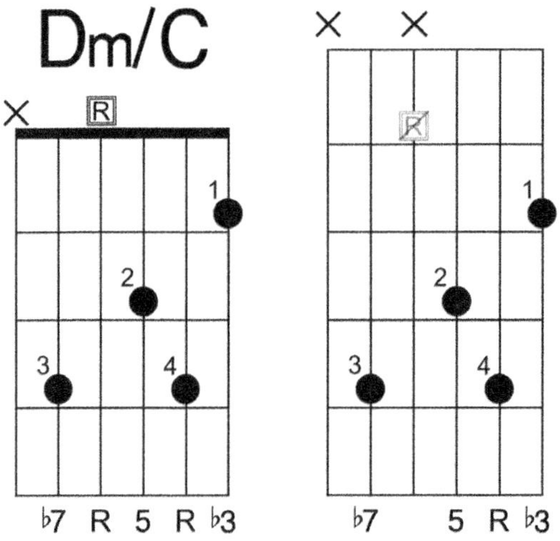

Answers

For the following answers, the fret on which the root note is located is indicated to the right of each fret-board diagram (apart from those where the chord is located near the nut).

Q1) Q2) Q3) Q4) Q5) Q6) Q7)

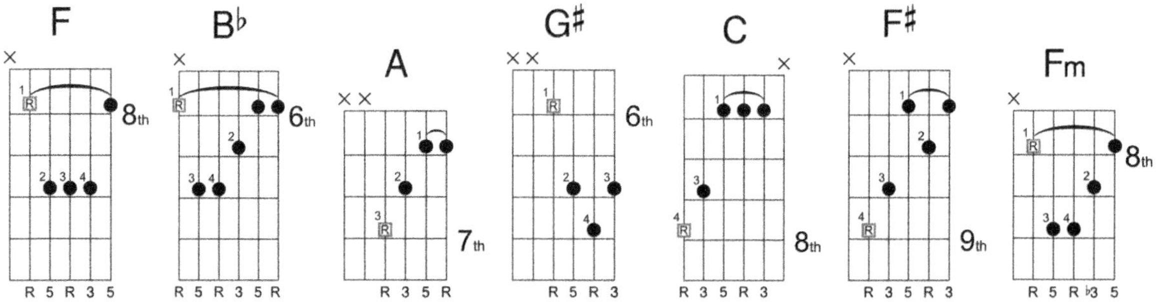

Q8)

D♯aug

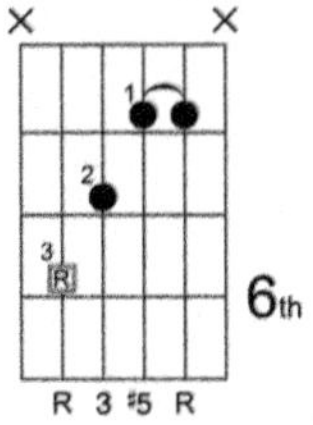

Q9)

Bdim

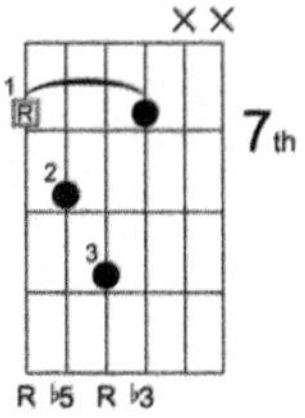

Q10)

Gsus4

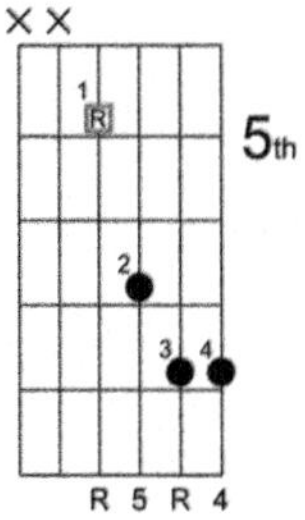

Q11)

B♭sus2

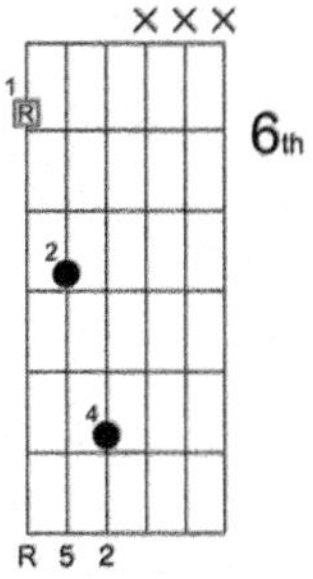

Q12)

F♯5

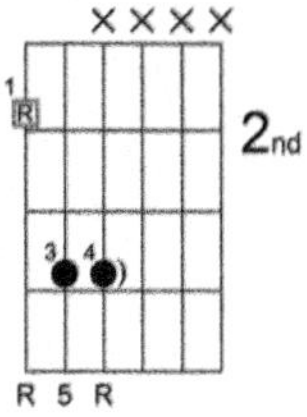

Q13)

Fmaj7

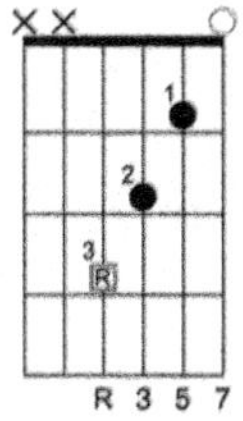

Q14)

C7

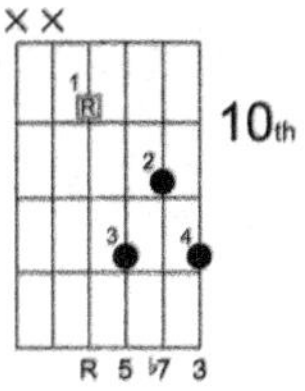

Q15)

D♭m7

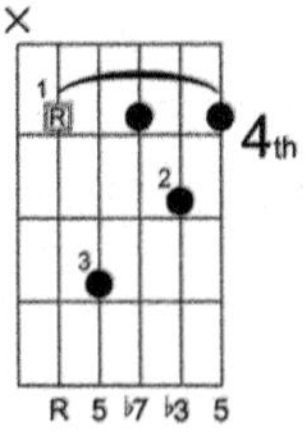

Q16)

Am7♭5

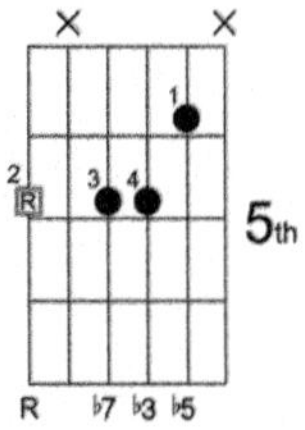

Q17)

Emaj9

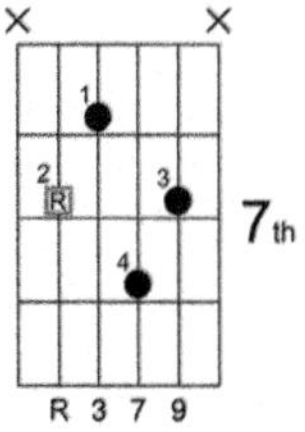

Q18)

G♯9

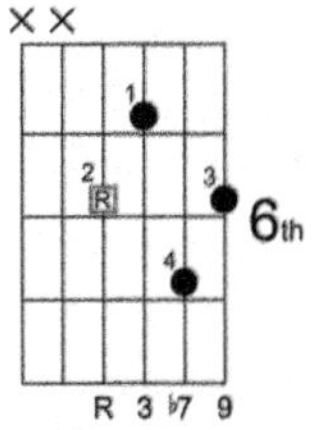

Q19)

Dm9

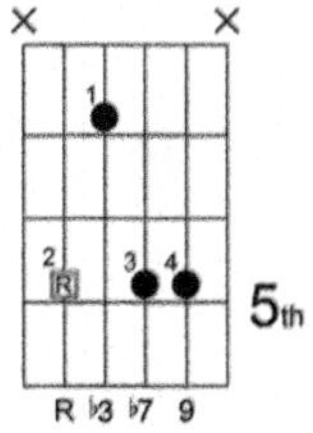

Q20)

E♭11

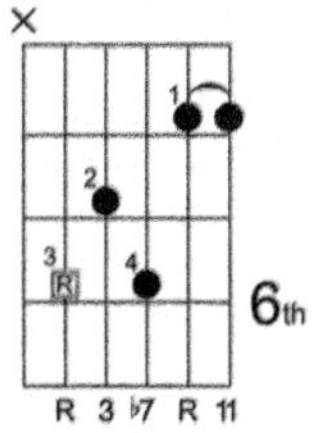

Q21)

Am11

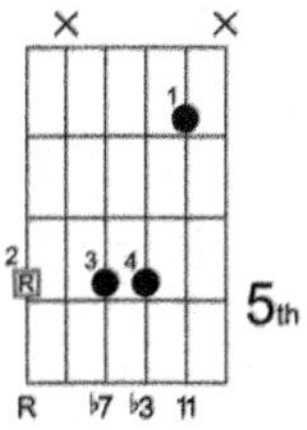

Q22)

Cmaj13

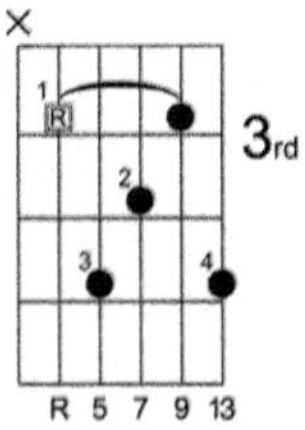

Q23)

B13

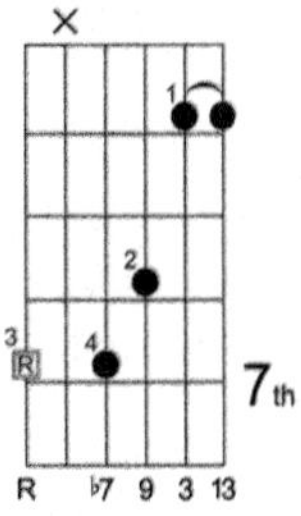

Q24)

A♯m13

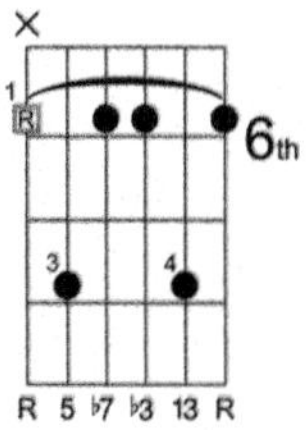

Q25)

C♯maj7♯5

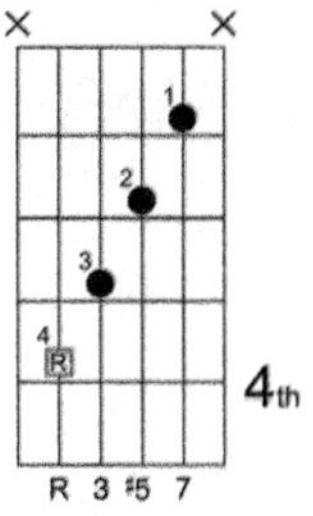

Q26)

Dmaj7♭5

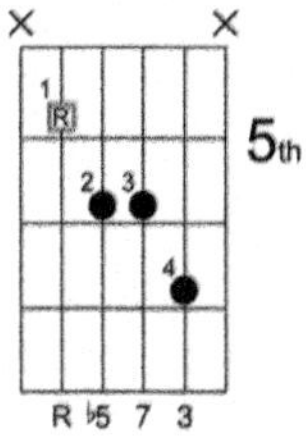

Q27)

G♭7♯5

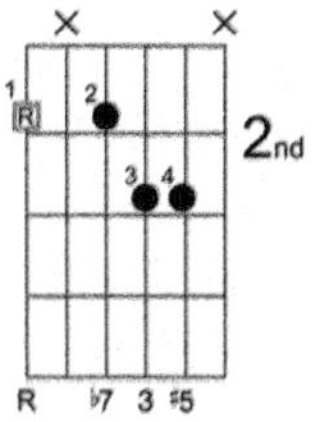

Q28)

E7♭5

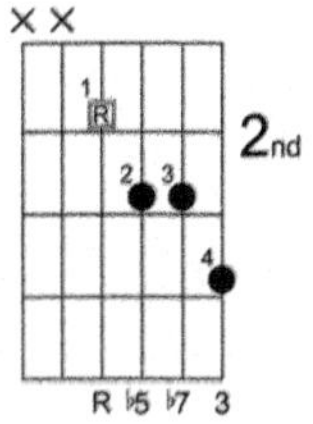

Q29)

A♭7♯9

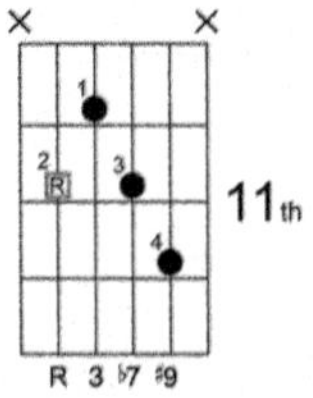

Q30)

B7♭9

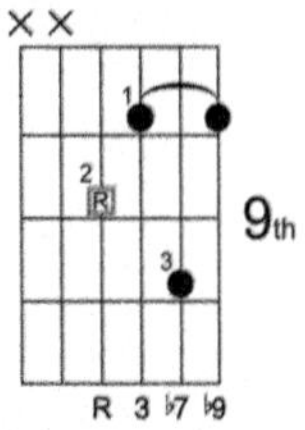

Q31)

Dm7♯5

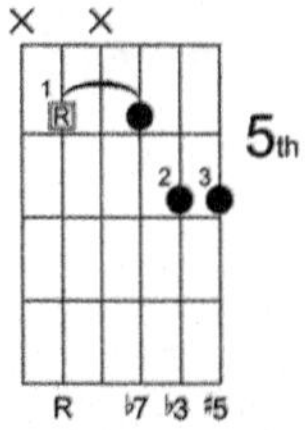

Q32)

F♯7sus4

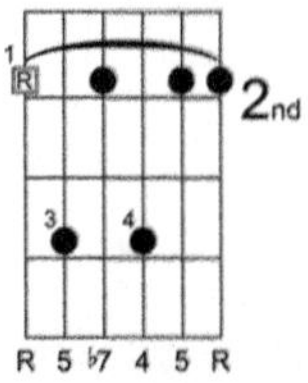

Q33)

B♭dim7

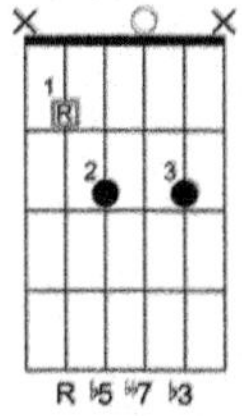

Q34)

D♭m(maj7)

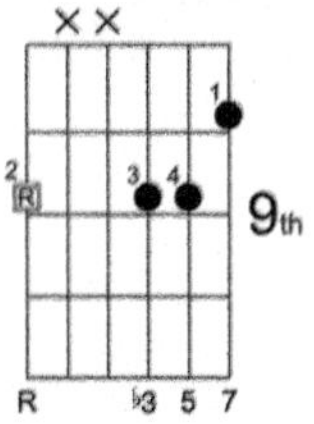

Q35)

G6

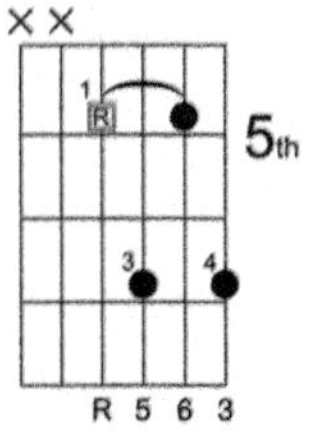

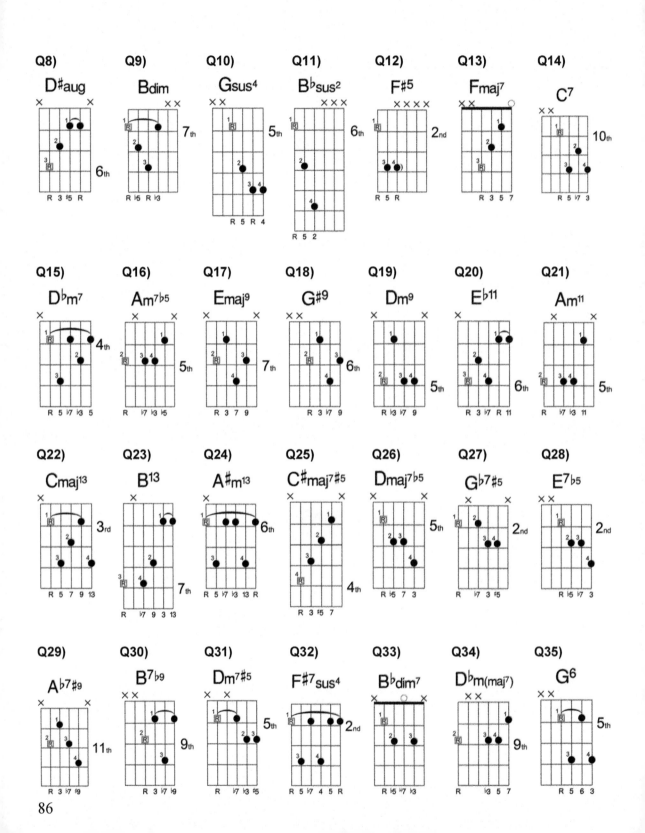

Q36)

Cm^6

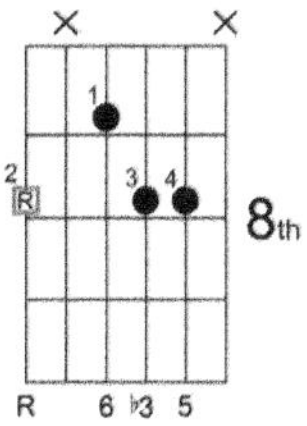

Q37)

$C^\sharp add^9$

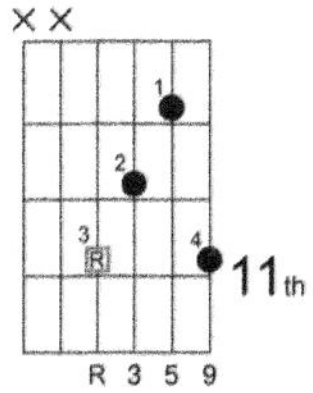

Q38)

$D^\sharp m_{(add^9)}$

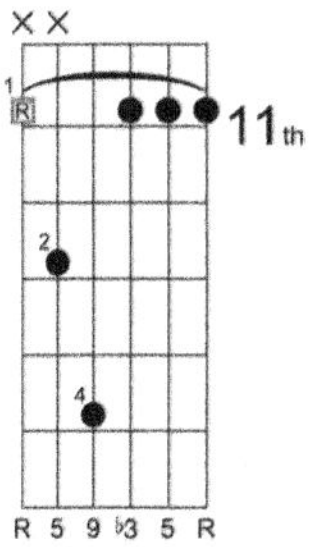

Q39)

$A^{\flat 7\flat 5(\flat 9)}$

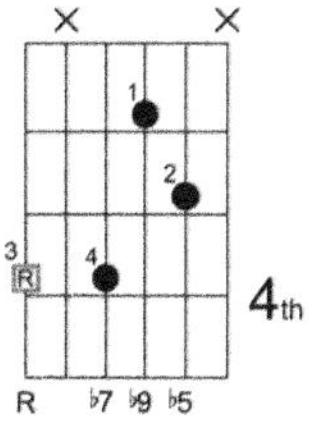

Q40)

$E^{7\sharp 5(\sharp 9)}$

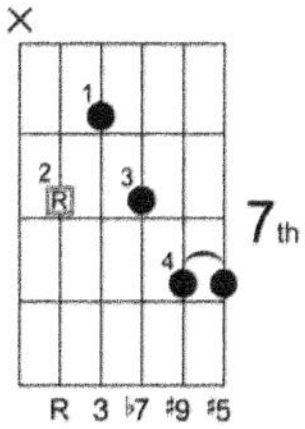

Q41)

$G^{\sharp 7\flat 5(\sharp 9)}$

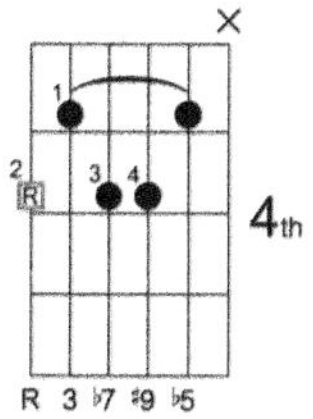

Q42)

$F^{7\sharp 5(\flat 9)}$

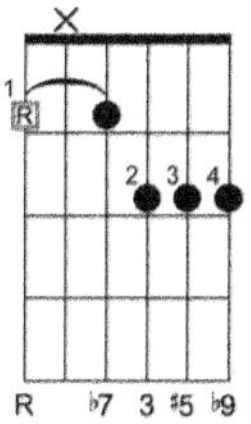

Q43)

$E^\flat maj^{9\sharp 11}$

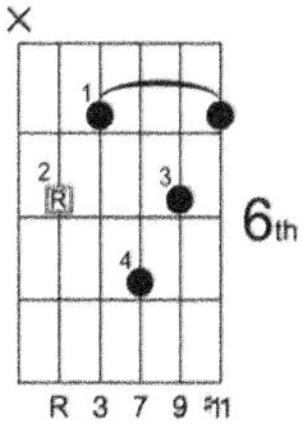

Q44)

$A^{\sharp 9\flat 5}$

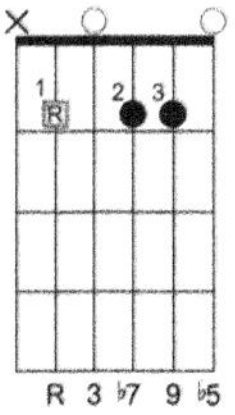

Q45)

$G^{9\sharp 5}$

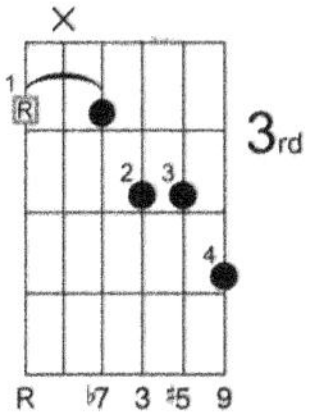

Q46)

$F^{\sharp 9}sus^4$

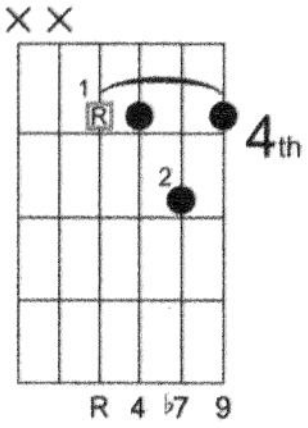

Q47)

$B^{\flat 6/9}$

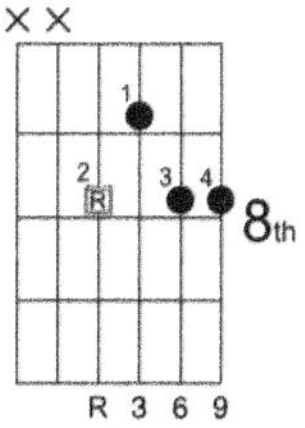

Q48)

$Em^{\flat 6}$

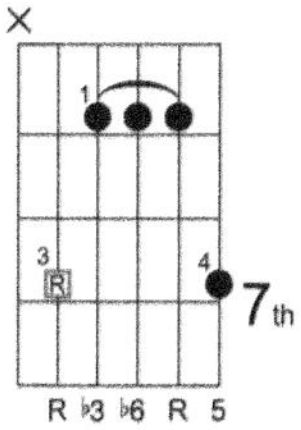

Q49)

$Fm^{6/9}$

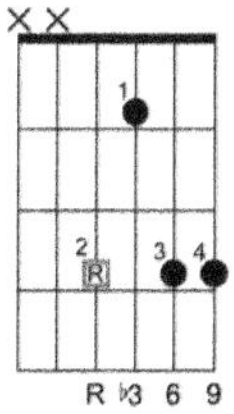

Q50)

$Cm^{9\sharp 5}$

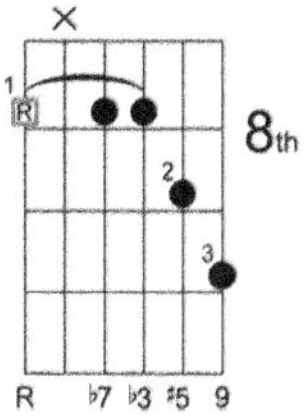

Q51)

$Dm^{9}_{(maj^7)}$

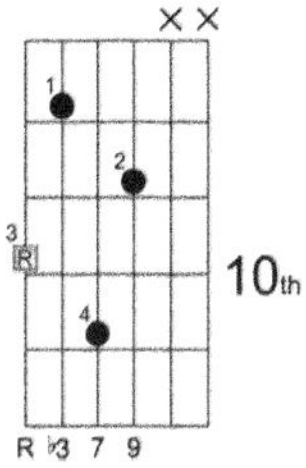

Q52)

$B^{13\flat 9}$

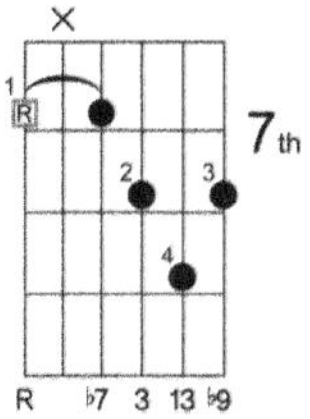

Q53)

$B^{13\sharp 9}$

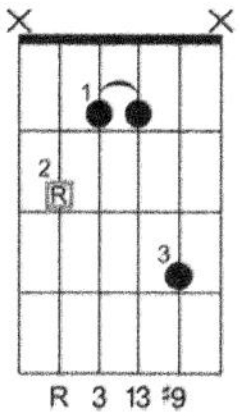

Q54)

$G^{\flat 13\sharp 11}$

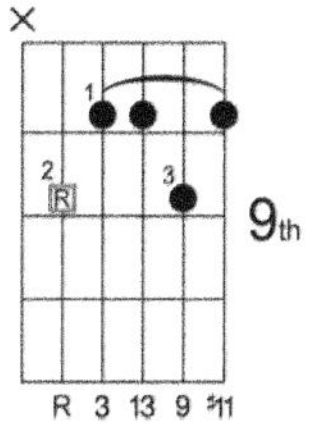

Q55)

$E^{13}sus^4$

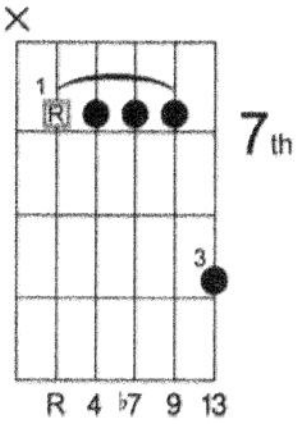

Q56)

C/E

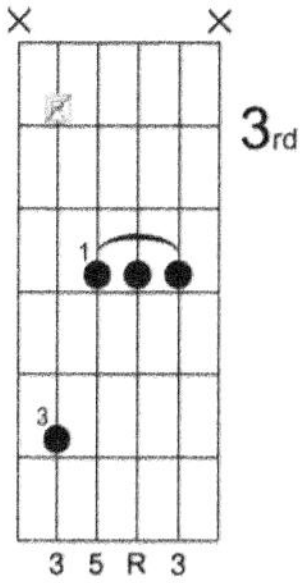

Q57)

B/F♯

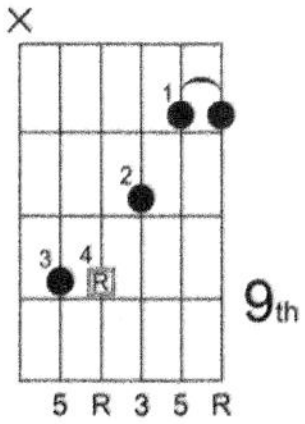

Q58)

Fm/A♭

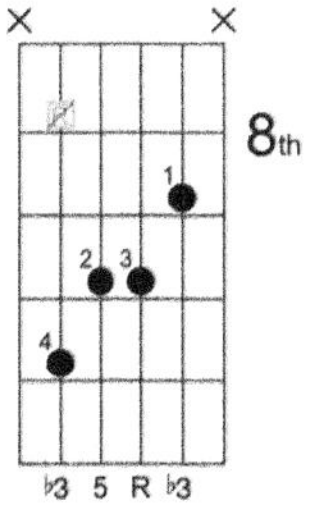

Q59)

E♭m/B♭

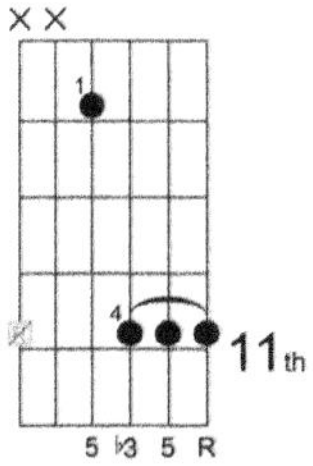

Q60)

G^7/F

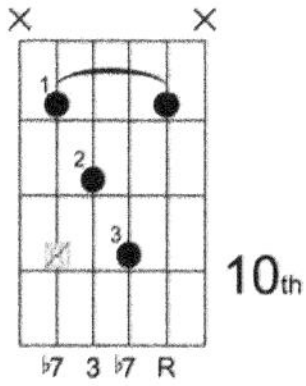

Q61)

E/F♯

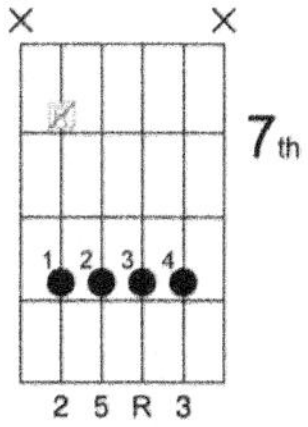

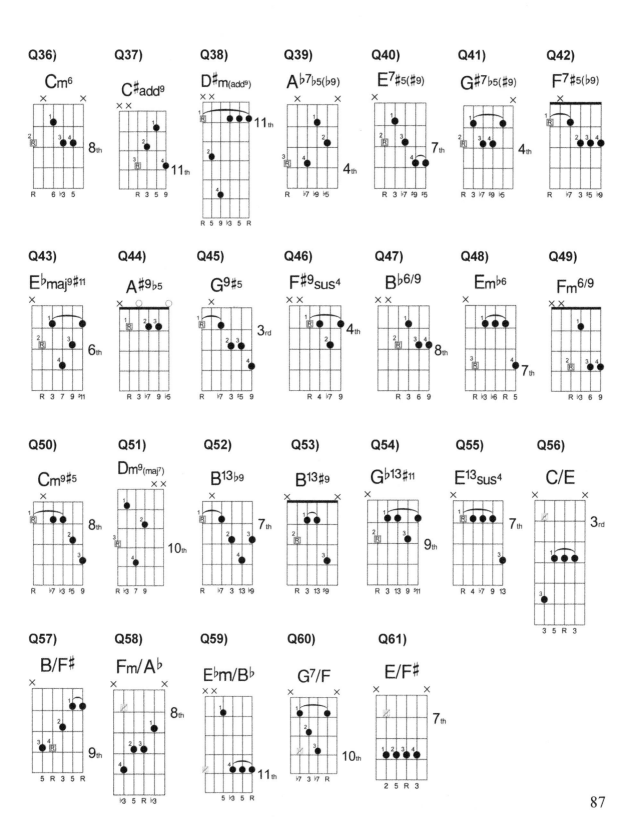

CPSIA information can be obtained
at www.ICGtesting.com
Printed in the USA
BVOW07s2225120317
478439BV00006B/109/P

9 780992 83431